Ernest Christopher Dowson, Arthur Collins Moore

Adrian Rome

Ernest Christopher Dowson, Arthur Collins Moore

Adrian Rome

ISBN/EAN: 9783744765268

Printed in Europe, USA, Canada, Australia, Japan

Cover: Foto ©ninafisch / pixelio.de

More available books at **www.hansebooks.com**

ADRIAN ROME

BY

ERNEST DOWSON AND ARTHUR MOORE
AUTHORS OF "A COMEDY OF MASKS"

METHUEN & CO.
36 ESSEX STREET, W.C.
LONDON
1899

ADRIAN ROME

CHAPTER I

ONE afternoon, near the close of a radiant July, a little party of four persons was assembled in the quiet, sunny garden of the vicarage of Underwoods. The house lay behind them: one of those low, rambling houses of uncertain architecture, so frequent in Berkshire, whose warm, red brick-work, and confusion of gables, of extravagant chimneys, gave it an air of not too remote antiquity; associations with Elizabeth, perhaps, or the earlier Stuarts. Before them stretched an expanse of smooth, spotless lawn, suggesting, like the sacred turf of college gardens, centuries of careful cultivation: and beyond that, visible only in a thin line of silver, piercing the willows, ran the meandering trout-stream, which bounded so pleasantly this pleasant domain. The extreme heat of the day had subsided as the sun passed westward; and, for two of the party, any superfluity of sunshine was effectually prevented by the large mulberry tree whose extensive shadow they enjoyed. They sat, in a silence which had probably followed protracted colloquy, in absent consideration of two youths, in white flannels and straw hats, who amused themselves some fifty yards away by throwing sticks for a vociferous terrier. And just then a trim maid-servant appeared, with an afternoon tea-tray, which she placed on the little wooden table between them. This diverted the attention of one of them, who appeared to be the elder, —they were both upon the further side of sixty,—and he glanced interestedly at the small silver teapot, and then tentatively, with a shade of diffidence in his mild, benignant eye, at his companion. By his clerical garb, and this incipient action, left incomplete through the other's absorption, of offering the hospitable cup, he was easily revealed as the present incumbent of the comfortable college living of Underwoods, and tenant (for life, as it seemed) of the old red vicarage and the river-bound garden. As visibly as the clergyman, however, Mr. Laurence Simeon's face and appearance betrayed the pedagogue—the don of an earlier generation. And the notion was sustained by his history, a long and uneventful service as fellow and tutor of his college, of which (though he had long ago retired, reaping this congenial reward) he still very perceptibly retained the aroma. His appearance was in the highest degree placid, a fact which, considering how his life had always flowed as gravely and sluggishly between the banks of unalterable conventions as some quiet, midland river, was hardly to be wondered at. A genial benevolence exhaled from him, although this was rather professional than clerical, —indeed, the pastoral office which his fellowship implied had always been highly embarrassing to him,—and his mild eye shone, if not with the light of wisdom, at least with the fainter radiance of scholarship. It was not in this attractive old gentleman's character to be violently disturbed by any circumstance, even the most disquieting: these occurred, of course, at times, but his displeasure took the form of deprecating timidity, towards the offending person or object, hardly of irritation. The offending person or thing removed, his equanimity returned to him. He reflected now, and the thought was a refreshing one,—it had indeed buoyed him up all through his vague unhappiness of the afternoon,—that in the present instance Lord Hildebrand could hardly remain much longer, if he wished to catch the train which would enable him to be in London within a measurable distance of dinner-time. For an invitation to dine with them at Underwoods—it had been a strain upon the clergyman's courtesy to give it—he had been good enough to refuse. Now that this visit was so nearly over, Mr. Simeon was inclined to plume himself upon his conduct. After all, few things more embarrassing than that had confronted him; that he should have spent an afternoon in the company of Lord Hildebrand, have offered him a cup of tea in the sanctuary of his own garden. He had been half afraid, when Mary brought down the tray, that his unwelcome guest might have launched some pleasantry—he had a vague notion that it would be a point of honour with a man of Lord Hildebrand's reputation to take indiscreet notice of a pretty maid-servant. But the Earl had not appeared to observe Mary, in spite of her Sunday ribbons: he still remained in silent consideration of the two boys on the lawn, watching them with that set smile which Mr. Simeon found so highly disagreeable. The latter took advantage of this absorption to glance across at his guest, not without trepidation, examining him more closely than he had ventured to do while they were conversing. It was a noticeable old face, older by at least a decade than its appearance, the clergyman reflected, although it retained no traces of the notorious beauty with which, nearly forty years ago, the Earl's name had been associated. What struck this shrinking observer most trenchantly now was the placidity of it, after so many years of presumably exhausting experience;—what had it not experienced that was disorderly, and licentious, and cruel? he was moved to ask, recalling a dozen scandalous stories which had leavened in time past the decorous tittle-tattle of his common-room. Life had left no writing upon it, had at most only marked it with vaguest hieroglyphics. It was like a waxen mask, unmoved and expressionless; the colour of his skin, drawn tightly like parchment over the cheekbones, over the thin aquiline nose, the close-shaven chin and mouth, bore out the resemblance. Only the eyes,—this too was in the manner of a mask,—when you chanced to meet them, brought expression into the whole face; illuminated—they were very bright and piercing, set in deep sockets—the immense irony of that compressed mouth. And Mr. Simeon showed no reluctance to escape them, when, after the boys had retreated to the river, the Earl turned to him, prefacing his speech with the production of a diminutive silver snuff-box.

"Then, Mr. Simeon, I understand you will find my arrangement a considerable satisfaction to you: it will relieve you of a pupil in whom you find cause for anxiety?"

The Vicar shifted a little nervously, unfolding for a moment his meek, fat hands.

"Lord Henry shows very great ability, considerable promise, I may say. I shall be most sorry to lose him."

The other interrupted him with a vague, deprecating gesture of one thin forefinger.

"Ah, for Lord Henry,—I have nothing to do with him. Not that!"

He took a pinch of snuff, expressively, shut the silver box with a little click before he continued—

"You understand, it is on account of my ward, not of my nephew, that I have troubled you with this visit.

It was about him, if I am not mistaken, that we were talking. I wish him to go to Oxford in the autumn. That is decided, whatever the result may be. However, as I am curious about the result, I ask you for your opinion upon him, upon his temperament. In answer, you tell me that my nephew, Henry Minaret, is a clever and amiable lad. Do you mean that my ward is an incurable fool?"

"Ah, my Lord!" expostulated Mr. Simeon with vague unhappiness. "You must not think that I had any intention of evading you—your question. Adrian—"

He paused, letting his eyes wander for a moment as if he found some difficulty in expressing himself: there was something very disconcerting in Lord Hildebrand's suggestion, in his expression of discreet mockery, of urbane expectancy.

The other relaxed the corners of his narrow mouth into a tolerant smile.

"I was going to say that your ward's character is somewhat complex; his temperament has a wider range. His successes are more brilliant, but his failures more frequent. He is a far better scholar than Lord Henry, but he has less—application."

"Oh, for application!" said Lord Hildebrand easily. "That generally goes with round shoulders and spectacles. Has he spirit—is he ambitious?"

Mr. Simeon paused. "I sometimes think so," he said, half apologetically. "Yes, I think Adrian is ambitious!"

Lord Hildebrand laughed. "Ah, well! he is brilliant, a scholar, and ambitious. That will do to begin with. If we have exhausted his virtues, let us proceed to his —to the other side of this complicated individuality. By the way, has he any social gifts? What is his reputation in the drawing-rooms of Underwoods?"

Mr. Simeon smiled uncomfortably.

"You do not seriously think that we have anything here which can be regarded as society? He—both my pupils are always spoken of as very gentlemanly, and so on, and they are invited to everything that goes on. You must remember, your ward is young."

Lord Hildebrand yawned covertly, glancing at his watch.

"Very gentlemanly, but too young to have a reputation, I gather. Happy boy! Has he—has he any other vices?"

The Vicar deposited his teacup on the tray at his side, and confronted his interlocutor for a moment with some dignity.

"My Lord," he said presently, still with the same stiffness, an unwonted attitude, which did not altogether suit his comfortable person. "If I had discovered your ward to be vicious, I should have felt it to be my duty to inform you. Moreover, if such were the case, I should hardly have permitted his intimacy with my other pupil, your nephew."

Having delivered himself of this mild protest, Mr. Simeon sank back in his basket-chair, letting his arms rest upon the commodious supports on either side. Then he continued, with less directness in his address, "I have known Adrian since his childhood—practically all his life, and, as you know, since his aunt's death he has lived with me, and I have never detected— never—"

"Found him out?" suggested the other, with a repetition of his humourless laugh. "A paragon, in fact,— except for his lamentable incapacity for application: an admirable companion for my nephew,—who, by the way, was expelled from school a year ago."

"I have not forgotten that unfortunate circumstance,"

said Mr. Simeon gravely. "But never was a boy expelled for a more venial offence: his headmaster—a very old friend of mine—assured me that the act was purely disciplinary, that he much regretted to lose Lord Henry. And I may add, this fact is fully recognised by the Christ Church authorities, who otherwise would surely have made some difficulty about receiving him."

Lord Hildebrand waved his hand with a gesture of deprecation. "Your pupils are very fortunate," he said urbanely, "very fortunate, to have so generous a champion. You must forgive me for asking so many questions: you will sympathise with my—my anxiety. And you will admit that hitherto I have not proved too exacting in my enquiries: this is the first time that I have troubled you, and it seems likely to be the last."

Mr. Simeon bowed, wondering a little nervously whether he might not have proved somewhat unreasonably intolerant of the examination to which he had been subjected.

"Quite so, my Lord. I can perfectly understand your anxiety, your feeling of—ah—almost parental responsibility. I am only sorry if I have—without the smallest intention to be so—appeared reticent. I assure you I have no reason; I know of nothing to conceal. And while we are on this subject, I hope you will allow me to assure you that I am in no way responsible for the somewhat peculiar education which your ward has hitherto received. Indeed, I always urged Miss Rome, on the rare occasions on which I saw her, to send her nephew to one of our public schools. But, as you are doubtless aware, Miss Rome was a woman of strong prejudices, and she would never hear of it. And as you appeared to be satisfied with the arrangement—"

Lord Hildebrand shrugged his shoulders. "Miss Rome was a—was certainly eccentric. The boy's uncle,

Sir Egbert, the doctor, was the only sane member of that family. I might have interfered, but—she always informed me," he continued hastily, remembering that in fact his guardianship had been almost forgotten for the many years which passed between the death of his ward's father and that of the lady whose eccentricities they had been discussing,—"she always gave me to understand that she was carrying out his father's express wishes. For myself, I certainly believe in sending boys to school—the earlier the better. However, we shall see; it will be all the more interesting."

Lord Hildebrand had risen with his last words, and stood in front of the chair which he had abandoned, leaning lightly on his ivory-headed, tasselled cane, consulting his little French watch.

"And now I must positively take my leave; I see that my train goes in less than half an hour,—though I suppose it will be late."

Mr. Simeon rose also, with an expression of relief, thinly veiled by a decorous regret which did not deceive the practised vision of his guest, and led the way towards the house. Lord Henry Minaret followed, at a little distance, carrying two racquets, on one of which six lawn-tennis balls were poised dexterously. The parting guest paused for a moment before entering the house, tapping his pockets delicately, as if to satisfy himself that he had not forgotten anything, his snuff-box, or his tortoise-shell-rimmed eyeglass.

"I suppose I had better say good-bye to you," he said, addressing his nephew. "I am going to the station, now."

"Yes," said his nephew, intent upon the mercurial tennis balls. "I shall have the pleasure of driving you there. There's plenty of time!"

The uncle cast a swift glance round the garden, and

then let his half-closed eyes rest for a moment on the narrow stream below, which seemed full to the brim of the orange and flame colour of the setting sun.

"Thank you," he said slowly. "By the way, I don't see Rome: I rather want to have a little further talk with him: perhaps the drive would be my opportunity?"

Mr. Simeon had disappeared in the dusk of the quiet house: Lord Henry stooped to pick up a ball which had escaped his vigilance, and succeeded in recovering it, at the expense of a majority of the other five.

"Rome was here a minute or two ago," he said vaguely. "Perhaps—perhaps he has walked down the road towards the station. The trap only holds two, you know."

"Yes," said Lord Hildebrand, with intention. "Precisely."

And then, after relieving himself of something between a cough and a laugh, he passed through the low doorway, garlanded with purple clematis, which led into the vicarage.

His nephew, after the avuncular back was turned, allowed a comprehensive grin to illumine his sunburnt, boyish countenance, a document in the lines of which one could already trace a tendency towards the humour which, while it was almost ceasing to be recognisable as such, so trenchantly characterised the features of his mother's brother. Here the resemblance began and ended: there was nothing to remind one of Lord Hildebrand in the expression of his candid eyes, in the rounded contours of cheek and chin, or the straight, short nose. He pushed his hat back, meditatively, exposing a capacious forehead, receding slightly at the base, and a wavy crop of brownish hair, of a tone somewhat lighter than the tan of his face, and of a quality more than ordinarily fine. Whistling gently, he deposited his burden of balls and racquets in their appointed place — he was eminently orderly in little things — in a small room opening out of the long, crooked, central passage; then with a glance out of the window into the empty garden: "Good old Rome!" he said softly; "Rome knows a thing or two, doesn't he?" Having delivered himself of this utterance, which, if it was inelegant, was also occultly expressive, Lord Henry somewhat disconsolately rejoined his uncle, whom he found already preparing to take his seat in the little pony-carriage which was to convey them to the railway station.

After casting a final interrogatory glance around the precincts of the vicarage, Lord Hildebrand devoted himself, during the few minutes which elapsed before their entry into the main road, to a delicate manipulation of his eyeglass, in which a spotless white silk handkerchief (his Lordship carried two, a piece of duplicity which struck Mr. Simeon as scarcely orthodox, and one at least was invariably spotless) played a prominent part. His nephew meanwhile allowed his spirits to rise, as he assured himself that they could hardly fail to catch the train, — he was not often so anxious about trains, — and he even found occasion for much secret merriment in speculating as to what they would say at home, at Towers, — what his "governor" the Duke would say, if it should become known that he had been brought so closely and intimately into contact with the black sheep (he was not considered less black because his hair had become white) of an ancient, and phenomenally respectable family. His uncle had enquired about his father's health (the Duke of Turretshire was a model of robust old age) in much the manner which a polite but disinterested foreigner might have adopted in a similar enquiry regarding the well-being of the Prime Minister, or the General of the Salvation Army. Really, it appeared to Lord Henry, his uncle was not quite sure that his brother-in-law still figured as an ornament of this world.

After Lord Hildebrand had polished his eyeglass to his satisfaction, and had buttoned a pair of loose but otherwise entirely unimpeachable grey kid gloves, he settled himself more comfortably in his seat, and relaxed his immobile features, first in a noiseless yawn, which displayed a set of suspiciously perfect teeth, and then into a smile at once indulgent and conciliatory.

"I don't see Rome," he said, as if he had expected to find his ward perched upon the fence. "You haven't quarrelled with him, I suppose?"

Lord Henry smiled a little uneasily, giving a shake to the reins, and fixing his blue eyes upon the shaggy mane of the Vicar's old pony.

"I don't know where he can be. We certainly haven't quarrelled. I think we get on very well together, considering."

"Considering?" echoed his uncle interrogatively.

"Well, you know, Rome hasn't been to school, and he's rather a queer sort in some ways."

"Do you mean that he's not like other boys—that he's rather a muff?"

"Oh, no," said the other reflectively. "It's not that, exactly. He's a nailing good shot, though he doesn't seem to care about shooting; and he rides a lot better than I do. Certainly, he knows about as much about cricket and football as—as that cow does about conjuring. But it isn't that, exactly."

Lord Hildebrand nodded gently. "His tastes, perhaps, are eccentric?" he suggested. "He has peculiar habits?"

"No, it's not exactly that," replied the other hopelessly. He's very fond of music,—Beethoven, you know, and that sort,—and he reads a lot; he's very literary—writes verses. And he sketches."

"The artistic temperament," said the uncle, half to himself. "I suppose he's pretty easy-going, and good-tempered now, isn't he?"

"Well, I don't know," answered the other candidly. "Hardly that, I should say. He's got a bit of temper; he can flare up pretty well, now and then!"

Lord Hildebrand suppressed another yawn. "How well you describe him! You must be an extremely close observer, Henry. By the way, you will probably have remarked that the Vicar's parlour-maid is rather pretty,—rather too good-looking, perhaps? Mr. Simeon must place great confidence in you—and in Rome."

Lord Henry looked up with an air of engaging innocence. "Did you find her pretty, sir?" he enquired a little maliciously. "I don't think she's considered a great beauty, in the village."

"Ah!" said Lord Hildebrand in a moment. "Then there must be at least one deuced pretty girl—in the village."

His nephew laughed, finding this the most convenient way of meeting the innuendo, while he wondered a little inwardly at the brilliant logic of which it had been the outcome.

CHAPTER II

OPPOSITE the gate of the vicarage there was a stile, which made the entrance of a field. Several elm-trees bounded this, and from out of them faint wreaths of blue smoke, rising perpendicularly in the clear, still air, suggested the presence of a village. It was towards this smoke that Adrian Rome, the younger of the two lads who were being educated by the placid Simeon, presently made his way. He walked rapidly, as if he had some definite object in view; but after he had crossed the meadow, and had turned into the little lane at the end of it, he allowed himself to loiter. Up the hill before him the village straggled steeply, a handful of white cottages, each with its trim garden, all ablaze with sunflowers and hollyhocks. One more pretentious house, on his right, lay back somewhat beside the sanctuary of its gated lawn,—a lawn it was by courtesy, although it had by no means the trim, urban aspect of Mr. Simeon's enclosure,—and before this house Adrian stopped for a moment. It was a long, low, white house, over the shuttered windows of which a vine that had long known exemption from the pruner's knife straggled riotously; a genteel house, even luxurious in comparison with its humbler neighbours, yet less fortunate than these, with an aspect singularly comfortless, cheerless, exhaling desolation. Its deserted air apart, it had no claim to be noticeable, and to Adrian at least, who passed it, on an average, three times a day, it was without the attraction of novelty. To-night, however, some impulse which he did not define induced him to linger there. It was not that the house was his property; a consideration so practical would have been the last to move him, even if he had not been still of an age when real property is of all possessions that which seems least to represent tangible value. It was rather that the incident of his guardian's visit had given him a glimpse into the future, and so had affected him, momentarily, with a desire to look back, to take hold, as it were, once more, for a little, of the past. And such past as he had, that rather melancholy house very largely represented. He debated in his mind upon the window of the particular room in which his aunt, three years ago, had drawn her last breath; hesitating a little, it was so long since he had thought of her, or indeed of the house, his house, which still seemed so essential of her quality. He drew a deep breath at last, reflecting how little, after all, it mattered. She was dead, and he could afford to be lenient to her memory; although she had been the terror of his childhood, and later, when his childhood had prematurely closed, the person whom in his life he had the most disliked,—at the last with an almost passionate hatred. He had nursed and cherished this antipathy in a manner peculiar to himself, although the reason of it was perhaps not very tangible. It was not to be supposed that the morose old woman's acerbity had been an intentional malice. It was her misfortune that she had been hard, and altogether without sympathy, with no capacity to perceive how disastrously her manner and her methods—her very temperament even, which was as keen as the blade of a knife—must have acted upon the nerves of a particularly sensitive child. It had been part of the evil which had come of it, that he had been led to discover that he had nerves at all, at an age when the self-consciousness of most boys has not extended further than their stomachs. It seemed to him that he had an immeasurable capacity for disliking, persons and things; that there were some of these which affected him as intolerably as an acute physical pain. Roughly, his temper was fastidious; so that his satisfactions were likely to be few, and fine ones. He was not yet sufficiently prone to self-analysis, or if the word seems preferable, sufficiently morbid, to be conscious of the full disability of these susceptible nerves of his organisation; but he was yet clever enough to be aware, that they might considerably handicap him. And, at times, he allowed himself the luxury of lacerating them. His dawdling here to-night, on his way to an encounter quite pleasurable, before a mildewy old house, which represented all the tedious things of life to him, was an instance of this.

He continued his interrupted course, after a while, following the tortuous line of the village; and his light, nervous step had still more the note of intention in it. Before almost the last cottage he stopped, hesitating a moment; then he pushed open the door,—a bell tinkled as he did so,—and entered. It was a little shop, of indeterminate character, half stationer's, half confectioner's, while the presence of a primitive desk, at one corner of the counter, suggested that in it also was performed the business of a post-office. A little, faded old woman with lavender ribbons in her cap, who sat at the receipt of custom, knitting, smiled placidly at him as he raised his straw hat.

"Can I get you anything, Master Adrian?"

"No, thanks, Mrs. Drew. I just looked in for a moment to see Sylvia. Is she about?"

"In the garden, Master Adrian. Would you mind stepping through?"

The lad made his way, with an air of familiarity, to the glazed door at the end of the shop, through which the glancing bough of a laburnum was faintly shadowed. With one hand upon the latch, he hesitated, turned back to her.

"My guardian has been here to-day, Mrs. Drew," he said. "I am to go to Oxford, to college, you know, in the autumn." Then he added abruptly, "I came round to tell her."

"Dear, dear!" said the old woman. "To think of that now! Well, the time passes, doesn't it, Master Adrian? We shall be sorry to lose you, sir. Sylvia will be real sorry."

He smiled vaguely, passed out into the garden, closing the door behind him, so quietly that his coming was not signified to a girl at the further end of it—it was a small though very pleasant domain—who busied herself, bending down over some flowers. Then he stood still, watching her, with a smile of amused admiration, waiting until some chance or other should inform her of his presence. She wore a large straw hat, and from under it—her back was turned to him—the mass of her dark hair fell in abundant ripples. When, from time to time, she moved an arm, or tossed back her rebellious tresses, as though she found them irksome to her occupation, her movements were extraordinarily graceful. And this was the more noticeable, in that she appeared to be of an age with which perfect grace is seldom associated. She might have been fifteen, or sixteen at the most; the short scantiness of her plain skirt promised the earlier age. When presently she changed her position, and gently flushed into consciousness of the intruder, the face which she turned to him —one was reminded by it instinctively of rosebuds, or the dew-drenched morning—was not the less charming because of its infantile roundness, a suggestion of immaturity, corroborated by the slim lines of her figure. It made her beauty (for the girl was beautiful,—one gave her advisedly the historic epithet) a thing rather of promise than of fulfilment. The curves of her face, delicious in its serene childishness, were singularly pure and noble. Only, one could afford to overlook this, in a certainty of the something more which would arrive. It was as though, thought Adrian just then, with a fantastic recollection, perhaps, of the fabled Galatea, the soul of her beauty still lay dormant within her, and awaited that last completing touch of life, of experience, to send it forth as the living, fateful power which it would surely become. As she came towards him, with her hands full of white marguerites, he was struck pictorially by the fitness of her companionship with such things. And, indeed, observers less interested than a lad of seventeen, who was a half-fledged poet already, and, after the manner of his kind, deeply in bondage to the delight of the eye, might have found something in this girl's carriage and movements akin to the natural waywardness of flowers.

"What are you going to do with all those?" he asked at last.

"I was just taking them indoors," she said. "Will you come?"

He shook his head smilingly.

"No, don't do that, Sylvia! Come and sit in the garden. You can bring the flowers with you. Yes, bring them, Sylvia! I want to talk."

"They will wither; it's so hot," the girl protested, but without appearing to consider that her objection was serious. And she followed him down the garden again, to a corner where was a little wooden table, and a bench, on which they sat. She held her nosegay in her lap, arranging a flower from time to time; and she looked out beyond them, at a plot blazoned with yellow marigolds and tawny nasturtiums, with her clear eyes that seemed unconscious of their own wistfulness.

"Poor dears! I have watered them once already this evening, and they look as thirsty as ever. It's very little good."

The boy nodded absently. "I've had a beastly day, Sylvia! Didn't I mean to come and help to water that precious garden of yours? Were you expecting me? Or did you hear how it was?"

"No—that is, I mean, I didn't expect you. Mrs. Brown's little girl told us you had company: she saw you, when she took down the bread. Thank you, all the same, Adrian!"

Her voice, when she spoke, was very sweet and low, breathing innate refinement; only about her speech, and, at times, her choice of words, something rustical hung. This seemed to Adrian, like her accent, which was faintly Doric, of the Midlands, hardly an error. It grated no whit upon his sensitive ear; if it was not right in the abstract, he was by no means sure that in this case, the case of a charming girl, it did not make a rectitude of its own.

"The company was my guardian, Lord Hildebrand," he explained. "I thought I should never get away. I made a clean bolt of it at last; crept off, and left Harry to drive him to the station. I wanted awfully to see you, Sylvia!"

"Oh, Adrian!" cried the young girl, in a soft, little whisper, as if the temerity of these proceedings, and a motive so inadequate, overpowered her. "And you could see me any time."

A curious cloud of moodiness darkened his face. It was a nervous, mobile face, striking and very pale: of the many fleeting changes of expression which came over it, this one was the most frequent of all.

"If I was only sure of that!" he said quickly.

She raised her long lashes, let her calm eyes rest upon him for a moment.

"You might always be sure," she said simply.

He was silent for a moment: he had taken a flower from her nosegay, and was absently, impatiently scattering its petals on the ground. Presently he continued slowly, rather as if he were alone—

"I have lived here so long, that it has seemed as if I should never leave this place. Of course I knew it would come to an end, that I should go to Oxford, or something like that,—do something or other in the world. I shouldn't want to stick here always. I have lots of ideas, projects, things I want to do—ambitions, I suppose, you would call them. And yet, I hate changes. Sometimes I don't know what I do want."

The girl said nothing for a while, during which she seemed to be giving his half-irritable outburst the consideration due to an abstract proposition.

"I think I always know what I want," she said at last.

"Yes, that is the way with women—girls. We are different."

"I want a great deal for you in the first place," she went on, slowly, dreamily.

"For me!" He looked up with a half-puzzled smile.

"Yes; an immense deal. I want you to be tremendously successful, and famous—with your verses, or to paint great pictures, or"—she hesitated a little, then completed her sentence with a blush, in humble confession of her feminine incompetence—he had sometimes twitted her with it—to synthesise upon Art—"or in some of the ways you have talked to me about."

"Dear Sylvia!" Then he went on with a quick, dark flush.

"I shall never paint great pictures. I draw detestably. My verses—oh, I daresay they are bad enough. No, they are good, some of them. But it isn't that: that is not what matters, not the success I want. Oh, I can't explain it! It's the feeling, a sort of way of looking at life: to give it scope, expression, to put it first always, that would be worth living for."

The girl looked at him without speaking: she hardly followed his imperfectly expressed explanation of the artistic conscience.

"You are very clever," she murmured softly, giving it up. "You can do anything you like."

He laughed a little mocking laugh.

"That remains to be proved, my dear! Well, it's beginning, anyhow. I am going away, Sylvia! I am going to Oxford next term."

"After all," she remarked, after a pause, which she devoted to the consideration of this news, "Oxford is not very far, it's not twenty miles."

"As if you cared," he flashed out, resenting the placidity of her tone. "It matters very little to you!"

She put out a small, sun-stained hand, and laid it upon his, which seemed by contrast the more white and girlish. It rested there, for the space of a few minutes, in perfect friendship and refutation of his petulant cry: he did not make any effort to clasp it, although he believed that she would not have resisted, but was none the less deeply conscious of the cool, consoling tenderness of the gesture.

"How silly!" she said at last, with a radiant smile, before which the last vestige of his ill-temper melted. "You know that I care."

"As you say, it is not very far," he summarised. "I

shall ride over and see you. I shall write—You will write, Sylvia?"

"If you would like it," said the girl simply. Then she went on with a sudden seriousness. "Wherever you go, Adrian! Whatever you do,—whether we write or not, even if—if you should forget me altogether, I shall go on thinking about you. I shall always remember these days."

"Forget you, Sylvia!" he repeated. "Whom should I remember, then? Aren't you about the oldest friend I have in the world? And, after all, I am not going yet: we have all the summer before us."

"Yes!" she answered lightly, "the harvest is only just begun. They are cutting the first wheat at Monkton Farm. The bearded wheat is blue—blue—it looked like the sea when I passed by this morning, the wind sent little ripples over it. It is so pretty, Adrian! But they won't cut it till the wheat is all harvested; it comes later, with the barley and the oats: those last of all. It will be a beautiful harvest, they say."

"A beautiful harvest!" he murmured absently. "Yes, I daresay."

He had but spoken the truth, when he had said that she was his oldest friend. In fact, their acquaintance dated from an extremely early period, when the speech, at least of Sylvia, had been indistinct; and Adrian, a picturesque little boy in a velvet suit, speaking a queer foreign English, full of liquid Italian words, was newly committed, in mourning for his father,—his mother had died when he was in arms,—to the severe tutelage of his aunt. If he had one faint feeling of tenderness to this lady's memory, it arose from her tolerance of the little Sylvia's presence in that funereal house. Such a humanity was so little to be expected from her, that one could only account for it on the theory that the expected course in any matter was always the last that she would pursue. There had been other children with whom Adrian might have been supposed more naturally to associate; not indeed at Underwoods, but at houses in the vicinity; but from the society of these he had been peremptorily excluded. This was perhaps only inevitable, in view of the open hostility which existed between their parents and the terrible old woman of the "White House," who received social overtures as if they had been offered in the spirit of physical assault. But when Adrian foregathered with the round-eyed little girl who lived in such close proximity to his gates, Miss Rome had tacitly acquiesced, and beneath her somewhat grim tolerance the intimacy had rapidly advanced. The post-mistress, Sylvia's mother, a foolish woman, with the traditions of faded gentility, popularly supposed in the village to have seen better days, had accepted the situation as a tardy tribute to the superior nature of her origin; the one subject upon which, in occasional gossips across the counter, she condescended to dilate. The children were always together; and, as they gradually grew up, the habit of their alliance had come to possess in the eyes of the village the sanction of an established thing. It seemed, indeed, as though Miss Rome, a woman who had never condescended to the weakness of an affection, had almost made an exception in favour of the pretty little girl whom Adrian was occasionally permitted to ask to tea. And once, when Sylvia had been invisible for a week, confined to the house with some childish ailment, the severe old woman had manifested sufficient interest to ask of Adrian, whom she encountered wandering disconsolately in the passages, what had become of the child with the great eyes.

Adrian's mind, as he sat silently beside her now, was busy with all this retrospect, in which she played so large a part,—and a little, perhaps, with a future which without her would seem curiously vague; although he had hardly as yet any determined vision of what her part in it would be. Presently he was recalled to the actual by the appearance of a third person—Lord Henry Minaret.

He came in through the door by which Rome had entered; and he wore for a moment, as he stood indecisively by it, not having discerned the two on their sheltered seat, a somewhat embarrassed air. He raised his hat, as Rome came towards him with Sylvia; then accepted, a little shyly, her frankly proffered hand.

"Mrs. Drew said I should find you here, Adrian, and I thought I would remind you that it is nearly dinner-time. Are you coming?"

"I know how you forget the time, old chap!" he remarked to his friend, a few minutes later, as they strolled down the hill together. "And I thought it would be as well that you shouldn't add the crowning sin of being late for dinner to all your other shortcomings of to-day!"

"Were they so many?" asked Rome carelessly.

Lord Henry laughed his pleasant, good-humoured laugh.

"Well, you ought to have driven the old boy to the station, you know. I think he expected it."

Then, as Rome seemed disinclined to justify his irregularities, he went on abruptly: "I am awfully glad that you are to come up to Oxford with me. Such an old ruffian as my precious uncle must be, from all accounts, would be capable of sending you to Cambridge."

The other smiled rather listlessly. "Isn't it very much the same?" he asked.

"Not in the least," said Lord Henry quickly. Then

he went on, discerning in his friend's speech that recurring accent, curiously remote, which often puzzled him.

"What a queer fellow you are, Adrian! One would think you didn't care, weren't glad to get out of this hole. You have often told me you hated it."

"There are worse places than this, very likely. The fishing is good."

The other laughed blithely.

"A lot you care for that! You had better go and live in that mouldy old house, when you've taken your degree; you will have time to fish then. You are awfully difficult to please! Hang it, man, you can get anything you want. You'll be beastly rich in a year or two; and you've got brains into the bargain. You'll be indecently rich, you beggar. And you have no people to interfere with you."

"I suppose I shall have enough money," his friend admitted.

"And yet you are not satisfied," said Lord Henry.

Then he went on with a rapid transition, which his friend found perhaps inconsequent.

"Sylvia seems to be growing up into a very pretty girl."

"Pretty," repeated Rome musingly. "Yes, I suppose she is."

"You seem to find her so. By the way, Rome," he lowered his voice confidentially, "are not you afraid of going there so much; I mean, that people will talk?"

Adrian flushed rather angrily.

"Idiots will always talk; let them. I have known her since she was three years old."

"Oh, so long as you don't care," said the other blandly. "But hang it, she *is* pretty, you know," he added, half to himself, as they reached the gate.

As Rome was still silent, however, after his scornful custom, repudiating the burden of justification, he dismissed the affair light-heartedly, saying to himself, as he tossed his hat down in the hall, "After all, it's no business of mine."

CHAPTER III

ADRIAN ROME'S rooms, on the first floor of the sunny side of the inner quadrangle of St. Cyr's, were certainly as pleasant as any to be found within the limits of that or any other college; and he had not been slow to appreciate the good fortune which had endowed him with them when he presented himself at the university as a candidate for matriculation. Yet, as he lounged, one evening, after dining in hall, on the disreputable but extremely sympathetic cushions in the window-seat beneath which lurked his so-called wine cellar, he felt, with a touch of regret, that now, after three years' residence, he was realising the charm of his surroundings to the full, for almost the first time. It was the nearness of the day when he would be compelled to abdicate, to remove his books from their shelves, his pictures and china from their places on the now familiar walls, which brought home to him the fact that, after all, in spite of petty restrictions (all the more vexatious to the spirit of a boy who had never known the discipline of a public school), in spite of the impertinent restraint placed upon a man's reading, and the offensiveness of the antiquated proctorial system,—notwithstanding, in short, all the limitations of an English university, there were still compensations—and this charming lodging was not the least of them—which made Oxford life a thing so truly enjoyable, that to turn one's back on it irrevocably, to take one's degree (in itself a secession from youth), to burn one's ships, could not be contemplated without a real regret, a wonder as to whether the world, even to the fortunate master of a liberal income, could offer anything more earnestly to be desired.

A ripple of light laughter, the tread of quick feet upon the close-packed gravel, invaded the quiet of the shadowy quadrangle: he turned on his seat, and leaning his elbows on the crumbling stone of the window-ledge, allowed his eyes to wander appreciatively over the grave, grey walls, with their decorous mantle of deep ivy, and luxuriant Virginian creeper. As he sat there in the twilight, throwing now and then a careless word or nod in answer to the sallies of the passers-by below, his face and the upper part of his body seemed to be framed, not inappropriately, in the sombre embrasure of the window.

The portrait thus presented was that of a boy who had almost entered upon manhood; he was within a few months of attaining his majority, and looked older than his years. If, at first sight, one would hardly have allowed that he was good-looking, the epithets which one would have selected, upon consideration, as more appropriate to his case, would have been in effect at least as complimentary, and certainly less commonplace. His face was too long, perhaps, and his hair, of a brown colour dark enough to border on black, disposed itself in lines too monotonously straight on either side of a wide, pale forehead, over which it formed almost a complete semicircle. His eyebrows, dark and horizontal, shaded a pair of restless eyes, over which they were placed rather high, and there was a faint, vertical furrow between them, which in certain lights, and particularly in moments of excitement, was much emphasised. The colour of his eyes was as hard to determine as that of the sea on a showery day in the spring: at some moments they were almost of the shade of his hair, dark and inscrutable, at others they were warmed and illumined until their dusky glow seemed scarcely less ruddy than the flame of a wine-coloured topaz. Moody and brilliant, wayward and sanguine, they sounded unmistakably the keynote of his temperament. His nose was a straight and well-cut member, of a length sufficient to make it fill its apportioned part of the rather unusual distance between brow and chin. His mouth was of a good shape, expressive and not too small; the upper lip, curving upwards at the corners, was covered lightly with a spare moustache, which did not promise to attain more than a moderate luxuriance. When he smiled, as he often did in speaking, a good set of teeth lent a momentary charm of brilliance to his expression, which, in repose at least, had little vivacity. The lines of his jaw were keenly marked, and sloped rather abruptly from ear to chin, without exhibiting the squareness which is generally accepted as indicating strength of purpose: his chin, somewhat deeply cleft, terminated in a flattened point, the apex of a triangle, of which his cheekbones, standing in higher relief than his slightly concave cheeks, very clearly marked the base. Of medium height, he passed for tall, owing to a certain lightness of build and length of limb; his arms hung loosely from a pair of square, well-knit shoulders, and the hands in which they terminated were broad, and shallow in the palm, with straight, taper fingers, capable and shapely.

A striking personality, and in many ways a puzzling one: it had been said of him with some shrewdness by a keen observer, that in whatever country he might find himself, he would pass for a foreigner: and yet— although this may sound inconsistent—there was in Adrian Rome, physically no less than morally, material for the making of a good cosmopolitan.

The clock in the little belfry above the college chapel chimed the hour, lingering on the notes with the gentle deliberation of old age, making its warning a hint rather than a command. It was half-past eight, and Rome reminded himself that he had invited one or two of his friends to take coffee with him. On nodding terms with most of the men of his college, he was intimate with few; he had not gone out of his way to make friends, and it was one of the defects (advantages, he might have said) of his education that he had had no early opportunities for forming juvenile intimacies, the chains of which university life would have welded more closely. He belonged to no camp; he could not have been classified either as an athlete or as a reading man; his set (if indeed he could have been assigned to anything so definite) was composed rather of the free-lances of college life, the men who made no great profession of ability, who did not regard themselves too seriously, who were tolerated, nervously, rather than approved by the authorities. He belonged to a literary society which showed symptoms of developing into a whist club; to a whist club which was suspected of being a society for the encouragement of poker. A member of the Union, he had been spurred by a moment, a mood, to deliver himself, nervously, of one brilliant, audacious speech; but he could never be induced to repeat the experiment, or even to propose a motion, although his friend Lord Henry Minaret, who had lately been elected an officer of the society, frequently remonstrated against this lamentable indifference towards the affairs of his country. Briefly, while general repute set him down as eccentric, (without thereby intending a compliment), the few men who knew him spoke of him as clever, and even as a genius. His friendship with Gerald Brooke had contributed much towards making him an object of curiosity and speculation in out-college circles : Brooke, the newly-elected Fellow of St. Jude's, the wit, the poet, the best-abused man in Oxford. They had encountered each other at Towers, where Rome was staying as Lord Henry Minaret's guest at the end of his first Long Vacation, and they had gradually become intimate on the basis of their common appreciation of Battersea enamel and Catullus.

It was precisely Brooke, among others, whom Rome was expecting to-night, and who presently arrived,—announcing himself with a *bon-mot* sandwiched between two puffs of tobacco-smoke, and casting himself with an air of infinite weariness into the largest easy-chair, among the cushions of which his meagre person was almost lost. He was small, to the verge of insignificance, and it was commonly reported that he had more than once been taken for a schoolboy up for a scholarship examination. It was only on closer scrutiny that one perceived the wrinkles at the corners of his cherubic eyes, and noted the set lines of his strangely immobile mouth. When he spoke, his hearers were apt to forget their first impressions in a wonder as to whether he had ever been really young. His lips seemed specially adapted for the utterance of charming things with a languid sting in them. Rome was not alone when Brooke knocked at his door; he had already been invaded by Corbyn, a Welshman, of his own year, who inhabited rooms on the next floor of the same staircase; and before the three had finished their first cigarettes quite a little party had assembled in the pleasant lamplit room, from the open windows of which their boyish voices and laughter, and the music which Corbyn extemporised softly upon the cottage piano, floated fitfully into the empty quadrangle.

"Don't stop," Brooke had said to Corbyn. " I shall

never deny that music has one great merit; it makes an admirable background for conversation; it fills up the interstices, and helps one to be suggestively unintelligible."

"Don't be unkind to Corbyn," said Rome lazily, from the depths of an easy-chair. "He's incapable of defending himself; he's just been ploughed in Pass Greats —in political economy, or something."

Brooke gazed for a minute thoughtfully at the back of the imperturbable musician, who broke into a defiant march.

"Ploughed," he said reflectively. "Ploughed! I wish it had occurred to me to be ploughed in something before it was too late. I'm sure it would have been a charming sensation. But I'm afraid I shouldn't have had the courage. I should really feel envious, if it wasn't so commonplace; there's nothing so distinguished as failure, except a really brilliant success! By the by," he added, turning to Rome, "haven't you been in the schools, too?"

"Yes," said Rome briefly, "I've achieved a grovelling pass. I wish I hadn't; I've got no decent excuse for staying up now. "No," he added, in answer to an enquiry, "I'm not going to take my B.A. now; it will be a good pretext for running up from town next term."

"Listen to him!" said a freshman admiringly. "And to think that I am always trying to find reasons for the reverse process!"

"I generally say I want to see my dentist," said Corbyn, wheeling round on the music-stool. "And last time the Dean—bless him!—asked me what his name was, and if I could recommend him."

"Well," said Barton, the freshman, "couldn't you? I should like to introduce the Dean to *my* dentist; he'd make the old beggar sit up!"

Corbyn smiled. "You see, as a matter of prosaic fact, I've never been to a dentist in town; my man lives at Carnarvon. So I had to invent a name, and say I'd forgotten the address. It didn't matter; I expect the old boy was only trying to make conversation."

"Imagine a man who would manufacture conversation about such a dreadful person," protested Brooke, puffing a voluminous cloud from his glossy briar pipe. "One might as well ask a convict if he could recommend his tailor."

"Ah," said Rome mischievously, "don't be hard on the Dean, he's old, you know; he knew better twenty years ago."

"People ought to be superannuated when they've reached thirty," said Brooke sententiously. "They ought to retire, to seclude themselves. They ought to be sent to—to America."

"Well," said Corbyn, in the middle of a brilliant cadenza, "what monastery do you think of selecting?"

"I?" replied Brooke, settling himself complacently among his cushions,—"I shall never be thirty; I shall draw the line at twenty-six. The resources of Art are inexhaustible; one need never be so *bourgeois* as to grow old."

"You should see my guardian," said Rome, shaking his head; "he isn't *bourgeois*, but he's old, old—he looks as old as Methuselah."

"Ah, well, a guardian! He has to look old; it's inseparable from the part. I hope you've been looking after him properly; it's a great responsibility, to be a ward."

"I wish I had a guardian!" sighed Barton. "It's so much more business-like. By Jove, the cheques I'd make him write!"

"I think I rather like some old men," continued

Rome reflectively, turning to Brooke, and speaking under cover of the laughter which Barton's simple aspiration had provoked. "Old men with white hair and bent shoulders, tremulous, and benignant. They look as if they had seen and known so much of life, as if the evil of the world was an open book for them. And yet they are so peaceful and simple,—the old men I mean,—so passionless, and powerless; they look as if they had regained the lost innocence of their childhood; they are like children, only their eyes have not that pathetic look of enquiry, of anticipation."

Brooke bowed his head gravely, raising his thin eyebrows a little. "Ah," he said presently, "let us be as old as you like, or as young as you like; but for Heaven's sake, let us give up being middle-aged! How I detest everything middling! Middle Classes! Middle Ages!— A fig for your Golden Mean! it's an invention worthy of a suburban grocer. Let us be extravagant, let us go to extremes; anything is better than moderation. To be moderate, isn't it another name for mediocrity?"

Just before the clock struck ten, the assembly suffered a diminution: Barton, who lived out of college, had recently been "gated," and was obliged to be in his lodgings before that hour (for the benefit of his health, he explained), and some of the other men were "in" for Honour Greats. Brooke had risen as if to take his leave, but Rome easily induced him to resume his occupation of the most comfortable chair in the room, and to fill another pipe. Corbyn also had deferred his departure: he was lying on a sofa, lazily sipping Maraschino from a small Venetian glass, every now and then throwing a word into the eddy of conversation, with a somnolent intelligence.

"You have quite decided to go down this summer?" said Brooke presently, addressing his host. "What do you intend to do? I wish we could go abroad together again. It was very delightful, that last Long!"

"Yes," assented Rome, smiling at the recollection of their pleasant wanderings in Brittany. "I wish you could come. I don't suppose I shall go abroad this summer—unless I run over to Paris to see the Salon."

"Ah, don't do that!" said Brooke. "If you want a dose—I use the word advisedly—a dose of Modern Art, Burlington House is much more accessible, and quite as inferior."

Rome shrugged his shoulders, laughing; while Corbyn was understood to remark that he knew nothing about Art, but found the Academy very edifying,—a sentiment which drew a rebuke from Brooke, who protested that he really shouldn't—he was young enough to know better.

"But what are you going to do?" he persisted, turning to Rome, "when you are not running over to Paris?"

"Oh, I'm going to fix myself up in town. I must find chambers somewhere, I suppose. And I'm afraid I shall have business with my solicitors; I shall be of age, you know, in a few weeks—in September."

"Accept my condolences," interposed Brooke gravely.

"And then I shall have to interview sundry publishers, and see my poems through the press."

"Ah, those charming verses!" said Brooke vaguely. "I'm glad you're going to publish them, though it's so indiscreet!"

"But don't you publish pretty often?" said Corbyn naïvely.

Brooke waved his hand lightly. "Oh, one has to sacrifice one's feelings sometimes. I publish; but I always feel like Lady Godiva about it."

"Do you mean," suggested Rome mischievously,—"do

you mean that people won't look at what you publish; that, except for an occasional Peeping Tom, they turn their heads away?"

Brooke coloured a little, laughing, acknowledged the hit.

"Nowadays," continued Rome, "Peeping Tom would have achieved distinction—as a critic!"

"Ah," said Brooke, "I have often wondered that it has never occurred to people that that objectionable person probably represented the Press: he clearly foreshadowed the American interviewer; he must have been on the staff of the *Coventry Herald*!"

There was a pause in the conversation. Corbyn got up slowly, and declared that he must go; he took a candlestick from the table, and, holding it in front of the bookcase, meditatively contemplated a long row of volumes bound in paper, green, lemon-coloured, grey, and white, subscribed with the names of publishers at Paris and Brussels. Presently he made a selection; it was Stendhal's *Chartreuse*; then he turned to the piano, and began to close it, half regretfully, fingering the notes.

"It's all settled then," said Brooke softly. "You go to London, you establish yourself,—do be careful about your wall-papers!—you publish your poems (excuse the transition — it's not unprecedented, you know),—you write other poems, I suppose, and—*après*?"

"Ah," said Rome, looking at him with a sudden access of fire in his dark eyes, "that's just what I would give anything to be able to tell you!"

Corbyn laughed satirically, rattling off a few bars of the "Wedding March," with intention. Rome smiled at the innuendo; but it seemed to Brooke, who was watching him from under his discreet, delicate eyelids, that the idea was not altogether one which pleased him.

There was a short silence, which Brooke was the first to interrupt.

"Your music has cast a gloom over us," he said, addressing Corbyn, but still watching his host. "The 'Wedding March' always reminds me of draughty churches, fashion-plate brides, ridiculous bridegrooms, and the necessity of effecting the disappearance of small, damp wedges of indigestible cake."

"Yes," admitted Corbyn apologetically, "and the unutterable difficulty one has in finding something original—appropriate—and cheap by way of a wedding present! I'm sorry my music isn't appreciated. But I'm going now; I'm as tired as a costermonger's donkey; I was up till four this morning."

"What, reading?" asked Rome absently as his guest opened the door.

"No," replied Corbyn as he vanished, with his tattered gown draped over one arm, and the pale green volume of Stendhal disposed under the other. "Whist!"

Before the sound of Corbyn's descending footsteps died away, the college clock struck half-past eleven; the atmosphere of the room, in spite of the open windows, was heavy with the faint perfume of the smoke of innumerable cigarettes, and the candles were flickering in their sockets.

"Well," said Brooke presently, "the lamp is going out, the candles are at their last gasp, and it's nearly midnight. I must take the hint; I must positively go. Come with me as far as the gate; see, how graciously the dainty moon looks down upon this solemn city!"

Rome had risen, and the two walked slowly down the creaking wooden staircase, and across the silent quadrangle, towards the narrow side-entrance, where the night-porter was nodding over a crumpled newspaper.

"You will come to see me in town?" said Rome as they parted. "Please say that you will! I need some assurance of that sort to keep my spirits up."

"My dear fellow," said Brooke, "of course I will; do I know too many people who can be relied on in the way of furniture? Be careful about your colours, and I will come and stay with you!"

"How would you like a magenta wall-paper, powdered with footprints in gold?" suggested Rome gravely.

"Heavens!" cried the other, raising his hands with a gesture of horror. "You oughtn't to joke about such things. I shall have to read my poems when I get back, by way of antidote, to keep off the nightmare."

Rome halted, when he reached the seclusion of the inner quadrangle: lights still shone from a few of the windows, and he had a vague idea of seeking companionship for a final pipe before going to bed. While he still hesitated, a door closed noisily, there was a sound of quick, descending footsteps, and two or three dark forms emerged from the obscurity of one of the staircases. As they passed him on their way towards the gate, the light of the dim lamp under which he was standing fell upon their faces, and he recognised one of them as his friend Lord Henry Minaret.

"The very man I wanted to see," he said, greeting him. "Did you get my note?"

"No," said the other; "I haven't been in my rooms since six. I've been dining in the common-room here, with one of your dons, a sort of cousin of mine."

"Oh, it doesn't matter," said Rome. "I wrote to ask if you could drive over to Underwoods with me, on the day after to-morrow?"

"To see old Simeon?" said the other, smiling. "I shall be delighted: I haven't seen the old boy since that summer three years ago, and I've been feeling rather guilty about it: I have never been able to go when you have asked me before."

"Good!" said the other; "I will call for you at Christ Church, then. It's a pretty drive, but I'm rather tired of doing it alone."

"I suppose you've been over a good many times," said Lord Henry, turning back, with a shrewd glance at his friend, as he passed through the narrow gateway. "Ah, well, of course it's different for you! Good-night: I've only just time to get into Peckwater before twelve."

CHAPTER IV

THERE was a somnolent old town some three miles from Underwoods, within an easy walk of it across the fields, and it was here that our two undergraduates chose to put up their horse and cart, in preference to throwing this extra burden upon the hospitality of their old tutor's not too commodious stable. When Henry Minaret joined his friend outside the vaulted courtyard of the "Bear"—he had preferred to smoke a cigarette while the other superintended the comfort of their steed —he found that Adrian's monosyllabic mood, as he sometimes jokingly designated it, which had largely prevailed during their uneventful drive, showed signs of disappearing.

"Let us go easily!" the latter had said, lighting a fresh cigarette from the stump of his old one. "We can talk as we go along. The later we get there, the shorter the interval before luncheon, the embarrassed interval in that grotesque drawing-room. Dear old Simeon's conversation is a trifle less tedious when he has had a glass of sherry."

"As you like," said the other. "I am not anxious to hurry. That mare pulls like a steam-engine. You shall drive her back, my friend!"

Adrian nodded his acquiescence.

"I don't mind," he said. "In the morning, I am not equal to driving, or to anything else. The morning is detestable;—as Gerald Brooke says, there is something indelicate about it: it's like calling on a woman before she has made a toilet. Driving back in the evening will be enchanting."

"Let us leave Brooke at Oxford," said Lord Henry, with a yawn. "One has enough of him there—people *will* quote you his *mots*, I mean. I don't often meet him, but—"

"Ah, you don't do him justice, Harry! No one has ever been so clever. He is clever enough to enjoy the sensation of letting a great number of people think him a fool. By the way, it was at your house that I met him."

"That was none of my doing. He was staying with Mrs. Vesper: she brought him over to Towers to dine. You know her, of course? I remember she was particularly anxious to meet you."

Rome reflected a moment; then he shook his head.

"Not that I remember. What is she like? Identify her for me."

"No good at all," murmured Minaret, struggling for a moment with the wind as he brought a deftly lit match down to the level of his pipe. "I am no hand at descriptions; besides, if you had met her, you would have remembered her. Ask Gerald Brooke to describe her for you. They are great friends; she has a mania for collecting people like that about her."

"It is from Brooke, then, that she has heard of me?" asked Adrian indifferently.

The other nodded. "Very probably that was it."

A moment later he corrected himself. "No, now I remember, of course; she was a friend of your people—of your father."

Rome looked up with a flash of interest.

"She must be an extraordinary woman. My people! there are none of them. My father knew nobody but

Lord Hildebrand, and—the *croupiers* at Monte Carlo. He only knew his brother—professionally!"

"Well, *she* knew him," said Lord Henry resolutely. "And your uncle, the doctor, Sir Egbert. Wasn't he your uncle? In any case you will be sure to come across her in time; she is constantly at Towers. By the way, I haven't the least idea of what your plans are, when you go down. I took it for granted that you knew we should be awfully glad if you would come to us."

"Thanks," said the other; "my plans are very much in the air. I must find some sort of abiding-place in London, I think, first; if it is only to house my belongings. I have thought of the Temple. Corbyn is after rooms there."

"Will you live in London?"

"I expect it is where I shall have the best chance."

"The best chance?"

"Of making a career."

"Oh, a career!" cried the other with his pleasant laugh. "Isn't it a sufficient career to inherit any amount of pounds sterling in a few months' time?"

"Not for me," said Rome, with a sudden flush.

Then he went on rather rapidly, as if he felt a delicacy in touching intimate topics.

"If you want details, I am thinking of my writing; that is the career I mean. I suppose you know that I write?"

His friend nodded.

"Of course I do, old chap. I am sure you write awfully well. Only—"

The other stopped him, with a little mocking gesture of one delicate hand.

"Ah, don't go on, Henry! I know so well what you are going to say; only—one shouldn't let such a trifling interest interfere with the order of one's life. I have heard it all before. Go in for politics seriously—the law, diplomacy, even trade. Be a serious *flâneur*, which is best of all. Take anything you like in the world seriously, except Art. My dear fellow, I will never be the sociable amateur; I will go to perdition first."

Lord Henry laughed with an air of good-natured bewilderment, knocking the ashes out of his pipe as they reached the familiar gate.

"Oh, I say, you can tell all that to Simeon!" he said. "I don't understand it. I don't want you to do anything you don't like; only, come to Towers in the autumn."

Then, as if he had been suddenly struck by something, he added a moment later—

"You will meet Mrs. Vesper there, too, by the way. If you feel like that, she is the very person you want."

They dropped any further consideration of Adrian's intentions as they were shown into the vicarage drawing-room, where they found their former tutor already awaiting them.

Adrian was able to gauge Mr. Simeon's nervousness—it had not been diminished, doubtless, by the fact that he had expected them somewhat earlier—by the eagerness with which he hurried them into the dining-room, where luncheon was immediately served. It reappeared from time to time even during the course of this meal, and was noticeable chiefly in his embarrassment as to the precise attitude which it was right to adopt towards his guests. He settled it, finally, by resuming his old part of the inveterate don, questioning the young men copiously about their lectures, and the result of their schools, permitting himself to show, not for the first time, a little mild surprise (it was hardly an expostulation) at Rome's unenterprising "pass." He had one pupil still, he went on to explain—an agreeable youth, who was now away for his holidays. It was through the Duke's recommendation that he had been sent there; he hoped Lord Henry would remember him to his father, that he enjoyed always the same wonderful health: he was under so many obligations to the Duke. And he turned to Adrian, by a sort of after-thought, to enquire after Lord Hildebrand, but was obviously relieved to discover that his former pupil's relations with the notorious old nobleman were still purely formal and impersonal, conducted through the safe channel of a banking account. He passed on to speak of his work, the monograph and exhaustive commentary on the fragments of Simonides, upon which he had been occupied for the last ten years, and which was still very far from completion. As he dilated upon it at great length, Adrian allowed his attention to wander, finding something which irritated him in the old gentleman's placid attitude towards time, which permitted him still serenely to contemplate postponement, at an age when most men are looking back upon accomplishment—or else have grown resigned to the lack of it,—of what was, after all, the absorbing labour of his life. He contrasted the old scholar's equanimity, not without a trace of envy, with his own eagerness and impatience, his quick impulses, and still quicker disgusts. He was already sensible that his own disabilities and qualifications were essentially different; his creative eagerness, already quickened within him, and, seeking expression in a laborious, almost painful effort after perfectly right form, was not stronger than his impulse towards the direct and concrete experiences of life. And his dissatisfactions in the way of art (he himself was his own severest critic) would necessarily be akin to his irritation against the æsthetically disappointing element in life, in which so many tedious things must always jostle one. No, he could not really envy Simeon; he chose deliberately the elements which, in a life such as Simeon's, had been rejected or ignored; they seemed essential of the most excellent choice. To be concerned with high passions, to live as fully and intensely as one could, rather than as long and as peacefully as one might,—it seemed to him that it was only under such conditions that the born artist could properly work out his salvation. The fulness of one's life, the fineness of one's impressions, the multiplicity of one's sensations; here, it seemed to him, was the rough material out of which grew magnificently the ultimate achievement of one's art. In a world where everything is priced, he was not ignorant that for a satisfaction so fine as this one might have heavily to pay. The price of it would be, largely, the exhaustion, the nerve distress which such a choice entails; it would be suffering, and ultimately, perhaps, the lassitude of an old age—supposing that old age was in the affair—not tempered by the calmly vegetable past, devoid of memories, which sustained Simeon.

The old gentleman had turned to Adrian, for the second time, enquiringly before the latter realised that a move was in contemplation, and that they had been waiting for his assent. He roused himself, with a visible effort, in time to excuse himself from accompanying the others to a church in the neighbourhood which had been recently restored, and which Minaret in the course of conversation had recklessly expressed a wish to see.

"The fact is," said Adrian, "I must go and set my house in order. I have hardly been in it since my aunt's death, and I think of trying to let it, when I come of age. It has struck me that there may be some of her papers which ought to be looked through."

Mr. Simeon acknowledged the necessity of this duty, with a decorous sigh, while Rome's friend glanced across at him, arching his eyebrows with an amused, half-sceptical smile.

"Don't be too long—taking the inventory, Adrian!" he said. "We must leave at a reasonable time."

Adrian smiled vaguely, remotely, with no appearance of deprecating the irony in his friend's tone. He had proffered his excuse, his decent pretext, as politeness required; and it was not in his temper to be troubled any further to consider whether people found it acceptable or not. It had been genuinely in his intention, moreover, to pay a visit to his old home; although the disposal of his aunt's papers had very little part in his motive: he had an appointment there,—it had not seemed to him necessary to explain that to Mr. Simeon, —but it was one which he had no mind to miss. When the other two left him at the gate, the house lying on their road, he found that it still wanted half an hour to the time at which he had asked Sylvia to meet him. He dangled the bunch of keys, which he had obtained from a cottage on the way, irresolutely in his hand for a moment, before he surmounted his curious reluctance to enter. A musty smell saluted him as he passed into the hall; the dining-room was quite dark, and reeked of damp and mildew: its sombreness was so essential of the room that it did not seem sensibly lighter, when he flung back the heavy shutters, and let the rich sunshine stream in through the long French window, which opened on to a garden even more neglected than the domain which bordered the front of the house. For some minutes he stood there, looking at it all, at the heavy, solid furniture, at the dark old pictures, family portraits and the like, which disputed with cobwebs the honourable places on the stained walls. It was at once full of a sort of disused familiarity, and oddly remote. After a time it gave him a feeling of oppression: it was as though the acrimony of his aunt had resisted disintegration, and remained permeating the air; there was an intangible odour of decay there which the sunshine could never touch. He stepped out into the garden, and wandered down, over the uneven grass, towards the time-worn sun-dial, in the shadow of which he threw himself down. And after a while he became conscious, as he had never been before, of how utterly his old life had passed away: it was too unreal and ghostly even to be remembered with dislike. Nothing remained of it but Sylvia, Sylvia Drew, the little girl with whom he had grown up. She would presently be with him. From his place where he lay on the daisies, he would see her coming across the field: the thought lent serenity to his meditations as he waited for her, conscious, not unpleasantly, of how deep a disappointment it would be to him if she should fail. Yes! the very blankness of his older past, his solitariness in the present, made it more delightful that the constant friendship of this child remained. He was not always thinking of her. Since he had been at Oxford, when a world of new sensations and ideas had opened out to him, when his aspirations and his ambitions had taken definite shape, she had been often forgotten; and then, suddenly, into the stress of his mental life (his intelligence just then was living an almost passionate life of its own) her image had intruded, and it seemed to him that she had never been less forgotten than when he had appeared to remember her least. And yet, the visible signs of their relation were very few and rare: fitfully they had corresponded; half a dozen times, in the passage of three years, he had ridden over to see her; and there was nothing in their letters, or in their meetings, which the world might not have seen. On almost the first of these visits, indeed, he became conscious that she had changed: she had greeted him, for the first time in their history, with shyness; so that, for a while, their talk, which had once been so spontaneous and direct, was complicated by a certain new reserve. And if there was some sorrow in this tacit recognition, which they made, of the passing of her childhood; if Adrian could not contemplate the loss of his frank comrade, to whom alone he had once confided his most intimate thoughts, without a pang, he was none the less sensible of certain sweet thrills, which were like omens of compensation in the future. From henceforth her memory came to him touched with exquisite possibilities, delightful in their vagueness, far too delightful to be defined. It was a memory which he liked to call up at incongruous seasons: it wrapped him away from the immediate occasion in a silence, which his company had come to accept as one of the eccentricities of a man whose extreme promise entitled his eccentricities to respect. And yet, in spite of the rare pleasure which he found in her company, he had not hitherto explicitly owned to himself that he was in love.

At the first glimpse of her light dress through the trees, he had risen to his feet; then he walked down rapidly to meet her. They shook hands in silence: he was hardly conscious of how long the greeting lasted, as he stood looking at her, finding in her face something more than the old charm; conveyed there by a touch of pallor, of tiredness, perhaps, "an hour's defect of the rose," which refined upon it, which seemed scarcely accountable, in that fine air, until she had explained, how her mother had been for a long time ailing, and she had been kept constantly by her side.

He directed their way towards a stone bench, and implicitly she followed him.

"It's very good of you to come, Sylvia! I felt sure that you would, though: especially, as it may be my last visit for some time to come. I told you that I am leaving Oxford for good? Won't you sit down?"

She took the place at his side, and for a little while there was silence. At last she said nervously—

"It is because it is very likely the last time that I am here. I don't know whether it's quite right to meet you in this way! It's too much like a secret meeting. I don't like that."

He took up one of her hands, which lay passively on her lap, and gently caressed it.

"Not secret," he said, "simply private. We are not hiding from anybody; we have nothing to hide: we merely don't wish to be interrupted. That is why I asked you to come here, instead of fetching you myself. Good heavens! aren't we old enough friends by this time to enjoy each other's company, without embarrassing ourselves with interlopers? Is it the first time we have been alone together?"

"It is different now," she persisted; "things are changed."

"Is our friendship changed? I thought that was to be a longer affair."

"No," said the girl simply, "that can't change, for my part. Only, our friendship ought to be old enough to be just as deep and true if we make up our minds that we can never see very much of one another."

"Why should we make up our minds to such an absurd thing? My dear girl, where have you found these ideas? They are quite new, and very bad at that. Do be reasonable, Sylvia! There are so many things I want to say, and such a little time to say them in. Minaret will be coming to fetch me, before I have begun."

She heard him passively, while he briefly unfolded his plans to her, his intention of throwing himself into the literary life, his residence in London, his projects of travel: and, in the midst of it all, he arranged that their meetings should be continued, whenever she would allow him to come down and see her at Underwoods, if it was only for an hour. He made a great point of these excursions, and, indeed, it was not only when, as now, he was actually under the charm of her personal presence, that life without her seemed impossible and cruel. But there was none the less a note of unreality in his words, of which he could not but be dimly conscious, and of which the consciousness irritated him, against society, against circumstance, against himself. Lightly as he glossed over them, there were difficulties in the way of this relation, differences which grew larger as one looked at them close. When he had finished, she came back to them with the same mild persistence. And he credited her for her good sense in that she recognised them, even while he resented her tranquillity, which held them for insurmountable, and acquiesced.

"Things are changed," she repeated. "Even if we are not, we must look at them. I have been thinking—"

He gave a little, half-mocking, half-tender laugh, which she answered by withdrawing the hand which he had retained. She locked her two hands together impulsively, and continued with an air of new seriousness which made her argument almost a prayer.

"Listen to me, Adrian! for both our sakes. Don't treat me as a child—I'm—I am not the little girl I was; I am a woman; I am thinking of your position, your place in the world. I can see things now, the difference between us. We are altogether different: even your way of talking is different to mine, and mother's. People would think it odd, to say the least, if they knew what friends we are. However you may like me, you would feel that, and be ashamed. Your friends would make you feel it. You are one of the gentry; and it's with them, with lords and ladies that you must mix. I'm—just a little country girl that you played with when we were children. Now, we are grown up, and we must go our different ways, with our own folk. It is better so! We can feel very kindly to each other still, but it must be apart."

His eyes had never left her face while she made this hasty little speech, the sense of which was apparent to him, although he hardly heard her words. His rapt attention was for her air, her grace, her beauty, which had never seemed to him more touching and pure. What impressed him in her little argument was not its substance, which seemed to him so inadequate, but a discovery which he made while she spoke, that her love for him was a vital thing with her, as unselfish as it was complete. Underneath her air of tranquillity, of resignation, with which she wished to reassure him, she was all the time intimately excited, was passionately pleading against herself. And all that gave him a singular insight into the issues which were at stake. All his life hung on a hair. The sentimental sops which his worldly prudence had induced him to throw himself, in vague promises, and still more indefinite procrastinations, had suddenly ceased to be satisfying; they were as dry as stale bread. She was a woman, as she had said; not a little girl, with whom one amicably philandered, but a woman, primitive of Eve, with a charm to him unsurpassed and unapproachable, for whom he had an absorbing passion; and it was heart for heart with them, and the worship of his whole body, henceforward, or nothing at all. He was conscious of those differences of which she spoke: she had never seemed more rustical, more separate from his own order and degree, than when she had enunciated them. Yes! there were even intonations in her voice, a selection in her words, which a "lady" (how furiously he despised himself for making the cheap comparison!) would not have used. But there was one thing of which he had a consciousness still more vivid—that she was a grand creature, far too precious to lose, that it was impossible to let her go.

It was amazing how far he had moved in a very few seconds, how much he had lived. The girl saw it in his face, which was visibly paler, as he leaned over towards her; and she shrank back, half afraid.

"Never, never! You must marry me, my darling! That is what I meant to say."

She shook her head imperatively, resisting his endeavour to draw her to him, but with a weakness which told him how much she distrusted her strength, until even her will melted to his triumph, and their lips leaped together. An instant later—to both of them it seemed far more than this—she had disengaged herself, and stood, rosy now to her finger tips, shivering with the incipient terror of a young girl who has looked, for the first time, upon the face of love.

"Ah, why did you do that? No, no, it was my fault, *I kissed you*." Her voice drooped to the shadow of a whisper, and as she faced him there, with her girlish head bowed, in virginal confusion, like a rose that the wind had touched too roughly, she seemed so adorable that he could only move towards her, with protests and asseverations, for a repetition of the offence.

But suddenly, by a common impulse, they drew apart.

A fresh baritone voice floated down the air to them, with the tag of an American student song that Adrian recognised—

> "There is a tavern, in a town, in a town,
> And there my true love sits him down, sits him down,
> And never thinks of me,
> And nev—er thinks of m—e."

Destiny, in the shape of Lord Henry Minaret, with a cigar in his mouth, and a reminder that twenty miles still separated them from home, had intervened. He bowed to Sylvia as he approached, and after giving Rome his message, turned at once on his heel, as though he had a delicacy in assisting at their *adieux*: in spite of this piece of tact, however, Adrian saw, and his face darkened ominously, that his friend had no intention of leaving them alone.

He could only hold the girl's hand for a moment, before he dropped it with a sigh; but it seemed to him that, into his silent pressure of it, he had cast the eloquence of many words. So that it was in answer to this greeting, rather than to his formal good-bye, that he took her whispered disclaimer.

"No, no! Do you want to kill me with shame? Forget that, Adrian! I would die sooner than hinder you, and I should—I should— It was our good-bye; that's all. Our real good-bye."

He did not answer, or restrain her; it was not till long afterwards that he could remind himself that in those words she had effectually given him his freedom. There were tears in her voice; and he could not trust himself to speak. He allowed her hastily to pass them; then he caught up his friend. Minaret glanced up at him, curiously—and held his peace. It was only an hour or so later, when they were well on their homeward road, that he ventured upon a comment. He had a horror of meddling, and was aware that there were many men upon whom the process might be more comfortably used than upon his difficult friend. But he too had received an illumination that afternoon; the thing was on his mind, and, after all, he liked Adrian well enough to risk his anger.

"My dear fellow!" he said at last, leaning towards him, lightly touching his arm—"Don't think me impertinent if I give you a bit of a warning,—upon my word, I speak from experience,—do, do take care!"

Adrian glanced at him with a look of intentional mystification.

"Do you mean, of the mare?"

"I know you are driving vilely; but I don't care for the mare. Oh, smash her up and the beastly trap too, if it relieves you. You can afford to pay for 'em. But for God's sake, don't play old Harry with your life, and another! I—I have nothing to gain by saying this. Throw up that little game at Underwoods: retreat with honour!"

He could see, in the vague flicker of the carriage lamps, the dark flush of anger which crossed his friend's face.

"It's not what you think. Sylvia—she's the best girl in the world! Please don't forget that!"

"I don't say a word against her—Heaven forbid! You misunderstand me. I am sure she is an excellent girl. Only—well, you must see, she is not your equal. It isn't even a kindness to marry her; it's damnation for both of you. Oh!" he went on after a moment, relieved at his friend's silence, believing in his good-natured density that he had made a point, "I know what I am talking of. Let me tell you the modern version of King Cophetua. You know Lord Altyshaw—"

But Rome interrupted him, bringing the lash of his whip down fiercely and repeatedly on the mare's flanks, until she leaped forward and the harness creaked. For a moment, as they scudded along over the uneven road, with its borders of yellowing bracken, covering a ditch on each side, the well-meaning adviser had enough to do to retain his seat. When the pace slackened, Adrian said sharply—Lord Henry could not be certain that he was not addressing the mare—"Be quiet, you fool!" A moment later he went on more calmly, as if he were ashamed of his irritation, but with an increasing lassitude.

"I know you mean well, Harry! But it's quite idle. You must leave me to settle this matter with my conscience, or consciences,—I have several which you know nothing about, and wouldn't understand. Don't suppose that half of myself is not dinning your suggestions into me with twenty times more force than you can do. They may be right, or they may be wrong, and in either case I may act upon them. And I daresay that will be the worst day's work I shall have done in my life."

"At least," asked Lord Henry, after a pause in which he seemed to be considering these statements without having struck any very lucid gleam from them,—"at least, you can tell me that you are not bound?"

The other shook his head.

"Upon your honour?"

Adrian reflected for some minutes silently.

"Upon my honour, I don't think I am bound."

CHAPTER V

LORD HILDEBRAND read Adrian's poems when they appeared: he found them lying at his elbow one evening, when he was taking coffee at his club: and there was something so attractive about the little volume, with its binding of apple-green linen, stamped with a design of daisies in pale gold, that he took it up almost involuntarily; and when he perceived the author's name upon the elaborate title-page, a kind of curiosity, stronger than his dislike for reading by artificial light, induced the old gentleman to draw his chair nearer to an electric lamp, and to glance at the first few pages, even to make hasty incursions among the last. Afterwards, when he had played his modest game of whist, and two or three more of picquet, and was strolling leisurely homewards through the cool lamplit solitude of St. James's Square, he was surprised to find himself unable to deny that, although his guardianship was happily at an end, he still took more than a passing interest in the boy (so he thought of him); that he felt himself somewhat weakly unable to turn his eyes away, to wash his hands of his career. That maundering old parson, the Rector—or Vicar, was he?—of Underwoods, had been right, then, the boy was clever: it was not everyone who could write verses with something more vital in them than vague aspirations on the subject of an unattainable mistress, or rhymed descriptions of Arcadian scenery. A poet! It was a long time since he had known such a being. And a poet with a grouse-moor, and a yacht, and a row of tin boxes at his bankers: such a person, with youth added to his other advantages, was assuredly not a bird to be found in every thicket.

Lord Hildebrand's first meeting with Adrian, more than three years ago, at Underwoods, had left him a vague, and speedily obliterated impression, of a somewhat ugly, uncommunicative boy, with a pair of curious eyes, and a habit of abstraction, which almost amounted to evasion. Their last interview—it had taken place only a few weeks ago, at Messrs. Featherstone's offices in Lincoln's Inn Fields—had to some extent revived the earlier impression, especially so far as the eyes and the abstraction were concerned. His Lordship, leaning forward in an easy-chair, at the side of Mr. Gregory Featherstone's table,—Mr. Featherstone was his co-trustee of Rupert Rome's will,—had found in his emancipated ward the only interesting object available for contemplation; for want of something better to do, he had devoted some twenty minutes to a discreet, side-long scrutiny of the boy, and he had ended by admitting to himself that the personality which he had been studying, while the sedate, voluble lawyer prosed with unction about rentals, and mortgages, and transfers of stocks and shares, was an extremely puzzling one, and defied his perspicuity.

"If you want to ask any questions," Lord Hildebrand had said, at the beginning of the interview, with a humorous glance at the boy, "If anything isn't quite clear to you, don't let scruples deter you from asking: I shan't be able to answer you, but Mr. Featherstone will: it's all far from clear to me; I never could understand accounts, and if I read everything I signed, as I believe well-regulated people do, I should never have time for anything else. I always sign anything which

Mr. Featherstone asks me to sign,—except cheques off my own account,—it comes to the same thing in the end, and saves trouble."

Rome smiled, admitting candidly that the neat documents and columns of figures which lay before him on the table, appeared to him entirely unintelligible; he was perfectly satisfied; he suggested that Mr. Featherstone should let him have a simple statement, showing roughly the amount of his income from all sources, and the deductions to be made for such outgoings as were beyond his immediate control.

"Unintelligible!" Lord Hildebrand had said, firing a parting shot from the doorway. "That's what the legal profession exists for,—to make things unintelligible, and to pretend to explain them!"

Mr. Featherstone laughed indulgently as the door closed upon the old gentleman and his snuff-box: it was nearly half a century since his father, the founder of the firm, had rescued Lord Hildebrand and his newly-acquired estates from an importunate horde of money-lenders, and the forty years had been a profitable period for Messrs. Featherstone: a client who lived slightly beyond a liberal income was likely, while he lasted, to be a good friend to his solicitors, and, in addition to answering this description, Lord Hildebrand had been the means of introducing to the firm an even more remunerative client in the shape of Adrian's father, Rupert Rome.

Lord Hildebrand's hilarity had modified itself into the semblance of grave complacency which he generally carried for the outer world before he reached the time-worn pavement of Lincoln's Inn Fields, and as he stepped delicately into his attendant brougham, he began to congratulate himself.

"I'm well out of that," he said. "Thank goodness,

his father didn't make the years of the boy's majority twenty-five! With eyes like that—his father's eyes, how well I remember them!—that youngster might have played the very devil, and let me—his anxious guardian—in for all sorts of bother. If he wants to now, he may—it might be amusing."

And now, as it appeared from very tangible proofs which lay upon club tables, and adorned the windows of purveyors of *belles-lettres*, Adrian Rome was a poet! Not a sentimental *amateur* who wrote sweet things in fashionable ladies' albums, but a professed verse-maker, a poet who was published. Lord Hildebrand was puzzled again; in spite of notable exceptions, instances to the contrary, he could not quite rid himself of the notion that, to be a professed artist in this department, one ought to live penuriously in a garret, and to be, socially, an impossible person.

It must not, however, be supposed that his Lordship allowed himself to take more than a desultory interest in Adrian Rome and his incipient career. Lord Hildebrand was really concerned about nobody except himself; his speculations as to the future of his old comrade's son, as foreshadowed by this last, and for him somewhat startling development (startling, though, after all, it was what one might have expected of the only son of the union of one of the most talented actresses with one of the most gentlemanly *roués* of the century),—his speculations on this subject were of the idlest, and most impartial nature. He wondered about Adrian, as a man, observing a cloud in a summer sky, might cast in his mind the probabilities of rain. Arrived at his lodging in Half-Moon Street, on this October evening, Lord Hildebrand forgot his former ward in a somnolent perusal of the latest betting on the Cambridgeshire; after which he made trial upon paper of a new martingale, with which he hoped, in the coming winter, to avenge himself upon the bank at Monte Carlo; and when, finally, the ancient peer retired to bed, armed with a well-worn volume of Voltaire, his placid dreams were not disturbed by any recurrence of the youthful poet's image.

A few days later, Rome, on his return from a short cruise in his newly-acquired yacht, found among the letters which had accumulated during his absence (they were chiefly polite offers from money-lenders in Cork Street) a note from Lord Hildebrand, an invitation to dinner at an early date. The recipient of this unexpected honour whistled softly, throwing the note across the table to his companion, Corbyn.

"That comes of not having your letters forwarded," said Corbyn, when he had grasped the situation. "If you had known of this, we might have stuck to the *Anonyma* for another week; we might have run over to Brittany, and dodged the venerable nobleman."

Rome looked at him for a moment, smiling absently.

"Yes," he admitted; "but how about term? Haven't you been rousing my envy by telling me that it begins to-morrow, that you have got to go up?"

Corbyn shrugged his shoulders loftily.

"Oh, that's a detail—of the slightest. I should have suggested to the Dean that we were detained in the Channel by contrary winds, or the king's enemies; that we had run aground on the Goodwin Sands, or been arrested for smuggling. Shall you go? He can't make you—he isn't your guardian now?"

Adrian smiled again. "He's very interesting—as a study, a document."

"Oh, well, I've never seen him, you know; my impressions of him are entirely derived from you. You didn't always love him! He probably wants to rook you at écarté, or to sell you a horse. By Jove!" added the ingenuous youth, sinking luxuriously into a capacious easy-chair. "What splendid rooms these are for being lazy in! One can see that Brooke had something to do with choosing them. I don't think I shall live in the Temple, after all; I couldn't read here, not even for the Bar; my only chance will be to get diggings in Bayswater, or Earl's Court, or some ghastly place of that sort."

Rome's expression was one of absent-minded tolerance, as he stood facing his indolent guest, in a favourite attitude, with his back to the fire, one foot on the brass fender, and his shoulders against the mantelshelf.

"Think of the people Lord Hildebrand must have known," he said softly. "Why, he owns to being sixty. I expect he's a perfect store-house of scandal about bygone heroes."

"And heroines," suggested Corbyn. "By all accounts, especially heroines. Yes, I daresay he's amusing if you can make him talk. But I shouldn't like to try. It would be like cross-examining a crocodile. What shall we do? Remember, I go up to-morrow — barring accidents. Let's dine somewhere, and go to see the Modern Actor,—at the El-Dorado, for choice. There's a new ballet; I must have something to talk about to my tutor, and he likes ballets."

The motion was carried without much discussion, and the two friends presently adjourned to exchange their yachting apparel for attire more suited to the requirements of the expedition which they had in view.

Now that he had published his poems, purchased and refitted his yacht, shaken off his guardian, and found a home for his *bibelots*, Rome was beginning to find time hang a little heavily on his hands. He could not quite make up his mind as to what the next move should be;

he had, in fact, a nervous horror of making up his mind; he expected the future to arrange itself for him without the necessity for cogitation on his part. It seemed to him that if he was to be called upon to do more than acquiesce, than glide with the current of events, his freedom was only slavery in disguise. It was the tyranny of little things which he found oppressive. To be able to choose one's path in life, broadly, without the fear of encountering inconvenient barriers,—that was certainly a glorious privilege; but how irksome it was to have to select a train for to-morrow's journey; to order one's dinner; to discuss trousers with one's tailor, rents with one's solicitor, politics with one's barber! Rome's attitude towards this side of life may perhaps be partially illuminated by saying that it seemed to him quite natural, and entirely commodious, that he should allow Corbyn to dispose of his evenings for him when they were together, just as he permitted Brooke to dictate to him on the colour of his hangings, the design of his wall-papers. It saved so much trouble.

Peter Corbyn was the first to reappear in the room in which they had been sitting. It was already growing dark, and the window out of which he bent his contemplative gaze was shaded by the almost intrusive branches of one of the tall plane-trees which stood in the court below. The rooms, with their low ceilings, dark, panelled walls, and florid, wooden chimney-pieces, were on the second floor of one of the oldest buildings in New Court, Middle Temple. Adrian had become enamoured of the view which they commanded,—the little, irregular terraces below, the solemn plane-trees, the whispering fountain, with its enclosure of unhappy laurels, the brown sixteenth-century dining-hall, and the grey, modern library, both so much like chapels; and, in pleasant contrast to all the sombre, soot-stained stone and brick, the green, brilliant garden, running down to the Embankment and the flashing river. There were seats under the largest plane-tree, that which shaded the windows, and the porter's children were playing about them, enjoying the immunity of a Long Vacation.

A door opened, and Rome entered the room, to signify, presently, that he was ready. The two sallied forth, and as they passed through the courtyard on their way into the Strand, Corbyn had an opportunity for observing that the porter's children were less charming than they had appeared from his post above.

Corbyn had a passion for things theatrical, which Rome only imperfectly shared. Corbyn read the *Era* with unfailing regularity; he was desperately in love with at least half a dozen charming actresses; and he even confessed to having waited, more than once, outside a gloomy portal, under a lamp labelled "Stage Door," to observe the passage of his divinities. He took a delight in studying members of the dramatic profession "off the stage," in being able to point them out in the streets, at public places. It was at his suggestion that the two friends, who had lunched at midday on board the yacht in Southampton Water, made choice of a populous restaurant in the Strand as the scene of their early dinner; the place and the hour alike being favourable for the gratification of his particular form of hero-worship. When they had appropriated one of the little tables which were grouped at the most favoured end of the vast, brilliant hall,—in the long proportions and elaborate decoration of which they found a striking resemblance to the saloon of a gigantic ocean steamer,— Corbyn was gratified to observe that they were positively surrounded by the boyish, smooth-faced men, and haggard, strangely attired women, pale and bright-eyed, in whom he took so great an interest;—all on pleasantly intimate terms with each other, and, as it seemed, on a hardly less friendly footing with the waiters. Rome lent a tolerant ear while his boon-companion, with something of the air of an enthusiastic collector before a case of butterflies, passed their neighbours discreetly in review, pointing out at this table the nightly exponent of injured virtue drinking Chianti with the villain of her own melodrama; at that, a lady who made the income of a Q.C. in good practice out of the humour of her winks and the artistic frenzy of her capers.

"I wish I could go on the stage!" sighed Corbyn presently, when they had reached the contemplative period of coffee and cigarettes. "I'd rather be a great actor than Solicitor-General or Lord Chancellor. Oh, it's easy enough to say, Why don't you? You don't know my people. In Wales they don't understand these things: they don't know how respectable the stage is, nowadays; its intimacy with the Church is not revealed to them; they would smile incredulously if you compared it favourably with the Bar. I've got an aunt—a very useful, dutiful sort of aunt—who would go into hysterics, and send for her solicitor, incontinently, if she knew that I was dining, from choice, in close proximity to a horde of miserable mummers: she wouldn't be more scandalised if she heard that I had been hobnobbing with the devil!"

Rome shrugged his shoulders. "I've thought of it, sometimes. But I don't think it would do: in these days of long runs it must be a frightful bore. No, I should prefer to write the plays, and see other people act them."

"Good!" said Corbyn; "you write a play and I'll make my *début* in it, as third villain, or a comic policeman:

so shall we achieve renown together. I'm glad to hear you talk about writing plays; it's all because I dragged you into this inspiring atmosphere. I was afraid you rather despised the theatre: for me, it's really the only thing which makes life worth living—'the blessed fictive world,' as Henry James makes somebody call it: I should like to have a permanent stall at every theatre in London, including the what d'you call 'ems, —the transpontines!"

"Then you'd better be a critic," suggested Rome; "you won't see any plays if you go on the stage!"

"Ah, I should never win laurels as a critic: I should be too complimentary: I should praise everything, and everybody, indiscriminately, like a country cousin at the Academy. It's the atmosphere, the association! I revel in the very aspect of the drop-scene, the sound of the first notes of the overture; and when the performance is over, I only half console myself by reflecting that I can come again!"

Adrian laughed gently, lighting a cigar and signalling to the waiter.

"Ah, well, then you must only criticise *my* plays: your panegyrics will have the distinction of being uncorroborated. No, let me square up for this. You shall pay for the supper. We will walk, it's not far, and the streets are so charming in the lamplight. It's only in the daytime that London is hard, prosaic, business-like: the nights give me an impression of a comfortable fairyland: there is something so restful and caressing about the jewelled, dusky vista of long streets. I am thinking, quite seriously, of making day my night, and breakfasting when the sun sets."

Corbyn sighed appreciatively, "Lucky devil, to be able to think of such things! How pleasant it would be to sleep away the vulgar, bustling daylight in the

Temple, waking now and then for an instant to pity, drowsily, the poor beggars toiling over briefs and consultations—conferences, don't they call them?—all around you!"

"They serve strange gods," said Rome, throwing back his head. "They can't help themselves, I suppose: I pity them; but I don't like to think of them."

"Dash it all," Corbyn protested, "we can't all be artists, poets, you know. You may pity me a little if you like, but I draw the line there."

The other laughed, taking his friend's arm, as they paused before crossing the wide road, full of a chaos of flying wheels, near Piccadilly Circus.

"Oh, you," he said vaguely, "you're not one of them yet: I'm going to make you go on the stage, or collaborate with me in a five-act tragedy. Say the word, and I'll take a theatre for you to-morrow!"

They passed quickly out of the narrow street, where a long line of heterogeneous vehicles waited near the stage door of the El-Dorado, into the resplendent corridor of the music hall, dazzled for a moment by the almost brutal brilliance of light and colour which pervaded everything, from the moulded ceiling to the thickly carpeted floor. They paid for two stalls, and presently found themselves in an atmosphere full of the smoke of cigars, the clamour of rollicking music, the hum of subdued conversation and louder laughter, and the roll of intermittent applause.

"By Jove," said Corbyn, glancing at a programme, "we're in luck; we've just missed those two people who knock each other about with thick sticks, by way of giving point to their inane attempts at humour."

"I know them!" said the other expressively. "Thank goodness! The ballet comes next, doesn't it? I like a ballet, one needn't pay any attention to it!"

When the curtain had fallen upon the last tableau of the ballet, and they had seen a disquieting gentleman tie himself into elaborate knots and sit upon his head, the two friends decided that, for the time being, their histrionic taste was satisfied. They adjourned, presently, to a neighbouring restaurant, where they found quite a small party of men of their acquaintance celebrating the close of the Long Vacation in midnight revelry; and it was not before the small hours of the morning had become numerically of some dignity that they sought their monastic bedrooms in New Court.

CHAPTER VI

THE French man-servant who admitted Adrian into the house in Half-Moon Street, where Lord Hildebrand occupied a small but unimpeachable flat, assured him that his Lordship would not be five minutes; and that period had barely elapsed when the Earl appeared, looking very old and delicate in his careful evening dress. Adrian had looked forward to this intimate dinner with the ambiguous old man with some curiosity; without knowing why, he believed it would be something of an occasion, that he would see his former guardian in a new light. To see him at all, he reflected, was an occasion of sufficient interest; for, whatever view one might take of him, the Earl had abundantly the faculty of appealing to one's curiosity. And his curiosity just then was Adrian's guiding principle: it was always eager and awake; an appetite which could not be sufficiently sated; and Lord Hildebrand was certainly the finest morsel which had yet been set before it. Adrian wondered, as he sat opposite him, at the brilliant little table (the dinner was at once exquisite and simple, like the manners of the host), if the old man knew how interesting he was,—he had so much the air of taking himself for granted, with the rest. Certainly, he was curiously unique; if it had not seemed a trifle absurd to attribute any share in his elaborate composition to nature, one had been tempted to say that nature, having produced him, had thrown away the mould. At least if there had been others of his type, he was the last who was left, the rest had gone their way, sacrificed to a more ethical though less picturesque civilisation, with gallantry, and the duello, highwaymen, and the peruke. He was so composed, and fragile, and rare: he had so eminently that well-bred assurance of a man who has been at home in the world from the first, that Adrian, knowing a little of his history, could hardly believe that he had always been against it, and was now literally under its ban. In the face of all that, his composure, the smooth impenetrable surface, like a cuirass of bright steel, that he presented to one, seemed the more admirable. Adrian wondered what was his secret, his principle of existence in a generation which had ceased to tolerate his traditions (whatever these might be, they were hardly those of to-day), and decided at last that it was only his irony which kept him alive. This was so pervasive, less perhaps in his speech, which was highly urbane, than in the impartiality of his mirthless smile, that the young man wondered if his interest, even when he seemed to be most interested, was ever sincere; whether it did not exist simply for the gratification of mental comparisons, for which his direct contact with the historic past offered him such scope. It might not be true, but at least it was well affected, he decided at last, as he found himself, before they had reached dessert, talking almost intimately with his host, who complimented him deftly on his muse, made discreet inquiries as to his plans, and listened to his answers with the respectful attention of a parliamentary candidate on his trial. Lord Hildebrand's faculty of conversation was notoriously great; but to-night he seemed for once to have suppressed it, to be actuated solely by a desire to make his companion talk. It was not until the Duke of

Turretshire was mentioned, and Adrian's projected visit to his son, that he allowed himself any latitude of comment.

"It is a very good house, though rather too political. The Duke is my brother-in-law, by the way, although I hardly know him. He is reported to take very serious views of life. A most worthy person."

His tone was impassive, but there was still an accent in it which compelled Adrian to stand a little on his defence.

"It is Henry Minaret whom I go to see. You remember, we were at Underwoods together. Besides, I have nowhere else in particular to go. I shall have a fortnight's cruise beforehand."

"You have a yacht?"

Adrian nodded.

"It was the first thing I thought of. I have always been immensely in love with the sea: and I determined to have a boat of my own. She is lying at Southampton."

"It is natural," said Lord Hildebrand, a little absently. "It's in your blood. It was a mania with your father —yachting." Then he asked—

"Where will you go?"

"I shall cruise in the Channel. I may run over to Guernsey, or St. Malo. Then I shall work round to Norfolk—to Towers."

"And after Towers?" Lord Hildebrand inquired.

Adrian glanced vaguely across the room; a sort of cloud passed over his face.

"I don't like making plans so far ahead. I shall probably travel: there are a good many places I want to see."

The silent man-servant brought in black coffee and liqueurs: he placed a box of cigarettes before Adrian, who lit one at the flame of a silver spirit-lamp, while Lord Hildebrand meditatively took snuff.

"Well," he said, when they were once more left alone together, "if your travels bring you to Paris, you must come and see me. That is where I may be said to live. They *must* take you to Paris, you know," he added, with his indefinable smile; "and if you don't want them to end there, as mine have done, it is from there that they had better begin. Will you travel alone, by the way, or with a friend—with Henry Minaret?"

Adrian remarked that he was afraid Minaret would be too much engrossed: he had his eye on the House already, was nursing a constituency.

Lord Hildebrand shrugged his shoulders with humorous tolerance; and his gesture alone would have told Adrian how greatly Paris had been his home.

"Ah, I forgot: that family is devoted to Parliament from their cradle; the younger sons too. Perhaps, though, you will follow his example, when you have travelled enough?"

"I think not," said Rome. "I fear it is hardly my vocation."

The old man smiled.

"I should have said that also, but I never pretend to be sure. You are very happily situated, *par exemple*: you have a fortune, and, I believe, very little land. You have no houses to keep up."

Adrian admitted that with the exception of his aunt's house and a few hundred acres at Underwoods, and some farms and shooting in Inverness, he was unhampered with real estate.

"I congratulate you," said Lord Hildebrand humorously. "I have my Irish estates. I believe they are very beautiful,—I know they are very expensive,—perhaps if you ever travel so far as that, you will visit them."

"You have never been to see them?" asked Adrian laughingly.

"Ah," said the Earl, taking another pinch of rappee, "in my time we hadn't your large ideas, we never went out of civilisation."

Presently he asked his guest if he played picquet or écarté, two games which, he regretted to say, the present generation had allowed to fall into disuse. He seemed delighted to find that the latter of the two was well known to Adrian.

The servant came in—his entrances, apparently at random, were always so opportune that Adrian wondered if amongst his accomplishments second sight had not to be included—and set out a little card-table before the fire, at which they established themselves. They played several rubbers, with varying fortune: the cards were generally with Adrian, and he felt that it was little to his credit that when he rose to take his departure his host was a rubber to the good. Certainly, he could admit that his attention had been less frequently given to the play than to the face and manner of his host, who seemed, in the glamour of the courtly game, with its urbane French expressions, more than ever to have slipped back into the past, into the century of Louis Quinze. Adrian indulged his fantasy (it was not difficult in that quiet room, lit only by the flickering fire, and the two fine wax candles on the low-legged card-table) until the sense even of his own modernity was diminished; and it was almost with a start of surprise that he met the Earl's valediction, his quick descent into the present, the personal.

"I suppose you will go on writing?" he asked.

A sudden light flashed into the young man's eyes, emphasised his assent.

The Earl considered him for a moment silently, oddly, with his cold bright eyes: then his mouth formed itself into the smile, curiously sardonic, which always complicated his speech, embellished it with an embarrassing richness of intent.

"You are very fortunate: you have position, and brains, and—and personality. And you have youth." He paused for a moment, took a pinch of snuff: then shutting the box, with a little emphatic snap, he continued—

"*Allons*, my young friend! You will no doubt meet a good many people of more or less esteem, who will give you a great deal of good advice. They will tell you that this is a good thing, and that that is something to look after. I do not deal in advice, but if you will permit me, I will also tell you something. To have youth and—what you have—*à la bonheur*! that is a good thing—the best."

He extended a white, thin hand to Adrian, bade him good-night; and as the door closed on the latter, he saw the old man shrug his shoulders once more, half absently; it seemed like an epitaph on the evening.

Less than a week later, that evening seemed to Adrian, as he tried vaguely to recall it from the deck of his yacht, already to have clothed itself in more than its just share of the mistiness of the past. He was glad, indeed, to put aside such civilised considerations, yielding himself more completely to the fresh delight which he always found in the sea; while a favourable, rough breeze sent the *Anonyma* scudding along the Solent. It was a rest which he had promised himself; and he was inclined to congratulate himself, that, contrary to his original intention, the cruise was to be a solitary one—

a friend whom he had asked to join him having at the last moment made excuse. So was he more entirely at liberty to follow the fantasy of the moment, to work, or to be idle as the whim seized him, and to meditate at leisure upon the various issues which concerned him. As he leaned, warmly clad, against the taffrail, watching the lights of Cowes slowly efface themselves, the physical good which he found in the birdlike motion through the darkness, the salt spray, and the wind in his face, seemed to be of the nature of a novel satisfaction. It was a refreshment: and his London life, short as it had been, and full of fascination, had given him the need of that, had tired him more than he was aware; so that he had already a foretaste of the yearning with which he might go to the sea, later, for solace of a lassitude become more ingrained and intolerable.

Brought face to face with the ancient sea, so cosmic and original, the accidents and factitious interest of his personal life fell into a proper perspective: its problems became more sanely soluble. Actually, he was two men: and such direct encounters with the lawlessness of elements released that second part of him, primitively poetic, which the life of cities, and society, even of his friends, at times irked and irritated. And it blew through his perversities, of the modern artist, through the charm of Brooke's paradoxes, and of Corbyn's pleasant cynicism, dispelling them like so many cobwebs. Incidentally, it sent him back to the image of Sylvia. It was not that he had ever forgotten her, or, indeed, ceased to consider her, in a relation which no other person could bear towards him. Only, when in the stress of his estranged life, the memory of this girl, whom he had loved, penetrated, the diversity between them seemed too intolerable, the difficulties of the relation insurmountable. More than mere leagues of country separated him from her garden of hollyhocks. Other women he had met now, with grace and intelligence, women in society, and girls too, the charm of whose girlhood had not been sensibly corroded by it, who were as beautiful as Sylvia, who had refinements which she lacked, and interests, dear to him, which she ignored. But here any such comparisons which he might have made, became at once false or insincere.

A wind-tossed shower of spray leaped in his face; and he retreated, laughing, to the shelter of the companion-hatch, to find a tarpaulin, and light a last pipe. They were leaving the shelter of the Wight: and the cutter lay to for a moment, plunging like a horse, while the crew ran aft noisily, and beneath the taciturn supervision of the skipper made a double reef in the mainsail, which catching just then the luminosity of the Needles' light, seemed immense, relieved against the blackness of the waters like the breast of some colossal swan. A moment later she swung to the wind again, and heeling over, leaped to the open channel, shaking the spray from her clean-cut bows, with a sort of human joyousness, heading straight for France. The stars above were plain: there was no light ahead; only the vague immensity of dark, heaving waters. With half a shiver, Adrian prepared to turn in. Certainly there was a huge cruelty about the sea, at least potential, even to its lovers. Life, too, he reflected, was of that quality: it lay before him, perhaps as dark and formidable, certainly more unknown; with an equal fascination, it might be capable of cruelties as profound. Human conventions, and gimcrack laws of society, seemed but a fallible compass. Was it not rather to some high ideal passion, sacramental, and primitive of sex, that one should turn, as to a guiding star, across the sea of one's limitations and one's ignorance? At least there seemed in that notion, half mystical, of the complete loss of oneself in another human person, a nearest approach to that absolute for which one yearned always, and which seemed now more necessary in one's utter loneliness with the waves and stars. So his fantasy ended, as it began, with Sylvia, and carried him to his berth.

CHAPTER VII

WITHIN a few miles of Towers, along the sandy Norfolk shore, the fishing town of Lowmouth, with its harbour, notable to all yachting men, had been fixed as the natural termination of Adrian's cruise. Hither, when there were guests at Towers, and the weather was propitious, Lord Henry Minaret drove such as were inclined for the expedition, in a capacious waggonette. Departing visitors were taken to the station; trains were met; expeditions were made for letters and the evening papers; the ladies sauntered on the pier, or did such light shopping as the rusticity of the town afforded; the men lounged an hour away in the yacht club.

Entering this building one afternoon in November, when the time of Adrian's visit was nearly approaching, Lord Henry found a belated telegram from his friend, who had worked up Channel along the French coast to Flushing, and announced that, the wind being favourable, he was on the point of sailing thence, direct to his destination. It sent him to the steward with inquiries; half expecting to find that the *Anonyma* was already in the harbour. She was not yet posted, however; but on a consideration of dates and winds, it appeared highly probable that she would be sighted in the course of the afternoon. A few moments later, he had betaken himself to the pier; hoping that, from the end of it, he might recognise, in some of the white sails which were discernible in the offing, his friend's craft. The Lowmouth pier, a somewhat dreary edifice, popular only in the height of the summer season, when a band played upon it, was almost deserted, on this particularly cheerless afternoon, when the season had long been a thing of the past; so that he had no difficulty in identifying two feminine figures, in blue serge, who already occupied the post of vantage which he had aimed at, as ladies of the party which he had driven over from Towers. They were leaning over the rusty bulwarks, gazing aimlessly at the waves. They glanced round at the sound of his step; and recognising him, the younger, slighter, more obviously pretty of the two, smiled, and then blushed, with a richness of suggestion, which seemed to her companion at least, who averted her handsome head with a certain haughty tolerance, to be reflected, as it were, in the sudden flash which came into Minaret's eyes.

"Have you exhausted the High Street shops already, Miss Lancaster?" he asked lightly.

The girl shook her head.

"I only wanted to match some silk, and they hadn't the right shade. They are going to send for it. It's very obliging of them, isn't it, Marion?"

Her voice, as she turned a charming profile to the elder girl, had a plaintive accent, sweetly appealing, to the charm of which other men than Minaret had fallen willing captives, without pausing to reflect upon the inadequacy of its cause. As with women often, who had a way of seeming cold to the inherent pathos of this girl's voice and eyes, he was half angry now with Marion Brabant, excellent friends as they were, for her irresponsiveness, ignoring the appeal.

"Marion has a soul above silks," he said. "You must expect no sympathy from her."

The girl, who had not spoken, desisted for a moment

from her contemplation of the sea, turning to Minaret —they were first cousins—a face which was a fine feminine copy of his own.

"Did you come for us?" she asked. "I am afraid we can't start before the time you arranged. Lady Lancaster has gone to pay a call: she has taken the carriage."

"Mamma will be just hours yet," put in the younger girl, smiling felicitously, "if the Dysarts are at home. We can't possibly start yet, can we, Marion?"

Minaret hastened to explain.

"It sounds very rude, but, really, I came here on my own account. I didn't know that you patronised piers. I haven't the least wish to hurry you—rather the other way. I have had a wire from Adrian Rome,—you have often heard me speak of him, Marion. He is about due. I came to have a look round. There are two or three yachts out there; if his boat happens to be one of these, we can drive him back with us, perhaps. May I borrow your glass?"

His cousin handed him a diminutive pair of field-glasses, and he considered through them, critically, the various sails in sight.

"Is that Mr. Rome's yacht?" asked Miss Brabant presently, as the nearest of the white-winged fleet swept down towards the harbour entrance.

He shook his head.

"No, that's a schooner; the others are too small. Stay! there's a big cutter right out at sea, which may be the *Anonyma*, but she is too far out to swear to."

The younger girl watched the schooner which had just passed within fifty yards of them, her speed diminishing as the snowy canvas was hauled in. She gave a sudden exclamation, coloured a little.

"Why, it's the *Andromeda*, General Verrinder's yacht!

We met him at Cowes last season. Mamma will be pleased."

The young man followed the direction of her eyes.

"I doubt if he's on board. Lady Lancaster will be disappointed. I expect she is only here to lie up."

"What a pity!" cried the girl. "Isn't it a pity, Marion? We might have made the General take us for a cruise."

"That can easily be arranged," said Lord Henry. "Rome will be delighted, and he is bound to be here soon."

Marion Brabant had taken the glass again, and held it steadily fixed upon the cutter which her cousin had pointed out, and which was no longer a speck upon the distance.

"It's a large yacht," she said presently; "it's moving very fast. It has a flag up, but I can't make it out. See if your eyes are better."

Minaret took the glass from her, and considered for a moment: then he dropped it with an exclamation.

"It's the Royal Thames burgee," he said, "and the *Anonyma*, without a doubt. I know her lines! Isn't she a beauty?"

"She has very white sails," said Miss Brabant indifferently. "How long will she take getting into the harbour?"

"Not very long, at this rate," Lord Henry replied admiringly, with his eyes still fixed upon the approaching white-winged phantom. "Not more than twenty minutes, I should say. If Rome doesn't run her on to the Chinkers!"

Miss Lancaster got up with an effective little shiver, stamping her feet, and displaying a neatly-gaitered ankle. "Are those the horrid rocks which we see sticking up at low tide? I hope he won't,—on a dreadful rough day like this, too! Don't you think you ought to warn him, Lord Henry?"

"Oh, I don't think we need man the lifeboat just yet," he responded lightly. "Rome has got a Norfolk skipper on board; they'll give the Chinkers a very wide berth: the *Anonyma's* heading away from them already; you'll see her go about in a minute or two. Hullo! isn't that the waggonette coming down the hill? I'm afraid Lady Lancaster can't have found the Dysarts at home."

"Poor mamma! I'm sorry she's been disappointed," said Miss Lancaster demurely. "I know she wanted to have a long talk with Mrs. Dysart."

"I'm disappointed," sighed Lord Henry. "I wanted to have a long talk with—"

"With your cousin?" suggested Miss Lancaster, interrupting him. "Shall I call her? see, she's at the other end of the pier. How charming she is! We have become great friends already."

"I know someone else who is a thousand times more charming," Lord Henry protested clumsily. Miss Lancaster gave no sign of having heard him. He could not see her face for the moment, but when she turned towards him there was no trace of resentment in her somewhat infantile blue eyes.

"Doesn't the sea always make you feel sentimental?" he continued.

The girl averted her eyes with a little movement and smile, which he took for acquiescence.

"Gracious!" she thought to herself. "What will he say next?—he'll be asking me if port wine doesn't make me feel sleepy."

"I'm sure you're a poet, Lord Henry," she said, turning her demure eyes suddenly upon him. "Now, confess! I used to write poetry when I was a little girl, until my governess found me out: she said it wasn't proper for little girls to write poetry." They had reached the end of the pier; Miss Lancaster turned.

"See," she said, "the carriage has stopped, and Marion is coming towards us."

"Yes," assented Lord Henry. "I suppose we mustn't keep Lady Lancaster waiting. I'm afraid Rome won't be ready to leave the yacht for another hour or so; he's such an enthusiast, he's sure to want to see her all snug at her moorings."

Miss Brabant, who had joined them, glanced at him for a moment enquiringly. "Don't you think we had better drive back with Lady Lancaster, and tell them to send another carriage down to fetch you and Mr. Rome? I confess that I've had almost enough of the sea-breeze for one day; it's getting rather *too* bracing."

Miss Lancaster assented,—somewhat reluctantly, Lord Henry flattered himself,—stipulating that she was to be allowed to drive; and Lord Henry escorted the two girls to the carriage, which was waiting on the desolate expanse known as the Parade, and despatched them, overwhelmed with rugs, on their three miles' drive inland to Towers. "Aren't you coming with us?" Lady Lancaster had said, addressing him. "Do you think Marjorie is to be trusted to drive, without you to keep an eye on her?"

Lord Henry glanced at Miss Lancaster with some perplexity, avoiding the faintly mocking gaze of his cousin's fine eyes.

"I'm awfully sorry!" he said. "You see, I'm obliged to wait for Mr. Rome. And Miss Lancaster drives as well as she does everything else. And there's Waters," he added, indicating the smart groom, "if the horses should be too much for her."

It was dark long before the dog-cart which had been

sent to fetch the two young men reached Towers on its homeward journey, and the house, as they approached it through the rustling obscurity of the park, presented only a vista of dark masses, a dusky, broken outline looming against the grey background of wind-scattered clouds; a nocturne in black, punctuated by the lights which shone broadly from a few uncurtained windows in the centre and one wing. The dressing-gong sounded as they entered the large inner hall, and Adrian, somewhat bewildered after his dark drive by the bright light and a crowd of unfamiliar faces, was glad to make it an excuse for curtailing his exchange of greetings with his host and hostess. Entering the drawing-room half an hour later, after dressing with unprecedented haste,—the tribute of a newly-arrived guest to the passion for punctuality which was not the least notorious of the Duke's innumerable virtues,—he found himself almost alone in a wilderness of furniture; there were so many empty chairs, presenting their seats to the discreetly moderated light of the electric chandelier, that he found his choice embarrassed. Sounds of music came to him from a recess at one side, where a girl was playing softly a capriccio of Tchaikowsky; an upholstered dowager was studying a photograph-album in front of the fire; and in the dimly lighted conservatory, which opened out of the further end of the room, he presently recognised Lord Henry, flitting from flower to flower with a pretty, fair-haired girl, whose face was strange to him.

As his eyes wandered idly round the room, noting the pictured panels and curious tapestries, they were caught by the reflection in a Venetian mirror of the profile of the girl at the piano; and the small head, well set on a graceful, rounded neck, the dark eyes, and the darker hair, disposed in a manner not greatly affected by the young ladies of the period, seemed to him vaguely familiar.

After a few moments of mystification, he identified the unconscious performer as the original of a variety of photographs which had embellished Lord Henry's rooms at Underwoods and Oxford; and he was pleased to find his conclusion confirmed, when, the Duchess presently introducing him, he learned that the girl was in fact her cousin, Miss Brabant.

Although he had been introduced to Miss Brabant, and the Duchess had intimated that he was to take her down to dinner, Adrian was not allowed to enjoy a monopoly of her society; the room was now full, in spite of its capacity; pheasants were plentiful this autumn in the ducal coverts, and the leaves being now well off the trees, quite an army of shooters had been invited to open the campaign. The duties of hospitality were somewhat onerous; and Miss Brabant, by virtue of her kinship, appeared to occupy more or less the position of a daughter of the house. Rome contented himself with watching her, finding something in the nature of a challenge to his powers of discrimination in the expression of her face,—a kind of impassive disdain, a reserve, of a quality extraordinarily subtile. A faint smile presently softened the curves of her lips, and lent a new brilliance to her eyes; he followed their direction, and was in time to see Lord Henry emerge from the conservatory with his fair-haired companion, who, blushing a little, was adjusting a feathery, copper-coloured chrysanthemum in the front of her white dress.

At dinner, Miss Brabant divided her conversational favours with great impartiality between Rome and Mr. Poindexter, the ex-Cabinet Minister, who sat upon her other side. She had owned to a passion for music. "It gives one an opportunity to relieve one's feelings without being indiscreet,—without being too intelligible," she explained.

Adrian assented.

"One can say a good deal, in music, without exceeding the narrow limits which propriety imposes upon one's ordinary conversation. A piano is like a typewriter in more ways than one: through the medium of your fingers your thoughts, or your interpretation of your composer's thoughts, are written—on the air!"

"Where not every one that runs may read," suggested Miss Brabant. "A composer can be even more obscure in expressing himself than a poet. I beg your pardon, —I did not mean to be allusive," she added a minute later, turning to Adrian, with a brilliant smile, in the middle of a conversational assault on the part of the politician. "Of course, I have read your verses; we have all been reading them; we have discussed them furiously."

Adrian's modest rejoinder was wasted upon his companion, who again turned her back to him. From his seat near the middle of the long table he could study the Duchess without making her feel uncomfortable, for she was too short-sighted to perceive that his eyes were fixed upon her. He found her interesting, on account of a curious resemblance to Lord Hildebrand. It seemed to him that the brother and sister were like two engravings struck from the same plate, but with a considerable interval,—the simile was carried out by the Earl's fifteen years' seniority,—during which the lines had become worn and blunted, so that the impression, in the sister's case, was fainter, less resilient. The Duchess, as he gathered from his observations and from common repute, was on the whole a happy woman; proud of her husband, though she was too clever herself to exalt him to a very high pinnacle of wisdom; and well content (in spite of the boyish escapade which had led to his expulsion from Winchester) with the prospects of her second son, Lord Henry Minaret. Her one sorrow was centred in the sense of responsibility which she felt for the moral obliquity of her firstborn, the Marquis of Towers; whose secession from the paths of virtue, which had been trodden for so many generations with unfaltering straightness by her husband and his ancestors, had for several years yielded paragraphs for Society journalists. The Marquis—he was ten years older than Lord Henry—was, in fact, a black sheep, of the inkiest possible description; and the Duchess of Turretshire, irreproachable as she felt herself to be, was uneasily conscious that she was still responsible for the introduction of the strain; if there was anything in heredity,—and she had been taught to believe in it as fervently as any latter-day dramatist,—Lord Hildebrand and his degenerate nephew, though it was only in their least amiable qualities that their characters tallied, were undoubtedly the products of a common ancestor, and the link could only be found in herself. It was a consolation to her that at least she could not be held accountable for her brother's misdeeds.

As for the Duke, it seemed to Adrian that Lord Hildebrand had described him with sufficient precision when he referred to him as "a most worthy person." Worthiness was, in fact, written in every line of his benevolent countenance, of his portly, comfortable figure. If he was bald, he had reached an age when baldness is scarcely to be resented: if he was, in plain language, fat, it did not interfere with his powers of independent locomotion, or prevent his personal supervision of the building of model cottages, his enjoyment of a long day's shooting. Adrian never looked at him without an inward chuckle, remembering a story which Lord Henry himself had irreverently conveyed to him, of how a guileless American, of tender years, and a great unconfessed respect for the British aristocracy, had mistaken him, in broad daylight, for his own butler. It was curious that Lord Hildebrand's somewhat patronising epithet should have been so exactly the word which one would have used with reference to a well-tried, virtuous menial: his Lordship, perhaps, would have been more surprised than flattered, if he had been told that an American—an American girl—had been capable of a judgment so precisely tantamount to his own.

Later in the evening, during the progress to a harrowing conclusion of an impassioned recitation, of which the drift was imperfectly revealed to him, Adrian found himself wedged into a corner behind two rustling, silk-clad dowagers, who addressed each other by their Christian names, and appeared to be sublimely unconscious of his presence, and of the fact that their impressive whispers were audible to him, as well as to several other persons in their vicinity. In spite of his endeavours to rivet his attention unreservedly upon the recitation,—as a stranger, with no one to talk to, this was his only resource,—he could not help becoming aware that the ladies were exchanging confidences on the subject of the eldest son of his host—the much-discussed Marquis of Towers.

"Such a sad break-down," said one of them complacently,—he recognised her, by her emeralds, as the dame who had been absorbed in a photograph-album when he entered the drawing-room before dinner,—"I'm afraid it's quite hopeless, my dear—living abroad, you know, with a—sort of companion."

"A ——?" queried the other.

"Oh, not *that* creature: I don't know anything about her. A kind of keeper, I meant. Yes, I believe it's as bad as that. Oh, I am told he's tolerably careful about appearances, now; you know Arabella, poor dear, hasn't been able to get a divorce yet! It does seem a shame, doesn't it? And they have no children, so it wouldn't matter. And she hasn't set eyes on him for years. It's a real miscarriage of justice,—though I am far from saying that she wasn't to blame."

"You are always so just, Selina!" murmured the other lady, with a pensive shake of her head that made her diamonds twinkle.

"And, you know, the Duke—poor man!—has quite declined to have any more to do with him; won't even pay his creditors— Rich American widow? Oh, but you see he can't marry again, unless— And there doesn't seem to be much chance of it. Otherwise—" Here the speaker cast an expressive glance in the direction of the ottoman on which Lord Henry was sitting with the fair-haired girl of the chrysanthemums.

"Ah, quite so," assented the other dowager meaningly. "Of course, it would make such a difference!—Dear Marjorie, how sweet she's looking to-night: how that white Empire gown becomes her! Crêpe de Chine, is it? You always dress your girls so well, Selina!"

Adrian did not find this conversation particularly edifying; he felt that he was forced into a position which had more than a suggestion of the indiscreet about it: certainly, there was nothing novel in the scandal about Lord Towers, whose affairs had for a considerable number of years been subjected to extreme publicity; but the discussion of the unhappy nobleman's prospects had, it seemed, involved a certain betrayal of maternal policy on the part of the more talkative lady, who, he gathered, was the mother of Lord Henry's inamorata; and he would have preferred a less surreptitious method of making himself master of the complications of this little comedy.

Escaping, when the recitation had come to an impressive end, and the lady who had been addressed as "Selina" had made her stately way across the room to play accompaniments for her daughter, who sang some little French songs with considerable grace and vivacity, Adrian found himself near Miss Brabant, and he took the opportunity of ascertaining from her that the singer was Miss Lancaster.

"And the lady accompanying her is her mother?" he suggested.

"Yes, that is Lady Lancaster,—how did you guess? Don't you think she's very pretty, Mr. Rome? The daughter, I mean, of course."

"The rules of friendship appear to demand that I should think so," he answered, with a glance towards Lord Henry. "Yes, she is certainly pretty,—and she sings very charmingly."

Miss Brabant smiled demurely,—Adrian decided that she was really very nice when she smiled,—and accused him of being a dangerously keen observer.

"But I suppose you are in my cousin's confidence: you and Henry are quite old friends, are you not?"

"I suppose I may call him my oldest friend, in a way,—the oldest friend I have,—the oldest among my coevals, certainly. But I am only in his confidence as to his political projects, which appear to be very tremendous! He will be in the House soon, I suppose: he is very ambitious."

"Poor Henry! I'm afraid he will be sorry that he wasted so much time at school."

Adrian shrugged his shoulders. "I confess," he said slowly, "I never quite understand what people mean by wasting time. So long as you're not asleep, what does it matter? What, after all, is the difference between wasting time, and killing time, or passing it?"

Miss Brabant, who in common with the other women now struggling towards the doorway, had risen from her seat, appeared to reflect for a moment.

"Ah, Mr. Rome," she said, glancing at him over a white and shapely shoulder, "I'm afraid you're terribly modern! You will have time to ponder that riddle, with a great many practical examples to help you, over your cigarettes in the billiard-room, to which I can see Henry is ready to conduct you. We keep early hours here, as you see. Good-night!"

CHAPTER VIII

ADRIAN was able to reflect, before he had been many days at Towers, that his guardian had been only right in warning him that he was going to an excessively political house. The warning had affected him less than it might have done, because he had been a guest on former occasions, when this quality had been less forcibly suggested to him. Then, there had been no considerable company; and the Duke, with his constant air of anxious absorption in public affairs, had been less in evidence than the Duchess, who, if she could be political enough on occasions, was always ready, with a certain bland satisfaction, which reminded the young man faintly of his guardian, to drop the *rôle* for that one, more congenial to her, of the charming hostess.

Henry Minaret also, in those earlier days, had not yet been explicitly trusted with the sacred torch of family tradition, to the worthy succession of which it was still remotely possible that his erring brother might be recalled. But now Lord Henry, it was easy to see, had entered into his inheritance. He had spoken at public meetings, and was the accepted Liberal candidate of a neighbouring borough, whose present member's resignation was a matter of the near future. And the consciousness of what was expected of the young man had matured him sensibly; he had already some of that grave assurance — it sat somewhat oddly upon his boyishness—which association with the management of a great nation, even when it is still prospective, indubitably secures. Sincere and thorough, however, as Lord Henry's concern with the national interests might be (and Adrian, who could not have explained why these admittedly great affairs should seem to him but a barren delight, was obliged to confess that his friend's temper towards them was not in the least factitious), it was noted by the contemplative poet, and pleasurably, that there was still room for matters more personal than the Irish question and the claims of Labour, in his friend's positive mind. His career engrossed him to the extent that he could forego his shooting for the tamer sport of running electors to earth: but the eternal feminine prevailed. He was rarely confidential; but Adrian smiled when, beneath a touch of spleen, what seemed a mere flirtation, was more particularly illuminated. The young men had come in from a ride, and they sat in a revel of procrastination before Adrian's seductive fire, until the first gong which heralded dinner should divide them to change their "cords" for the less picturesque garb of civilisation.

And Minaret broke in, almost fiercely, on a desultory sketch of his friend's projected travels, with the exclamation, "Thank the gods, you are not a younger son!"

"Does the shoe pinch there?" said Rome, unfastening one of his leggings. "You will get over that."

"My brother — you mean?" Minaret went on impetuously, misinterpreting him: then, scenting his error, he flushed furiously, but did not interrupt his vein.

"It's his head which is weak, not his health. I speak brutally, but when has he ever considered me — us? Besides, she may get a divorce,—goodness knows, she has reason!—and he will marry some monstrous woman, out of spite. A fellow like that! Oh, my people don't hear the worst; no, not even the Society papers,—or they don't print it. It's a mad blackguard."

Adrian picked up the thread of his suggestion, buried in this outburst.

"I meant that matters would arrange themselves," he said skilfully. "Does the lady ask so much? Forgive me, but I can't help having eyes!" He was proud of his tact; a quality inherent in him, like a subtile, sixth sense; and never more than when, as now, he seemed to violate it, was consciously indiscreet. For he knew how the conventional, behind their mask of convention, implore dubiously to be unmasked. So does a fine player of whist, versed in Cavendish, discard his book at the critical moment; playing, as it were, by instinct of the game.

"You mean—you mean that I am in love?" Lord Henry queried, after a moment's silence. "Very likely."

Then he gave a little nervous laugh.

"Why should I humbug you? Of course I am. I have proposed to Miss Lancaster. Do you admire her?"

Adrian smiled; though, honestly, the charm of the little, blonde girl, like an angel in Dresden china, hardly moved him. In these matters of attraction, however, were not the inexplicable, the exceptional, the only laws? And he was too conscious of how defenceless to outside criticism lay predilections of his own, to be other than acquiescent in any freak of a lover's choice. "She is exceedingly pretty. Am I to congratulate you?"

"She has been good enough to accept me."

Finding, perhaps, that his friend showed some surprise at the lack of enthusiasm with which this announcement was made, Lord Henry went on hastily, sketching the situation.

"It is the mother who has to be reckoned with. She

will hear of no definite engagement; though I have the girl's promise. She will not have it published, so that she can slip out of it—if she can do better. She deprecates the scandal of my brother's possible divorce. She plays fast and loose."

"But Miss Lancaster is firm?"

"While I am there to support her; but away from me, a reed in the wind. She seems wax to a strong will; and that woman stamps upon her. At least, I fear so."

"What does she want,—the mother, I mean?" Adrian asked.

Minaret smiled contemptuously, throwing out his hands, with an explicit gesture. "Money, money, any amount of it: her debts paid, to begin with. I listen to the old women talking, and that much I am certain of. Do you know Verrinder—General Verrinder?"

"I know him as a name," said Adrian vaguely, "little more of him. Isn't he a yachting man?"

"It is the same man. He owns half Eastshire, and is enormously rich, besides. He had a million, they say, with his first wife, who fell in love with his V.C. Now he is a widower of sixty; gouty, and—a *parti*! Pshaw! the idea is blasphemous."

"Lady Lancaster stalks him?" Adrian asked, to supply the hiatus in his friend's words. The other had risen as the first, deep notes of a gong began to throb through the house; and he stood, caressing his fair moustache, his broad shoulders resting against the mantelpiece, vaguely disquieted.

"I must be moving," he said, but still remained; then he went on abruptly—

"So it stands: I have Marjorie's word; but the mother is shifty and a harridan. She may be playing me against the millionaire, to egg him on. With the title, perhaps, I am preferred ;—but a bird in the hand, —a fortune, and such a fortune—"

He left his sentence unfinished, gazing out rather moodily at the dancing reflection of the light upon the furniture and walls. Then he glanced at his watch, exclaimed at his tardiness, and was at the door; where he looked back, by an afterthought, to remark to Rome, that Mrs. Vesper would be at dinner, had arrived that afternoon.

Descending into the drawing-room, twenty minutes later, Adrian Rome seemed to identify this lady, in whose name he was just dimly conscious that he was interested, in one of two ladies who conversed apart, where a sort of alcove, rendered discreet by curtains, made, when these were drawn, almost a separate apartment. The second of the two ladies, Marion Brabant, had corroborated this recognition by briefly mentioning his name, and the name of Mrs. Vesper, before he had time to waver from it. She acknowledged the presentation vaguely; then turned, and continued her talk with Miss Brabant. The manner of their discourse, rather than its matter, which concerned persons strange to him, appeared intimate; so that when he had learnt that Mrs. Vesper fell to him at the dinner-table, Adrian was content to stand aside, absently turning the leaves of an illustrated paper, while at the same time he collected, at some advantage, his impressions of the new arrival. She was slight, and slim, and past middle age; the simplicity of her dress struck the young man as conveying almost a note of exaggeration,—as though she wished to accentuate the fact, that she had long ago lost the justifications of coquetry,—until he reflected that the plainness of this garb (to be sure, it was tremendously fashionable, *simplex munditiis*!) sprang largely from contrast with the magnificence of her companion. He had noticed before that Miss Brabant affected a certain richness of apparel, a splendour of adornment, which seemed to him, who, like most men of his temper, associated the candour of maidenhood with pearls and white muslin, at the least an audacity. A happy audacity perhaps; for her figure, tall and statuesque, deserved liberal drapery. So that he would have hesitated to declare that this young lady's preference for trailing, imperial clothes, brocades, even, and velvets, confessed a flaw of taste: there might be even a subtilty in its suggestion of what he seemed already to have discovered, that, girl as she was, she was, none the less, the most mature of women. Watching her now half surreptitiously; in juxtaposition with the sedate, little lady, with her bright eyes, and compressed mouth, and her immense composure; he was surprised to discover what animation she could on occasion exhibit. Indeed, the singular coldness of this girl, with whom his acquaintance halted, had sensibly repelled him; the more so in that he made sure she was clever, and suspected that she was cultivated; and so, could ascribe her chilling haughtiness neither to shyness nor to stupidity, so much as to arrogance, of the superior person; an attitude unpardonable for him in women. His discovery now, that she could glow with a quite girlish ardour, could be really nice, as he phrased it, as her eyes, which were certainly fine, wandering in his direction once or twice, seemed to include him in her sudden graciousness; was provocative less of a desire to dwell on itself than to probe the immediate cause of it. Had this plain, little, elderly woman, then, the great gift, to which Lord Hildebrand attached the last charm, describing it dubiously, as personality; a force to be reckoned with? Certainly, Marion Brabant seemed to be moved and altered by it. He remembered hearing—it might have been from

Gerald Brooke—that Mrs. **Vesper was** inimitable; and suddenly, with little reason, perhaps,—for she had hardly addressed him,—he felt that rumour was right. He was conscious of a vague **pleasure,** which, it seemed to him, was reflected in the quick scrutiny with which now and again **she** favoured him,—a scrutiny which promised much—treasures of intimacy.

They sat down **to this** meal, a comfortable **dozen;** for many **of the** shooting party had dispersed; and Adrian was hardly surprised to find that the new guest knew everyone, **and was known to all.** This quality threw him at first, **for social sustenance, on** his left-hand neighbour, **the** Dresden-china **damsel, into** whose confidences, indirectly, through **the** admissions of Minaret, he seemed recently to have penetrated. Her conversational **resources were not** extensive, but she could talk about nothing prettily, after **the manner of her** class; and Adrian, without feeling **bound to be** remarkably attentive, considered her more closely than he had done before. **He had** turned away **from her at last; Mrs. Vesper's** talk with **her** neighbour, Dalrymple Green, a young political journalist, who was supposed to have a brilliant future, having lapsed; **with** a shadowy sense of pity. He had **never seen anybody who** seemed to him **so soft, so pliable by circumstances;** it was a comfort to reflect, **that if her destined tears** were numerous, they would all **be very easily dried.** Just then a conversational battle **waged at the top of the** table, between the **Duke** and **Sir** Rufus **Hake,** whose property bordered upon **Towers; a** Tory of the **most** rigid cut. It was their eternal feud, Free **Trade against** Protection, which broke out **whenever they met,** excellent friends **as** they were, **of thirty** years' standing. The words, "retaliation," "**corn** laws," "Peel," party **cries of a** bygone generation, floated down the table.

"Where are they gone? What were they?" asked Mrs. Vesper. Dalrymple Green smiled.

"Out of practical politics; impossible in the present state of the franchise."

"I believe in retaliation," grumbled a gentleman facing them, "We are flooded with foreign goods, and they meet us with prohibitive duties. We should discriminate between agricultural products and manufactures. I don't want the corn laws back again; but a reasonable tariff."

"The heresy of Fair Trade," put in Lord Henry, with a smile. "Don't compromise me, by preaching it on the platform."

"Fair Trade! What is Fair Trade?" asked a pretty, dark girl sitting next to him.

Lady Lancaster said it sounded reasonable. "Besides, it would stop all those horrid, cheap things made in Germany."

Dalrymple, scenting his pet abomination, burst in with a definition.

"The wolf Protection, in a most transparent lambskin."

Under cover of the laugh, Mrs. Vesper turned to Adrian.

"Are you of Lord Henry's way of thinking, Mr. Rome?"

Adrian confessed that his friend's Radical enthusiasm went too far.

"Is he Radical?" she asked whimsically; "or too good a Conservative to desert the principles of his family?"

They admitted to each other their scant interest in questions of policy, while an accompaniment of voices, in which Dalrymple Green's high, nervous tones dominated, discussed universal suffrage.

"I agree with Balzac," **Adrian** murmured into the ear of his tolerant neighbour. "Universal suffrage means government by the masses, which is the most irresponsible tyranny in the world."

"Treason in a Whig house!" **Mrs.** Vesper laughed. "But I agree with you, if you hate democracy."

"I think I am afraid of it. Yes, seriously, I am afraid of it. It threatens the only things I care about in the world."

"There speaks the artist. Well, you have my sympathy. Possibly I am an artist myself. Oh, I don't mean that I paint or write, but in my own way. Some day I will tell you my medium."

She smiled at the young man's mystified air. "I have read your book. I can't say how it struck me. You must come and see me in London."

Adrian expressed his pleasure at the prospect, and she went on.

"You seem hardly a stranger to me, Rupert Rome's son."

"You knew my father?"

"You are remarkably like him."

Her phrase was sufficiently deliberate to be an answer in the affirmative.

"You have no brother, have you?" She asked after a moment, "Is your aunt—" She half paused, as if she anticipated his announcement, that that aged woman was no longer in the flesh. "You must be the last of them all," she concluded. "Well, that is rather sad."

Adrian gave a little nervous laugh.

"Some people might say it was rather fortunate."

He imagined that he should embarrass her; but she appeared to be impervious to that emotion: at least, her prompt reply revealed no trace of it.

"People are very stupid. If one has character, if one

is not like the rest of the world ; roundly, they call one mad. At least," she added, after a moment's pause, in which her eye caught the Duchess' signal for retreat— " I find no people like them now."

His last impression of her, as she passed out with the stream of ladies, by the side of Marion Brabant, was that she was clever, and that she had charm. His impression of her cleverness, it may be said, was a permanent one, although there came days when he could question her charm ; and long after that dinner, he remembered with a singular sense of irony, that it was in connection with Miss Brabant that both of these qualities had first been revealed to him.

CHAPTER IX

CORBYN astonished himself and his friends by satisfying the Oxford examiners before the end of the Michaelmas term, and when the Spring came he was already a B.A. of some months' standing, and, casting Herodotus and Aristotle behind him, had familiarised himself with the backs at least of the ponderous volumes which filled the shelves of the eminent counsel, who, for a pecuniary consideration, allowed him and a few other aspirants towards forensic honours to enjoy the run of his chambers in King's Bench Walk. Returning, after the week's sojourn in the sunshine of Oxford, for which it had not been difficult to find a pretext, to his somewhat gloomy attic in New Court, he discovered, buried among the pressing appeals from university tradesmen which had accumulated during his absence, one of Adrian Rome's cards, with a few words scribbled on it in pencil, announcing his return to London. Casting the bills light-heartedly into the waste-paper basket,—a receptacle only too familiar with such documents,—Corbyn made haste to accomplish the descent of his staircase and the ascent of the lower half of the next, on which his friend's rooms were situated, and he was fortunate enough to find Adrian at home, on the point of setting out in search of dinner. Their greetings were cordial and brief.

"What a chap you are!" Corbyn expostulated, as they emerged a few minutes later into the Strand. "I haven't seen you for nearly six months, and you've only written about twice. If it hadn't been for your name at the foot of the staircase, I should long ago have concluded that you were the creature of my fertile imagination—a beautiful dream."

"I ought to have written oftener," Rome admitted apologetically, "but I can't write letters; it's such a grind. You weren't in town when I set out on my travels; I started rather suddenly, before Christmas, meaning to have a little cruise in the Mediterranean, and somehow the cruise protracted itself; and I have only been back two days. I couldn't make up my mind to leave the sunshine; it was so delightful, after all the winters I've spent in England."

"I wonder you came back at all," said Corbyn enviously. "I shouldn't; only I should miss the theatres," he added, with an affectionate glance at the portals of the Gaiety which they were passing. "How jolly sunburnt you are! you look preposterously fit. Where have you been?"

Adrian shrugged his shoulders. "Where haven't I been? Nice, Corfu, Venice, Florence, Verona, Rome, Algiers—and half the ports on the Mediterranean. I didn't stay anywhere long: I moved on when my fellow-countrymen became too conversational. I have developed quite a passion for the road: I think nature must have intended me for a *commis voyageur*."

Corbyn smiled. "I wonder what the dickens she intended me for? Whatever it was, it was something in the contemplative line, and she spoiled it by forgetting the money part of the qualification. But weren't you awfully lonely? Especially if, as you say, you dodged your fellow-countrymen."

"I was—rather," admitted the other. "But I wanted to be alone. I had quite enough society in Italy, chiefly of the Bostonian order. I have been working pretty hard. I have written a play, and started on a novel. Lord Hildebrand was with me for a week or two at Nice, and Brooke paid me a flying visit at Rome. Henry Minaret was to have joined me soon after Christmas, for a cruise; but his sister-in-law died—Lady Towers, you know."

"Yes," said Corbyn; "very sudden, wasn't it? The man I am reading with held a brief for the lady, in her divorce case. Poor thing, she was very badly treated! And they say that Lord Towers is likely to marry again!"

"I shouldn't be surprised," said Rome. "I saw him a week or two ago at Mentone, dangling in the train of a colonial lady,—a person with emeralds like chandelier drops, and everything else, including an accent, on the same scale. I don't envy either of them. But its rough on Minaret."

Chatting indifferently, the two men made their way along the Strand, teeming just then with its eastward stream of pleasure-seekers, and westward tide of home-faring men of business; across Trafalgar Square, where they paused for a moment, beneath the shadow of the National Gallery, to gaze admiringly at the medley of delicate lights, gleaming across the sombre square and converging roadways, like tall daffodils in a wood; thence, turning their backs on the gloomy pools and statues, they passed into Regent Street. Rome had proposed that they should dine at the Café Imperial, and Corbyn, tapping his pockets a little ruefully, assented: it was an occasion; for once, he would be extravagant. "We will celebrate the return of the prodigal," he said, laughing. "I confess that I am getting very tired of cheap dinners. You don't know how the poor live, my boy! I feel that I could write a blue-book on cheap restaurants: I know where to find a dinner—a substantial dinner—for a shilling, and I habitually lunch for half that sum. And yet, I can't economise! I don't know how it is: I don't gamble, my tastes are simple, and I keep accounts—or try to; but every month I find myself a sovereign or two out—on the wrong side; and they have to go down as "Tobacco, etc.," or, more vaguely still, as "Incidental expenses." It's the very devil!"

Rome sighed, looking at his companion across the table a little wistfully, while the nimble waiter bustled about them with forks and spoons.

"I don't see what you have got to sigh about," said Corbyn captiously. "For Heaven's sake, don't say that you envy me—that you would like to be a pauper. That would be playing the part of the pompous idiot, who gives away the prizes, on speech days, and wishes that he was back at school. I know I don't! Talking about parts, tell me about your play: you said you had written one. I'm awfully glad. When is it to be produced?"

"Goodness knows!" said Rome, colouring a little. "I haven't sent it to anyone yet; when I do, I shall be told that it isn't suited for the stage. I daresay it isn't."

"Oh, skittles!" said Corbyn airily. "I expect it's awfully good. I drink to its success! What is it? Comedy, I hope."

"Yes, it's a comedy, I suppose. It certainly isn't intended for tragedy or farce. You shall read it, if you will criticise it. But you won't: that's the worst of friends,—they can't be candid, except in little things. And afterwards, when the book has been cut up, the play damned, they exchange mysterious glances, and tell each other that they only expected it."

"Oh, I'll abuse it," said Corbyn cheerfully. "I'll go

through it with a big blue pencil. I rather fancy myself as a stage-manager, you know. By the way, you probably don't know—I write for the *Outcry*. Have you ever heard of it? Oh, it's a most influential organ, though its circulation has latterly become somewhat limited. It's edited by a cousin of Barton's; he introduced me to him. He takes me to the theatre with him now and then, and sends me tickets for the less important Private Views. Rather a—well, in short, a bounder; but we get on pretty well, so far. Chiefly, I expect, because my services are gratuitous. I write about the Drama, with a big D, and (whatever you do, don't tell Brooke!) Art, with a very big A. You should see how I pitch into the R.A.'s. I came across the President the other day, and I felt quite ashamed of myself: he looked such a venerable and imposing old gentleman."

"Oh, they're all very respectable," said Rome, "and certainly imposing—like their pictures. I should think the Private Views would be rather a bore; but I suppose that you appreciate the theatre tickets?"

"It's not bad. But I don't get many tickets: I'm only a kind of understudy, you know. They generally send me to the music halls, and the Surrey-side places. When I do go to a decent theatre, I have to accompany the editor. I find that rather trying. I'm not sure that I don't prefer the independence of the pit. The gratuitous stall savours of bribery and corruption."

"I'm glad to observe that journalism hasn't blunted your artistic conscience. I can understand too, that if a confiding manager sends you a ticket for his show (isn't that the correct term?), you don't like to go home and revile it. Haven't I heard of a critic who won't accept complimentary tickets, but pays his half-crown at the pit door, so that he may have a free hand—instead of a free seat?"

"Yes," said Corbyn. "He must be a man of means! I don't think one ought to pamper one's conscience like that; mine would wax fat and kick in no time."

"You think conscience is like a wife,—a thing to be openly obeyed and covertly coerced."

"There is a certain resemblance. But you have some choice in the matter of a wife: you needn't saddle yourself with one unless you like."

"I hope not!" said Rome. "But it's so difficult to know what one really does like."

"Unless one has tried, you mean? That's the worst of it,—matrimony is such a devil of a plunge. In spite of the Divorce Court, there's practically no retreat. But you—you have Art for your mistress!"

"And you: haven't you become the Mentor of playwrights? I don't say of painters, for I imagine that there you don't take yourself quite seriously?"

"Gracious!" cried Corbyn, in burlesque alarm. "Have you, by chance, been reading the *Outcry*? It isn't my fault. I admit that as a writer I'm a hopeless duffer. But if I don't trouble myself about the painters and pictures, it's because Brooke and you have told me so often that they aren't worth it. Now, the Drama,— I do take that seriously: if one can't say much for the plays, at least the actors are interesting; one can write about them. And your play—I'm sure that will inspire me: I shan't have to fall back on saying that it's admirably acted, magnificently staged."

"I hope it will be well acted, if it's acted at all," said Adrian, emptying his coffee cup, and leaning back to watch the thin smoke of his cigarette floating towards the painted and gilded splendour of the ceiling. "As for the staging, I don't care. It isn't spectacular; its success won't depend on scenery and supernumeraries. I don't bring Cleopatra's Barge, or the Scotch Express, upon the stage. It's the presentment of a temperament, of a condition of soul, of nerves—"

"Like an American novel?" queried Corbyn, interrupting him. "Be careful; they don't dramatise well!"

"Like an American novel? Well, we'll call it the play of manners, if you like; that is, to put it shortly, what I have been trying to write. In these days action is so commonplace; physical situations have become so hackneyed; the fifty ways of committing a murder, of rescuing a heroine; aren't they more than threadbare? These devices are almost as stupid as the inevitable second act of the modern farce, when the scene presents an interminable array of doorways, which the author employs as so many bolt-holes, to get himself out of difficulties."

"And to get his characters into them," suggested Corbyn. "When the maiden aunt gets locked into the bathroom with the butler, and the key has been dropped down somebody else's back! Oh, I always know there's going to be some fun when I see those doors. They're adapted from the French!"

"Precisely! Isn't it time that we changed that? What I want to write—I don't imagine for a single instant that I have written it—is a play which shall be readable as well as actable, a play which shall present an interesting life-scene, with style, form, literary finish, dignity,—in a word, a work of art, not a skeleton for a star actor to clothe with mannerisms. Oh, you may smile: I admit that I am ambitious!"

"It's refreshing to hear you talk!" said Corbyn. "An original play is all I want. What I complain of is, that as soon as I have read the programme, I know what's coming. If the properties were scheduled, like the actors, I have little doubt that I could reconstruct the play—evolve it out of them."

Rome laughed contemptuously, assenting. One had only to look at the theatrical advertisements, he said, to gauge the state of things: a long list of announcements of melodramas, professed and in disguise; comic operas translated and adapted from the French; farces obviously hailing from the same source, though their authors (save the mark) generally hadn't the decency to own as much.

From this well-worn topic their conversation drifted into more pleasant channels, as for an hour or more they sat, smoking and watching their neighbours, amid the tedious clatter of dominoes and the surge of voluble voices: it seemed scarcely possible that there could be a greater percentage of Frenchmen in any *café* on the Boulevard des Italiens. Rome grew eloquent upon the subject of his wanderings, inspiring his companion with feelings which were frankly envious; and presently they deserted the behaviour of the yacht, the blue shadows of Algiers, to fall into the familiar discussion of aims and aspirations, discoveries and disillusionments.

As the hands of the clock over the bar advanced, and the more serious business of dining came to an end, the *café* grew fuller and noisier: the clamour of voices ceased to form a background for their conversation, and assailed them bewilderingly, like the wide-eyed electric light which was reflected, unshaded, from the mirrored walls, and from the gilded ceiling, with its posturing, painted nymphs. On the suggestion of Rome, who complained that he was beginning to imagine himself in a *bonbonnière* full of madmen, they made their escape; and the adjournment to the cooler air and comparative quiet of the street seemed pleasant, in spite of the hovering fog, while for a time they wandered under the vague panoply of the sky, which they could not see.

Later, when they sat in meditative enjoyment of their

cigars and the contents of tall tumblers, in the billiard-room of the club which numbered him among its members, Adrian, in the frequent pauses in their conversation which occurred when Corbyn's interest in a complicated cannon or a brilliant break held him silent, often felt himself vaguely troubled by some ill-defined uneasiness, the ghost of some forgotten aberration, which was all the more baffling, because his conscience told him that it must be trivial. It was only after the feeling had been many times peremptorily dismissed, and as often timidly recalled (after the fashion of a maiden playing with her lover), that the ghost embodied itself in a regret that he had not bestowed more consideration upon her last letter. (It is perhaps worthy of note that Sylvia Drew was the only woman who figured in his thoughts after this manner, in the familiar domino of a pronoun, anonymously.) Her last letter; it came to him while he was in town before Christmas, in answer to the one which he had written to her just before leaving Towers, and he had treated it with little ceremony; he remembered, with a blush, that he had even gone the length of crumpling the careful writing and lighting his pipe with it, cynically. During his wanderings abroad, this scruple had not assailed him: wounded pride at first had held him aloof from the thought; and the frequent change of scene, the unfamiliar environment, the long-anticipated pleasures which now found fulfilment: all operated to turn his eyes to the future rather than to the past, to wean him from his weakness for introspection. But now the key had been changed, the scene shifted. The Temple, where her photograph lurked in a pigeon-hole over his writing-table; Corbyn; the club; the foggy London night outside: it was natural that 'his mind should clothe itself with its old habits, and even that it should feel more at its ease so clad. What had he written to her? What had been her reply to him? He could only remember that his letter had been the result of careful deliberation, that it had been copied and recopied, that it had impressed him, in its final shape, as diplomatic without ceasing to be loverlike, loverlike without being ridiculous. He had intended, he remembered clearly, to bring matters to a definite issue, to explain his position, his point of view, to Sylvia; to inform her that he was ready to follow to an honourable end the path upon which they had entered so light-heartedly. But he had also asked for some assurance; it was not in his nature to feel certain about anything or anybody; he had pleaded (and perhaps that was where his tact had failed him) for the removal of certain uncomfortable doubts.

If pride had held him silent afterwards, it was pride no less which had dictated Sylvia's answer: and when friends or lovers withdraw themselves to separate pinnacles, estrangement follows as a matter of course.

It was a confession difficult to make, but Adrian's subtilty had been at fault: he had not given this village maiden credit for pride. His clearer vision of to-day showed him that he had been guilty of the folly of regarding this passion as his lordly prerogative: he recognised his mistake.

He wished that he could remember exactly what she had written; he could only recall his impressions on reading her letter,—a sense of coldness, a feeling that he was being rebuked, misinterpreted, held at arm's length. At the time, if he had been compelled to give voice to his thoughts, he would have complained that he had been snubbed,—an affront which of all others his temperament found it hard to assimilate.

He awoke from his reverie presently, to find his friend regarding him curiously through a mist of tobacco smoke.

"What is it now, old man?" said Corbyn pleasantly. "Why those frowns, symptoms of brain-racking? Are you hammering at a *villanelle*, to celebrate your return to London, or pondering on your mistress' shoe-lace, or what?"

"I beg your pardon," said Rome. "Have you been talking to me? I'm afraid my attention was wandering. Isn't it late? Shall we walk back to the Temple?"

"Late?" replied Corbyn pityingly; "no, it's early. I'm just beginning to feel alive. You don't want to look in at the Eden, or the Dorado? No? Well, let's make for the Temple,—and so to bed, as Pepys would say."

"We might walk along the Embankment," Adrian suggested, as they passed into Piccadilly. "The river has always a new charm for me, especially at night; it quite amounts to a fascination. I'm almost afraid of it, when I'm alone. It's so silent, mysterious, beautiful. After all, there's nothing like it in this world—not even Venice."

"Yes," said the other; "but don't let it fascinate you too much. I like to see the lights, and moonbeams, and stars, and things struggling and drowning in it; but I should be very sorry to follow their example."

"I'm afraid," continued Rome, "that some night I shall see a poor wretch— I suppose one would have to make a fool of oneself, and jump in after him—or her."

"I don't know," said Corbyn. "I think it would be rather rough luck to be hauled out when one was once in,—and probably slanged next morning by an unsympathetic beak. Candidly, I think I should run away, like blazes, if I heard an ominous splash. After all, people don't do such things without making up their minds!"

"Perhaps it's well for some people that they can't make up their minds," suggested the other, with a short laugh. "I can't!"

"What about?" queried Corbyn. "Not that!—Girls, I suppose? Are you between two bundles of hay? Let them slide: they aren't worth bothering about. But seriously," he continued, after a pause, "you're not in love, are you? There wasn't anything in that little flirtation down at Underwoods, was there? If you go marrying, and so on, what's to become of me?"

"In love," said Rome, slowly letting his eyes wander along the river-front, where the electric light shone through the fog like a necklace of moonstones and opals. "I don't know! Perhaps I am not. Well, confound women: I'm a confirmed bachelor—at least, I think so!"

Corbyn whistled softly. "This looks bad, my friend. It's no business of mine; but I see that I shall have to begin to look for a wedding present. Are you coming up to my rooms? I've got some whisky, of the old brand: you'd better come up and smoke a few last pipes. I'm awfully glad you've come back: the Temple is very charming, especially New Court; but it's devilish lonely at night. I don't like being alone in a big place like this: it makes one feel so insignificant!"

An hour later, when Adrian reached his own rooms, he found on the table a letter, which, to judge from the postmarks, had been pursuing him over half the Continent. It was from Lord Henry Minaret, and Rome smiled a little scornfully when he read the brief announcement of Miss Lancaster's engagement to General Verrinder.

"Poor Harry," he said; "I don't suppose he knows that he is well out of it!"

CHAPTER X

Mrs. Vesper's little house in Mayfair, and Mrs. Vesper's little dinner parties, at which no one who was not worth knowing ever sat down, had been for so long a feature of the London season, that any wonder at the extent of her vogue would have seemed provincial or underbred. Adrian Rome almost felt convicted of these deficiencies, or at least of a deplorable *naïveté*, when he had, once or twice, questioned some of the more fashionable of his club acquaintance as to the lady's standing, and had been met with a tolerant but superior smile. Yet he doubted, on reflection, whether any of them could actually have told him more than he himself, in the course of two visits, had grasped: that Mrs. Vesper was, in London society, a person to be accounted, perhaps even a power to be felt. Whatever there might be ambiguous about her (in attaching this epithet to her it must not be inferred that he gave it a detrimental sense), of one thing he felt that he could, without undue vanity, be certain, her genuine goodwill towards himself. She had extended her benevolence so far as to ask him to disregard the formality of her days, and to call when he felt inclined, adding, smilingly (in an undertone, for certain of her guests still lingered), that she knew how to treat artists, creatures of impulse and mood, with whom the wind of social intention blew very much where it listed;—the stated period was good enough for diplomatists and men of affairs.

Adrian thanked her; and a few days later, when he availed himself of the licence, had the luck to find her alone.

The smile with which she welcomed him banished any scruple which he might have felt as to having taken her invitation too literally. He wondered afresh, after half an hour's converse with her, how, without personal beauty or the advantage of youth, she managed to be so charming. To her voice he decided, which reminded him, in its silvery modulations, of that of a great French actress, just then at the height of her fame, she owed much, and a little, perhaps, to her surroundings—the discreet and sober elegance of her house. When he left her, he was hardly sensible of how she had imposed herself on him. He found himself pledged to read his play to her on an early occasion, half surprised himself at the ease with which the promise had been extracted.

"And by the way," she had added, "would you mind a small audience, and make it Thursday? I expect one or two people to dine; your friend Gerald Brooke is coming, and I want you to be one of the party."

He went back to the Temple to spend an absorbed, distressed evening over his manuscript—emending, correcting, excising, until, to his confusion of ideas, the play came to seem to him a monstrosity of imperfection, and he cast it aside in despair. This result was the more disheartening, in that he could recall how, when he wrote the last page in the cabin of the *Anonyma* at Algiers, he had gone through it with less of that inevitable disgust with which, to a certain extent, always at the moment of completion, he needs must contrast achievement with the evasive beauty of his idea. He had thought it a strong play, exposing lucidly, in several dramatic movements, a forcible story.

Less than ever before, too, he had reproached himself with offences against his passion for style, believing that he had, in a measure, succeeded in his constant endeavour to be classically fine, without "preciousness," or merely ornate writing; to be simple, inevitable, precise. In his present mood, his characters grew puppets of melodrama, the deliberate simplicity of his dialogue, ineffectual reporting.

Though in the sober morning he could take a more lenient view of his effort,—he was maintained in this judgment by Corbyn, to whom the play was shown, and who was loud in its praises,—it was not without sundry trepidations that he rendered himself, with his manuscript, on the appointed evening, at Mrs. Vesper's house. He found that her small audience was still large enough to make a considerable show round a dinner-table that was, nevertheless, of respectable size. He felt vaguely puzzled during the uncomfortable interval in the drawing-room (happily he was a little late), for though the majority of the guests were strange to him, he seemed so familiar with their faces, that he felt as if he ought to have known them. It was not till Mrs. Vesper had mentioned the names of two or three of them that he could account for this sentiment; they figured too often in the chronicles of the world of Art for the most absent peripatetic to have missed their photographs in the shop windows of Regent Street. When he discerned the face of Miss Brabant amongst them, he hailed her by contrast as an old friend; was sensibly relieved at discovering, when they had exchanged greetings of some cordiality, that he was to take her down to dinner. One of her allusions, while they waited, to the promised morsel of the evening, the reading of his play, disconcerted him. He gathered that the fact was published, the match already laid to the train; and a project, which had half formed itself in his mind, of evasion, of retreat, was shattered. His unhappiness—he had seldom felt so disorganised—drove him to the girl for sympathy, and before dinner had made much progress he had confessed his scruples, his tremors. Her laugh was benevolent and sanguine.

"You remind me of my cousin Henry, when he was going to address his constituents. He was terribly nervous. But you need not be afraid; your poems were so good, that I feel certain of your play. Besides, it will not be so formidable—some of these people will have gone on to the Foreign Office."

Rome had heard of his friend's victory—of course, it had been a foregone conclusion—at a bye-election a month ago. Had he spoken yet?

"I see very little of him," the girl replied. "I am staying here for the present. The Duchess is not in town."

There was a trace of reticence in her tone, and he wondered how far she was in his friend's confidence; or it might refer simply to the continued obloquy of the eldest son of the house, which was making the Duchess more and more a votary of country seclusion; precisely, a paragraph he had read half an hour before in an evening paper seemed to corroborate this; a rumour of an approaching alliance between the noble Marquis and the Australian lady, with whom his name was so constantly coupled—an impossible person!

Mrs. Vesper interpolated a remark just then, strategically seeking to make the conversation general.

Gerald Brooke, whose smile of good-humoured self-appreciation reassured the young dramatist over a rampart of exotic flowers and glass, seconded her with an epigram. And he leaned back, while the laugh rippled round him, with the air of a man who had plenty more in stock, and was disposed to be generously lavish with them.

It was upon conversation, indeed, that the conversation trenched; and more than one lady turned to this past-master of the practice for an opinion. He declared it a lost art, cultivated by the fewest, at least in England; he was in favour of a parliamentary committee to enquire into the cause of this.

Dalrymple Green, as a prominent lobbyist, protested against the tribunal; they heard so much bad talk in the House, that their judgment must be warped. Mrs. Vesper alluded to the new enterprise of an enterprising purveyor of all things, who supplied entertaining guests to the *nouveaux riches* for a consideration.

Lady Adela Moon, a lady with a passion for barbarous experiences, who was only in civilisation to publish a book of her last travels in Central China, commended the idea. "If ever I have a house again, I will entertain on that principle."

"The objection would be," put in Brooke, "that your best talker depends upon his atmosphere; he can only flourish under the choicest conditions."

"That is the worst of bores," Adrian hazarded; "they are not only dull themselves, but they make you dull: their vice is catching."

"Exactly," went on Brooke, with genial egoism. "I tremble to think of the oceans of dulness I might pour out, if I were hired for, say—a Nonconformist breakfast-table."

The incongruity of the notion provoked hilarity.

"A Nonconformist breakfast-table! The mere mention of such a gathering is depressing," Mrs. Vesper declared. "What would it be like?"

Dalrymple Green repudiated knowledge of it, though he admitted his acquaintance with its conscience.

"You keep it, don't you, Green?" asked Lorimer, the editor of a famous monthly review,—"the Nonconformist conscience?"

Brooke bent forward with his suavely malicious smile, answering for him.

"Dalrymple tickles it in his leaders—as they tickle trout—to catch votes."

"One must catch them when one can," said the journalist cynically.

And the stream of pointed talk, of bright, apposite impromptu, or of more deliberate phrases, uttered with the air of impromptu, flowed into other channels.

Adrian, the youngest, least-known man present, weighted, moreover, by disagreeable anticipations, was content for the most part to be a silent listener, admiring especially the deft management of his hostess, to whose nice tact he attributed it, that the effect of brilliance was so general, with no privileged wit or predominant monologue. She had her table in hand, and moved it harmoniously, as the born conductor his orchestra. They rose soon after nine, and almost immediately the men followed the ladies into the drawing-room. And there were leave-takings from the persons who were pledged elsewhere, hardly numerous enough for Adrian, whose nervousness, when he saw the little table with its pair of stately candlesticks already set for him, had reached its climax. Actually, however, when he had seated himself, and with a last, appealing glance round the room, opened his manuscript, most of the strangers had departed.

It was but a vague circle of arm-chairs that confronted him, for the large, handsome room was dimly lighted. The well-bred hush which ensued amongst the indistinguishable guests, after a few preliminary murmurs, struck Adrian cold, and he plunged at his title, at the list of his characters, desperately, with a voice that trembled. But a moment later, with the opening of his first act, his disorder had passed away. A sudden determination to do his work justice, mingled with a renewed confidence in it, had restored him. When he turned the first page, he read, until he came to the end, in a low, distinct voice, full of subtile modulations, with composure and conviction; he had forgotten his audience. People listened, watched him with an increasing curiosity; they were disposed to be interested, finding his long, oval face, rather pale, with its vivid eyes against the background of shadow, a picture impressive and striking.

The Opportunists: a Comedy, he called his play, the category striking at least one of his listeners, before the reading had very far progressed, as a trifle arbitrary. Certainly, in spite of not a few passages of effective wit in the first act, which opened in full sunshine, upon a return of the newly-married, there was little of the genial spirit of old comedy in this somewhat relentless piece of dramatic observation. In some dialogue with the husband, full of literary charm, the character of the heroine revealed itself: a vivid, girlish figure, wisely innocent, cherishing her dignified ideals, "the fair sum of six thousand years' traditions of civility," defending them all most passionately from the playful attacks of a friend, older by some years, Mrs. Helvellyn, who viewed marriage ("if one doesn't begin by forgiving one's husband, one ends by divorcing him") more cynically; who meets Cynthia Mallory's impetuous denial that she has married a husband who needs forgiveness, with the shrug of superior knowledge. More subtilely, the character of Mallory was exposed: a weak, well-meaning, handsome fellow, "the average sensual man," or more so, keenly appreciative of his wife, yet a little bored already, after a six weeks' honeymoon, with the odd part she casts him for. Half amused, but a trifle exhausted, he sketches the situation to his cousin, Captain Romilly, in a scene which the author had treated with a discretion quite masterly, and which brought the act to an end. The situation had the germs of tragical, or, at least, of ironical development; and Marion Brabant was prepared for the hardly mirthful note which pervaded the subsequent scenes, of the heroine's successive awakenings. Is that operation, so dear to the heart of woman, of washing the Ethiopian, ever really successful? This was a question, among others, which Adrian's play seemed to suggest to the audience; though, certainly, he had avoided the error of answering too definitely this or other questions. At least, in the second act,—an interval of some months had elapsed,—Mallory has returned to the fleshpots of Egypt. A discovery, inexorably convincing, of the clay in her idol, has estranged Cynthia from her husband, and in a scene, with some art only touched upon in retrospect, she has coldly dismissed him. In his absence, Captain Romilly, superficial, adroit, inflammable, misses no opportunity of consoling a beautiful inconsolable; and with all the skill of a past-master of gallantry, he widens the breach between the disenchanted couple, for his own purpose. The masque of the highminded, chivalrous lover imposes on the disillusioned wife, and, with her youthful hunger for the ideal still unsatisfied and exorbitant, she draws the inference which Romilly desires. It is but from one high horse to another that this gentle amateur in the difficult art of loving steps. And an artful dialogue, in which Romilly, with some casuistry, argues with Cynthia for a woman's right to avenge her husband's notorious infidelities in kind, paves the way for his declaration. Between a noble lover, and a husband, who is, at the best, a good-natured profligate, choice is difficult and involved. Her very hatred of compromise; the legitimate recklessness of a fine nature, wantonly outraged, are advocates of his cause; and the curtain falls almost upon her consent. And it was here Adrian scored his first triumph, retaining his audience's sympathy for a heroine capable of such weakness—of an abdication which had at least its roots in nobility. The sequel, and the precise *Deus ex machina* to save Cynthia from social shipwreck, resumed the key of lighter comedy. At the point of flight with Captain Romilly, the irresolute woman, attacked by her friend, Mrs. Helvellyn, whom old acquaintance with Captain Romilly has rendered suspicious, is reduced to explain, to justify herself. The scene which followed between the two, when from a few deft revelations Cynthia learns that her lover's record is less creditable even than her husband's own, provoked applause. Her dismissal of him, characterised by a certain cold disdain rather than her old fire of indignation, signalised her defeat. Mrs. Helvellyn's pitying reminder, "One doesn't make one's life, my child! one arranges it, puts up with it: it's compromise one makes"; the defeated, doubly defeated woman's rejoinder, "One pays dearest for one's aspirations," prepare for the reconciliation between Cynthia and her husband, privately summoned by Mrs. Helvellyn. As she makes her exit, leaving them with the benediction of a good-hearted *mondaine*, who has killed a scandal, Cynthia, with half a sigh burying her girlhood, is a convert to opportunism. The finale, the half-hearted reconciliation of the intimately divided pair, sought with a curious lassitude by the wife, met with good-natured acquiescence by the husband,—at heart he is plainly impenitent,—came upon the audience as a surprise of cynicism. There was a minute's silence, before they were sufficiently certain that the reading had come to an end to seal it with a little polite applause. On the whole, however, they had been diverted, although their urbane praises probably concealed a variety of opinions.

There was a quick shuffle of chairs; people split up into little groups; some were taking leave. Adrian, as he moved towards his hostess, was afflicted with a return of shamefacedness, of disgust at his part of the entertainment, was anxious only to get away.

But Brooke stopped him for a moment, to introduce him to a tall, thin, close-shaven man, with restless eyes; Cyrus Holmes, an actor, who was also a manager, and who was reported to be less prone than most of his fraternity to time-honoured reproductions, to have a taste for dramatic novelties. Stammering a little, smiling rather foolishly,—his perfect self-possession on the stage being in odd contrast to his extreme nervousness in private life,—he asked Adrian if he might have the pleasure of reading the manuscript; it had struck him very much, he wanted to find something new.

"He means, that he wants to produce you," Brooke interpolated.

"I think—I think I might very likely be able to make you an offer," the actor went on. "Your play is very strong."

Adrian professed himself delighted; he had feared that perhaps it had not the elements of a popular success.

"Oh, the public is waking up," said Cyrus Holmes placidly.

"So you have scored a point!" Brooke remarked a few minutes later, as they stopped beneath a gas-lamp, lighting cigarettes. "Holmes talks like a schoolgirl, but he is far too good a man of business to compromise himself. You will be produced, and very well produced, and I congratulate you in advance. Your play, my dear fellow, is charming, but it's horrible. Your people are quite too absurdly vulgar and real; they are people out of the street, they lack atmosphere and grace."

"You are an impenitent romantic," laughed Adrian; "you would like to dress my persons in seventeenth-century clothes."

"Yes," admitted the other, as they separated, "I am a very impenitent romantic. I am going away to devise a beautiful Oriental ballet: it is much less tedious than writing plays."

Left alone, Adrian paused for a few moments at the street corner, gazing vacantly at his watch, in search of inspiration. He felt restless, disinclined for his own society; vaguely dissatisfied, and at the same time exhilarated. He remembered suddenly that the hour was one at which he would almost certainly find Corbyn at a neighbouring club, and his yearning for sympathy prompted him to bend his steps thither. The club was one where the university element largely predominated, and the little group which he joined on his arrival was augmented shortly after midnight by Lord Henry Minaret, who had come up from the House. A pleasant hour ensued, full of reminiscence and the exchange of personal news.

"You have heard, of course, about poor old Simeon?" said Lord Henry, as they parted later in Piccadilly, turning abruptly to his friend. "I'm sorry!" he added quickly, perceiving that Adrian's expression exhibited the note of enquiry rather than assent.

"I thought you would have seen it in to-day's *Times*."

"He's—dead?" said Rome softly.

The other nodded gravely, and after a moment's expressive silence they separated.

CHAPTER XI

THE train which conveyed Adrian and a few other friends and kinsmen of his old tutor from London to Underwoods did not time its arrival with any consideration for the hour of the funeral, and, finding that he had plenty of time to cover the short three miles on foot, Adrian preferred to allow his companions to drive off without him in the rusty, hired carriage which had been sent to meet them. For a while he stood on the platform, exchanging a few words with the station-master, who did not fail to recognise him as a former inhabitant of the place; watching, while he waited, the carriage creeping between the hedgerows, with its dusky load of mourners, whose black coats and hats seemed an affront to the tender beauty of the fresh spring landscape. So soon as he felt that he had nothing to fear from the dust of their wheels, he set out after them, walking on the short grass by the roadside, with an eye for the peeping primrose in the hedge-bottom, the delicate shimmer of blue-bells and wind-flowers in the spinney. When he came in sight of the little village, it seemed to him, gazing upon it from his post of vantage on the top of the hill, to be almost buried in a sea of apple-blossom, which clung like a white surf round the red gables, the tiled and thatched roofs, and the crooked chimney-stacks; the place was hardly less silent than the bright spring sky, which spread its cloud-flecked dome above. The fugual cawing of the rooks in the elm-trees, the challenge of the cuckoo in the copse, the distant bleating of the lambs on the hillside; these were the only sounds that broke the perfect stillness: one might have fancied the village uninhabited, or the villagers asleep.

While he waited, leaning his elbows on the top rail of a gate which, as a boy, he had often climbed, the church clock struck, and the familiar sound carried him still further back into the days of his childhood, recalling, amongst other memories pleasant and bitter, the little girl at the post-office, at an age when she had not (to him at least) presented anything so disagreeable as a problem, a difficulty. He sighed presently; but the emotion of which this may be imagined the expression was not due solely and singly to the change in his, or Sylvia's, estate, but rather to a general feeling of present discomfort: a funeral was a function which his soul abhorred, and he often felt that this, and certain other attendant circumstances, rather than the actual passing from life, were the attributes which made the thought of death so ugly. As he descended the hill, feeling glad on the whole that his road to the vicarage did not lie through the village or past the post-office, he promised himself that he would make a will which should enjoin upon his executors, in the strictest possible terms, his desire that his death should not be made the occasion of the ordinary dismal ceremonies. He passed his own house quickly, almost without a glance; he did not even know whether it held a tenant; and coming within sight of the vicarage which for so long had been his home, the scene of a bondage which he recognised now as certainly beneficent, he fell to thinking, a little self-reproachfully, of the many kindnesses which had come to him from the hands of his old tutor, the dear old pedant, whom he had so often laughed at, though at heart he revered him as a single-minded man, and loved him as a kindly foster-father.

The weary waiting in the darkened parlour, the slow procession of bareheaded men to the sunny churchyard, the hospitality which he found himself bound to accept at the hands of the Vicar's sister-in-law, whom he remembered as a frequent visitor to the house in his boyhood,—all those irksome ceremonies dragged at last to an end; and, with something like elation, he found himself once more on the outer side of the vicarage gate, with only his black clothes to remind him of the ordeal to which he had been subjected.

Consulting his watch, after surreptitiously flinging his black gloves behind the hedge, he found that it was nearly four o'clock, and he remembered that there was no available train to London before half-past six. Circumstances seemed to dictate that he should take the familiar short-cut along the river to the post-office, and his inclination, though at first somewhat feebly, abetted them. He felt that, after all, he could not afford to quarrel with Sylvia: when all was said, the fact remained that she was a beautiful and charming girl, the only friend of his boyhood, the most pleasant feature of a period from which, if he did not altogether wish to return to it, he had no desire entirely to sever himself. He had not recognised her among the little group of villagers who stood, somewhat apart from his fellow-mourners, in the churchyard; but it was possible that she was there; nor would there have been anything startling in her absence, for he well knew that of late years Mrs. Drew had become a confirmed invalid, needing constant attendance. He had no fear lest he should not find Sylvia in the queer little house which was her home, or possibly in the pleasant garden, which he had so often helped her to weed and water; for his voluble friend the station-master had informed him as to the mental and bodily estate and whereabouts of all the dwellers in Underwoods, and her name had not figured among the absentees.

The little shop, shuttered on account of the funeral, was empty when Adrian entered it; but a small boy, appearing in obedience to the summons of the tinkling bell, which his entry had startled into spasmodic eloquence, informed him that Mrs. Drew was within. He found the old lady (with a person whom he correctly denominated as her younger sister) in occupation of the prim, festal parlour, in which he had sometimes taken tea when he was a child. The windows were closed, and a fire crackled in the grate, in spite of the warmth of the vernal afternoon; and it struck him at once that Mrs. Drew had aged very fast, that she had become old, decrepid. She recognised his voice, she told him, and his manner of knocking at the door: she quavered out various polite little speeches, and presently, when the conversation flagged, reminded him strangely of the old days by sinking back into her arm-chair, with a nod in the direction of the low bay-window. "Sylvia's in the garden, Mr. Adrian; she will be right glad to see you. It's pleasanter there, for young people." Her intimation conveyed no news to him: his first swift glance through the window had confirmed his anticipation; he had seen, with a quick thrill, that Sylvia was outside, in the sunlight, standing in front of the old arbour, with her back towards the house. Her occupation was not so promptly revealed to him: something in her pose, her movements, seemed to indicate that she was holding animated converse with an invisible interlocutor, who might be concealed within the arbour: once, when she turned slightly, with a dramatic gesture, he caught a glimpse of a buff-coloured book, held in one outstretched hand.

Mrs. Drew, observing his hesitation, reassured him; it was all right, he wouldn't be interrupting anything; Sylvia was only reading to her cousin. Whereupon Rome smilingly took his leave of the old lady; recalling, with a laugh at his own stupidity, that Sylvia had always shown a weakness for helping small boys with their lessons; she was probably engaged in this way now.

As soon as his footsteps sounded on the red tiles which were set before the garden door, Sylvia came quickly down the path to meet him, blushing a little, and putting up one hand in restraint of vagrant tresses. If their greeting was a little formal, lacking in the old frank simplicity, it must be remembered that they had not seen each other for at least six months; a period which, in the country at least, is a long one, and may well work many changes in a maiden's manners, even though it leaves her heart unscathed: moreover, their last exchange of letters had imposed vague burdens on their consciences.

Sylvia wore a black dress, almost entirely covered by the apron, of a faded blue, which formed part of her garden apparel: when her blushes died away, he noticed that she was rather thin and pale, and that her beauty gained thereby an added charm of delicacy.

"I saw you in the churchyard," she said softly, growing restless under the gaze of his eyes. "Poor old gentleman, we shall miss him in Underwoods! They say he died very peacefully."

"Yes," said Adrian, "he did everything very peacefully, dear old man! I think my guardian was the only person that ever ruffled him."

"And the Salvation Army!" suggested Sylvia. "Yes, we shall miss him!"

Adrian watched her, while she stooped to pick a dead blossom off a flame-coloured wall-flower: revelling in the rapid grace of her movements, the curves of her hand and wrist.

"You will miss him, Sylvia! I wonder, do you ever miss me?"

"Of course we miss you!" she answered brightly. "The whole village has missed you, ever since that summer when you went to Oxford."

"Oh, the village!" said Rome. "I didn't realise that I was so important a member of the community. But you—you yourself: do you ever think of the old days?"

"You were very kind," said the girl, still intent upon her flowers. "You used to help me water my garden, and read to me. I should be very ungrateful if I didn't think of you sometimes," she continued bravely, turning towards him. "I'm afraid I made you waste your time: you must forgive me, I was only a child."

"Your precious garden! I wish I might never waste time less pleasantly. I should like to help you water it now. Do you remember, you used to make me a buttonhole, by way of reward, and even . . ."

"Oh no," said Sylvia hurriedly, "that would never do! You mustn't think I don't know what a celebrated person you have become. Of course, I knew you would! We read the newspaper here, you know, and I have seen what a deal they think of your poems. We were very glad, mother and I."

"Ah," said Adrian softly, "I would give it all—it's not worth much, it has been only a little bubble—for one of the summer days when we sat and talked by the old sun-dial! Why can't they come again, those old days? I haven't changed, Sylvia."

"Everything has changed!" cried the girl. "They were all wrong, those old days. If they were pleasant,—and

I'm sure I thought **so then,—so** much **the better**; but they are gone—we can't be children again. **I was**—we were very foolish."

"**And are we so wise now?** I don't like your wisdom; **I liked** you better when you were foolish . . . I wish **I wasn't** obliged **to go** back to town to-night. I should like **to** stop **here all my** days. **I feel** quite another **being when I'm in your garden; I think it must** be enchanted!"

"**Poor garden!**" she said, gazing away from him **across** the green grass-plot, where the blossoms of the old **pear-tree lay** like sprinkled snowflakes. "Who **can have** enchanted **it? Isn't that** another reason why you **ought never to** come **here? Haven't** you read **to** me, **out of your wonderful books—Homer,** wasn't it?—what **happens to** people who linger **in** enchanted places? Yes, **that's it, it** has **an evil** influence, **my** garden; it makes **you forget your ambitions,—the figure you are** to make **in the great world. Have you** forgotten how you **used to** talk **to me, about your plans?**"

"Forget—forget! **does one ever forget? And I** thought you wanted **me to,—you know,** you said we **were** foolish **then, Sylvia.**"

"I think **we were very wise, sometimes.**"

"I'm sure I was very **wise—until I went away.** That **strikes** me now **as** the beginning of **all my** follies."

She sighed, smiling a little wearily. "**It was the end, I hope.**"

Adrian echoed her sigh: it reminded him that he was **weary, in body and mind.** He had wandered into Sylvia's domain in the **hope of** finding **an** oasis **in the desert of** controversy: an **attack of feminine** logic was **not at** all **what he** had bargained **for. He** wanted to **tell** this immensely charming, but provokingly perverse damsel,—whose **rusticity, he was** relieved to find, had

(at least while he was under the spell) absolutely no
terrors for him,—that he adored her, that she was a
thousand times prettier than she had ever been before,
that he was a fool for having written her that stupid,
prosy letter, of which her reply was, after all, only the
natural consequence; that he was, in short, her slave,
humble and devoted. But she seemed to be hedged
about with scruples, bristling with secrecy, conventional,
discouraging. For a moment, whimsically, he was
inclined to attribute his defeat to his funereal appearance: after all he was hardly dressed for the lover's
part; he was better calculated to produce a nervous
attack than an access of tenderness. He wished he had
the courage to ask for a flower—something bright, a
pansy, or one of those little yellow things—for his
coat; but catching a glimpse of his reflected image in
the glass door of the diminutive greenhouse, he at once
dismissed the idea, as hardly decorous. His efforts,
which he did not at once abandon, to establish a greater
degree of ease, to bridge the gulf of time, of misunderstanding, which seemed to lie between them, met with
scant success. So long as their talk ran in safe channels,
clear and shallow, she was the pleasant Sylvia of old
days; but any attempt on his part to court the swift
danger of the rapids, to fathom the deep pools which
formerly she had shown no anxiety to avoid, seemed to
lead inevitably to his discomfiture.

"Adrian," she said suddenly, after a silence which had
been broken only by the tramp of his feet upon the
gravel, the carol of the blackbird in the pear-tree. "I
wish you would promise me something!"

"And I wish you would promise me—something!" he
interrupted, with a look which made her turn away
passionately, with a cry, a protest that he was cruel.

"I'm sorry," he said. "Only, I don't know what I've

done. Forgive me, trample on me, anything—only don't turn your back on me: your face is so much prettier!"

The girl uttered a little despairing moan, and then turned to him, laying one hand (how well he remembered that dimple, between garden-glove and sleeve, on the sunburnt wrist!) upon his arm.

"Promise me that you won't come here any more, for a long time,—that you won't!"

"My dear child!" he murmured, caressing the little hand as it lay upon his black sleeve. "What are you afraid of?"

"I'm not a child!" she broke out, tearing her hand away and walking on. "It's you who are a child—a mischievous child! Take care; you don't know what you are driving me to. Haven't I been patient enough?"

Adrian frowned, biting his lip with a hasty protest, as he followed her along the narrow path, noticing again the charming contours of her neck and shoulders; the easy carriage of her arms, of which her scanty sleeves revealed the modelling; the radiant coils of her wonderful hair. He began to realise that it was true, that things had changed: there was to be no more of the old, frank love-making, when there was no need to count the kisses, to think of the morrow. Sylvia had of a sudden become desperately practical, surprisingly worldly. He had gone out into the world, it seemed, while she had stayed at home and garnered its wisdom. A Sylvia with whom one had to pick and choose one's words; to be on one's guard: he found the development somewhat disconcerting. She had never looked so charming, she had never treated him so unkindly. He was desperately in love with the creature (he withdrew the "desperately" later, on his way home), but he was bewildered, tired, uncomfortable. What did she mean? he asked himself. If it had not been done so often before, by every lover that he had read about, he would have enquired whether there was anyone else—if he had a rival? She turned, presently, (the silence had been, in fact, of brief duration), and he was agreeably disappointed when, instead of making some further unreasonable demand of him, she suggested, naïvely, that if he was going by the 6.30 train it was time that she should see about getting him a cup of tea.

Strolling together along the winding paths, between the nodding columbines and golden leopard's-bane, they had hitherto, by tacit, mutual consent, avoided the vicinity of the summer-house; but now they drew near to this retreat, Sylvia leading the way, and Rome was soon in a position to observe that its occupant, of whose presence he had been vaguely aware, was a good-looking youth, a little older than himself, dressed in flannels, lounging in a basket-chair, lazily intent upon a novel, yellow-backed, by Carrie Morella. His careless conclusion as to the little boy and the lesson-book had, it seemed, fallen somewhat short of the mark. He wondered, for an instant, what Sylvia had been reading to this gentleman, and whether his presence was the key to her incomprehensible attitude. Presently he perceived that he was being eyed in turn; and, when the three were already at close range, the stranger rose deliberately from his comfortable seat, and stood, stooping, in the low doorway of the arbour, caressing a fluent, well-ordered moustache, regarding the approaching couple with lazy curiosity. Sylvia coloured a little, and after glancing askance at her companion, murmured a few words of introduction.

"George, this is Mr. Rome; Mr. Rome, my cousin, Mr. George Winter."

"That happens to be my name," supplemented the stranger, bowing graciously, with a flourish of his smart straw hat; "but I am better known as Montague Villiers. Anyway, I'm very pleased to make your acquaintance, Mr. Rome."

Adrian bowed, a little stiffly, in spite of his wish to avoid such an attitude. It had never occurred to him that Sylvia numbered among her kinsfolk a cousin so urbane, genteel: he was aware that she had relations on her mother's side, but he had been quite in the dark as to their social pretensions: in the days when he dwelt there, they had not visited Underwoods. So Sylvia had a cousin with an assumed name; he felt somewhat curious as to the motives which had prompted the man to abandon the appellation (he had forgotten what it was) which Sylvia had murmured, and which was presumably the gift of his godfathers and godmothers; while, at the same time, he felt that after all the substitution had been singularly judicious: the Montague Villiers (had he heard the name before?) was so unmistakably impressed upon the cut of his handsome features, the fashion of his coloured flannel jacket, (disposed so as to allow a liberal display of a gaily striped shirt-front), his smart be-ribboned hat, his staring yellow Russian-leather shoes.

Sylvia, begging the gentlemen to excuse her, hastened towards the house on an errand connected with the promised tea: her cousin meanwhile (he appeared to be of a conversational disposition) explained to Rome that his presence at Underwoods was due to his mother's desire to visit her sister, Mrs. Drew.

"My aunt's in failing health, you know, Mr. Rome; not expected to live long: the old lady's not so young as she was. And I thought a week in the country wouldn't be so bad for me. Town takes it out of one, doesn't it?"

Adrian assented, lighting a cigarette and offering his

case to Mr. Villiers, who was encouraged thereby to profess his contempt for tea, and regret that he was unable to provide Mr. Rome with a whisky-and-soda.

"I've been telling my cousin that she ought to go on the stage," he continued confidentially. "With a little teaching and experience she'd do first-rate. You know, I'm in that line myself: if you read the *Era* you have probably seen my name. Yes? Theatrical agency, you know. Do a bit myself, sometimes. Take a show round the provinces, you know. Oh, I'm certain Sylvia's got it in her, the right stuff. I know it well enough, when I see it. And she's pretty, too; there's no doubt she'd knock 'em, even if she wasn't so clever. Oh, she'd knock 'em all right."

"Does your cousin favour the idea?" asked Rome, frowning a little unconsciously, "I imagine that Miss Drew has had no experience of any kind: surely it must be a little difficult, even for an expert like yourself, to estimate her capacity?"

"Oh," said the other airily, "it was her own notion in the first place. She wrote to me about it some time ago, and I didn't encourage her, I assure you, Mr. Rome. I told her it wasn't all beer and skittles and big salaries, and that there were vanloads of girls all over the country fancying themselves Ellen Terrys and Sarah Bernhardts on the strength of an encore at a Penny Reading. But she's been studying up some things on the quiet,—I sent her down acting copies of a few of Robertson's plays, and so on; and she knows a good bit already. She was reading over Polly Eccles' lines to me just before you came: it wasn't half bad. As her cousin, I don't want her to go on the stage; but Art, Mr. Rome, Art has no consideration for one's feelings!"

Rome expressed his appreciation of this sentiment; and, somewhat to his relief, further discussion was arrested by the advent of Sylvia herself with the tea-tray: he was relieved, for although he could not reasonably resent Mr. Villiers' choice of a topic, he would have preferred that his enlightenment as to Sylvia's possible projects should have emanated from her own lips. Before taking his leave, as he presently did, in order to catch the London train, he found an opportunity of questioning Sylvia briefly as to her supposed histrionic ambition, to which her cousin had again made allusion over the tea-table; and he accepted as reassuring her reply, that she had not considered the matter seriously, that she certainly had no intention of doing anything of the kind during her mother's lifetime.

CHAPTER XII

LADY LANCASTER'S summer dance had come to be regarded as a "fixture" no less invariable than the Henley Regatta or the 'Varsity cricket match; events with which it was, in point of time, very closely associated. As a general rule, it was a well-attended gathering. People ordered their carriages to drive to the plain, commodious house in the unlovely square to the north of Oxford Street, not because they expected to find collected there a brilliant assembly, graced perhaps by the presence of Royalty, or the latest discovery in skirt-dancers, but rather on account of a certain dumb reluctance to forego a ceremony which appealed so strongly to that conservative habit of life, that love of the treadmill routine, to which everyone is at heart a victim.

Moreover, the daughters were pretty, and (crowning virtue) easy to talk to; versed in the dangerous wiles of the ballroom, the seductive arts of conservatory and staircase: if this was an argument which smiled not upon the mothers of marriageable but less attractive daughters, to the irresponsible butterfly of the clubs, to that rare bird, the dancing man, it appealed with considerable force. Now, it was true, Lady Lancaster had (to use a metaphor of the garden) planted out two of the four charming seedlings which had originally adorned her nursery; only Marjorie and Phyllis remained—practically only Phyllis, for it will be remembered that Marjorie was already the destined bride of that famous warrior, General Sir Cuthbert Verrinder; but the tradition clung to the house; the girls were pretty, and if it was not smart, one met very decent people there. On this particular night, in the second week of June, Lady Lancaster had the pleasure of opening her doors to the customary throng of damsels and dowagers (in the proportion of four to one); budding politicians and diplomatists; tall youths from Aldershot and Oxford; and country cousins, easily identified by their complexions and their preference for Irving and the Academicians,—a somewhat solid agglomeration, discreetly leavened by a pinch of what the astute hostess regarded as reclaimed Bohemianism, in the shape of a few young painters who could display letters after their names (Marjorie had already been immortalised on the walls of Burlington House, and a "Portrait of Miss Phyllis Lancaster" by Sir Richard Lightmark, R.A., was one of the features of the current exhibition), two or three men whom one associated vaguely with the austerer paths of literature, a newly-returned explorer, and a successful novelist.

Adrian Rome, who came under the wing of Lord Henry Minaret, represented for their hostess a fine example of those invaluable social units who are catalogued by strategicians of her order as eligibles, a category under which Lord Henry also fell. And Lady Lancaster's welcome of the two young men was as gracious as circumstances (such as an elbowing crowd, a hot room, an elaborate toilet) would allow. One of them (Mr. Rome, for choice) would do so admirably for Phyllis, if the Marquis of Glendougal failed to come up to the scratch. She bore Lord Henry no malice on Marjorie's account; indeed, she regarded him as an important feature of her triumph; she could afford to pity him, to feel, gratefully, that he had been instrumental in hastening General Verrinder's decision.

This enviable old gentleman had posted himself at Lady Lancaster's elbow, blushing quite boyishly under the congratulations which were showered upon him. His behaviour throughout had been all that a prospective mother-in-law could wish; he had displayed a princely liberality in the matter of settlements; and the recklessness with which he had laid his Surrey rosebeds and hothouses under contribution for the greater glory of this festivity had brought tears to the eyes of his Scotch head-gardener.

For a time, Adrian allowed himself to be towed about the crowded rooms in the wake of one of the indefatigable daughters of the house, winning golden opinions by the urbane impartiality with which he asked every girl to whom he was introduced if he might have the pleasure of dancing with her. It was more by chance than by design that, somewhat late in the evening, he found that he had left himself without partners for two consecutive numbers, and was so enabled, without breach of contract, to take Miss Brabant down to supper at the end of the waltz which he had begged from her.

"I'm engaged for the next dance," she explained, as they made their way down the wide staircase, between the banks of fragrant roses. "But only to Henry: he won't mind. One always has to take one's chance with the supper dances. Really, one might imagine oneself at a flower-show!"

The girl was looking singularly well, Adrian reflected, as he glanced at her across the little table at which they found places. The music, the heat, the rapid motion, had lent a colour to her cheeks, a brilliance to her eyes; even a charm to her voice, and a certain languorous grace to her movements. She was Diana masquerading as Venus; the part suited her indifferently, but the step was in the right direction. As she talked, inconsequently, and a little breathlessly,—protesting that she didn't want any supper, she had only come down because it was the right thing to do, to reassure her chaperon,—he forgot that she could be cold and irresponsive; he felt, more than ever, that he had begun by doing her an injustice.

He caught up her reference to the roses, glancing at the petals, deep red and copper-pink, which had fallen from a tall vase upon the table at which they sat.

"Quite a wonderful display: one feels like Heliogabalus. I didn't know there were so many roses in England. Lady Lancaster must have imported them, from Bulgaria or Provence."

The girl smiled, with a little air of mystery.

"Not from Bulgaria, I think,—unless that is the name of General Verrinder's place in Surrey."

"Ah, I see!" said the other reflectively. "I wasn't in the secret. Poor Harry!"

Miss Brabant shrugged her white shoulders imperceptibly.

"Poor Harry, indeed! I'm afraid he's very obstinate. He won't own that he's beaten, even now."

"He has taken a lesson from politics," suggested Rome; "that's the way seats are won, Miss Brabant. Pardon the comparison!"

"It's not what I should have expected—of a poet!" the girl admitted, with a smile.

"Ah, that's too great a name for me," said Adrian modestly; "for a maker of indifferent rhymes."

Miss Brabant protested. "You should hear Mrs. Vesper talk about your poems—and your play. And I regard her as an authority, of the highest."

"Mrs. Vesper is my guardian angel, my fairy godmother!" declared the other gravely. "I am learning to go to her in all my difficulties; she is really extraordinarily gifted! Last week, for instance, I suddenly remembered that I had taken an enormous house-boat for Henley, and I hadn't the remotest idea as to what to do with it. In this extremity—"

"You repaired to your fairy godmother, and she undertook to get up a party for you."

"Precisely! And if she has been clever enough to secure you, I shall regard her as—as a veritable *Deus ex machina*."

"The house-boat being the 'machine,' I suppose," laughed the girl. "Mrs. Vesper has been good enough to ask me; in fact, she has enlisted me as a kind of lieutenant. We are going to take down all sorts of people!"

"The dear creature!" murmured Rome. "I hope you haven't had much trouble about it?"

"Oh, I ought to thank you!" said Miss Brabant. "Otherwise, I expect I should have missed Henley altogether. The Duchess isn't going this year."

"And do you care much about it?"

The girl hesitated for a moment. "Candidly, no. It's always the same. I haven't missed the Regatta for three or four years now, and, so far as my experience goes, it always rains on two days out of the three: there are always the same people, the same house-boats, the same tents and flowers on the lawns; and if the same crews don't win every year, at least they are so much alike that an ignoramus like myself can't tell the difference."

Adrian laughed, admitting the truth of Miss Brabant's summary.

"I was there last year, for the first time. St. Cyr's—my college—had a crew in for something or other—the Ladies' Plate, I think. They didn't win. I remember I felt quite depressed about it. I think it must have been much pleasanter in the old days, when it was less formal, before it put on the smartness of Hurlingham and Ascot, and became a great social festival."

Miss Brabant nodded. "It certainly must have been nicer when one didn't have to think so much about one's gown."

Adrian glanced quickly at the extremely becoming robe of stately corded silk, ivory white, with a trimming of silver lace and moonstones, which she was wearing.

"Ah," he said, smiling; "decidedly I shall have reason to be proud of my party! Or perhaps I ought to call it, Mrs. Vesper's party?"

Miss Brabant echoed his smile faintly, buttoning her long glove, and bending over the programme which was fastened to her fan. "I think you may consider it your party," she said indifferently.

It seemed to Adrian that the flickering flame, which he was not vain enough to imagine that he had kindled, but which he had hoped to encourage, was rapidly dying out; that his Galatea was unregretfully returning to her pedestal. Outwardly calm, discussing lightly subjects persistently trivial, he was still at his wits' end to think of an expedient to stay the inevitable moment when he would experience the chagrin of seeing Miss Brabant relapse into that state of impassive frigidity which she could wear so becomingly, and which yet constituted, so indubitably, a blow to his self-respect. He felt himself singularly barren of ideas; his incompetence to rise to the occasion struck him as almost ludicrous. For an instant, when they made their escape together from the ballroom, just before the voluptuous waltz rallied into its last bars, he had flattered himself that the barrier, which it had become quite an inveterate habit for him to attempt to climb, had of a sudden fallen to the ground; he imagined, vainly, that the fortress had capitulated, that at last he was on the other side, within the walls;—

with Mrs. Vesper, whom he had so often envied when he had seen the two ladies exchanging rapid glances expressive of a privileged intimacy, or chatting, confidentially, with frank, sociable enthusiasm. His want of success presented itself as a signal reproach to his address, an impeachment of his tact. The game had ended by interesting him more than he would have acknowledged. He was piqued, in short, attracted by the unattainable in proportion to its remoteness: the predicament was not less perilous for the reason that it was, after all, indigenous to his temperament.

If inspiration came at all, it came too late. He was presently obliged to surrender Miss Brabant to one of the claimants whose names appeared upon her programme; and as he wandered homeward in the pleasant, mellow coolness of the June midnight (he had basely deserted Lord Henry, whose passion for dancing ran far beyond his own), he was able to console himself only by reflecting that, if he had not advanced, at least he had not lost ground, and Henley seemed to promise a field upon which he might retrieve his laurels.

It must be admitted that when Miss Brabant denounced her cousin as obstinate, incapable of retiring gracefully from the inglorious field, it was no unfounded charge that she laid at his door. His presence, and in particular his tactics, at the dance this evening, had prompted her. Hoping, in common with such of his other friends as were in the secret, that the House would serve to draw the young politician's attention to worthier interests, she could not help reproaching him (womanlike, a little pitifully), when she saw that he had deserted the debate on Bimetallism to dangle after the girl who had rejected him.

Miss Marjorie Lancaster, to whom Lord Henry appealed on the first opportunity for a dance, professed herself unable to comply with his request; later, perhaps,—she could not promise; her duties as daughter of the house were too onerous to allow her to enjoy herself at present. She protested, demurely, that in her own house she couldn't think of dancing while there were other girls in want of partners.

"Won't you dance with Miss Carnaby?" she suggested. "You don't know her? Then I will introduce you at once. And if you don't tread on them (you'll know what I mean presently!), it will prove that you are in good form, and perhaps—only perhaps, mind!—you shall be allowed to dance with me. Miss Carnaby, if your card is not *quite* full, may I introduce Lord Henry Minaret?"

Lord Henry bowed, glancing a little reproachfully at his retreating hostess. "Ah . . . I should really feel quite ashamed of myself if I victimised you by making you dance this, Miss Carnaby. I'm sure you must be tired, and the room is so full, isn't it? Do let me get you an ice!"

"But I relented," he explained afterwards to Miss Lancaster. "It wasn't a nice thing to do—in spite of my provocation; and she seemed to feel rather sorry for herself when we went out of the ballroom, and I caught her shivering over the ice! So I concluded that she hadn't been dancing much, and we went upstairs in a hurry, and danced the polka, recklessly regardless of each other's feet, the music, and our neighbours. Now, haven't I done my duty? Haven't I earned my reward?"

"You've been an angel!" she admitted, glancing down at the tip of a little foot, shod in the neatest of gilded shoes. "You know, we're going to Henley; I don't want to miss that!"

"I couldn't tread on them if I tried!" protested the

other. "Besides, do you think I don't want you to go to Henley? I'm going down with Adrian Rome; he's got a house-boat, and we mean to sleep on it."

"We're going to stay at Rose Court," said Miss Lancaster. "I tell you, so that you may avoid it!"

"All right," nodded Lord Henry. "I'll come and look for you on the first day, after lunch. What a delicious waltz this is!"

"Yes," said the girl softly, letting her eyes rest on his for a moment as they swung round, her light weight thrown on the support of his encircling right arm. "But I ought not to be dancing with you; you don't know how angry mamma will be!"

Lord Henry bit his lip, and they danced for a while without speaking. He tried to think calmly, to be reasonable; but his thoughts were invaded by the rustle of the silken skirt of Marjorie's Empire gown, the faint perfume of the spray of violets, blue and white, which so charmingly relieved the fairness of her neck and lifting bosom. It was not possible even for a statesman to be calm within kissing distance of her golden hair, her dainty eyes. Beginning to dream a little, to lose himself in the plaintive rapture of the waltz, (a state of mind incompatible with the alertness, mental and bodily, without which, in full measure, it is difficult to find a clear course in a London ballroom), he was recalled to himself by the shock of a slight collision, and a little surprised protest from his partner. He apologised, and for a few seconds devoted himself to making amends by swift, skilful pilotage.

"General Verrinder does not dance, I think?" he said presently, with a transparent air of indifference.

"No," said the girl demurely, tapping his arm with one of the slender fingers which rested upon it. "But that doesn't matter, you know. One doesn't dance with one's—one's husband."

"Husband!" he echoed, in a savage whisper. "Marjorie, you can't, you won't! It isn't too late—say that you won't! that it's a horrible mistake, and I'll speak to Lady Lancaster to-morrow!"

She glanced at him, pouting a little, and relaxing the clasp of her left hand.

"Don't be so horrid! Of course it's too late; it's all settled, and—and the wedding presents are coming in. Why can't you be sensible? You shall dance with me afterwards, as much as you like. What more can you want? You aren't a bit nice!"

Lord Henry could only find relief for his emotion in a smothered groan. This self-possessed young lady bore very little resemblance to the tearful maiden who had bidden him farewell in the conservatory at Towers. On that occasion—a hurried interview in the twilight, among the palm-trees and azaleas—she had posed as a victim. Now, under the chastened brilliance of the electric light, she wore an air of contentment with her lot; her tears had been succeeded by a complacency, a lightness of heart which her lover viewed with suspicion and resentment.

"Marjorie," he said quickly, as they sank down on the low seat which stood in a dim recess half-way up the staircase, "you don't really care for him?"

The girl fixed her eyes on her slim third finger, where the shape of a jewelled ring defined itself suggestively through her pale suède glove.

"He's really very nice to me," she murmured, still without looking at her companion. "He has sent me a present every day since our engagement was announced, including Sundays. This bangle—isn't it pretty?—came to-night."

Lord Henry clenched his teeth viciously, but vouchsafed no answer.

"Jargoons and aquamarines set alternately, you see, with a daisy for a clasp. Wasn't it clever of him to think of the daisy?"

"You are cruel," he said, after a silence which she had broken by a little sigh. "I don't know you."

"No," put in the girl quickly. "You wouldn't want to marry me if you did. I am a wretch. You ought to be glad."

There was a note of sincerity in her words, and the gaiety of the charming, childlike eyes was eclipsed for the moment by a more passionate fire. He could hear the rustle of her bodice as her breath came fast. But if she was touched, it was only for an instant. Her next words sounded the keynote of the old mood.

"I've no patience with you," she said, turning to him with a pretty air of reproach and a daintily wrinkled brow. "You, a man, crying for the moon—no, not even the moon, only a bit of a girl. Now promise not to do it any more. Let's kiss and be friends—oh! figuratively, of course. Quick, there's the music; say that we'll be friends."

Lord Henry shook his head, then wavered, protesting ruefully, with a puzzled look in his honest eyes, that he was bewildered—he didn't know what he was saying.

"Gracious!" said the girl, rising lightly, like a bubble, from her seat, and stooping to gather up her flowers and her fan. "Then it's time I went back to the ballroom. Poor Lord Henry! I know I'm horrid; but, come, give me your arm; we will be friends—you shall have this white violet as a pledge. If it is to be war, you must give it back to me at Henley."

During the remainder of the evening, Lord Henry was obliged to console himself by gazing upon his charmer

from afar; his eyes followed her through the maze of
every dance, in spite of himself; and it is to be feared
that his successive partners had cause for complaining
that the attention he bestowed on them was incommensurate with their claims. Once, as Marjorie passed him
on the staircase, leaning lightly on the arm of General
Verrinder, who was escorting her to the supper-room,
she threw him a glance which a woman might have read,
but which only served to increase his perplexity; later,
when he took his leave, one of a stream of departing
guests, he found her smile, the frank pressure of her
little hand, equally unsatisfactory.

CHAPTER XIII

CORBYN, pipe in mouth, looked on with eyes sleepily observant at the progress of Adrian's toilet, (he was by way of destroying his third unsuccessful tie), the later stages of which were being accomplished, for greater convenience, in the sitting-room, before an old Renaissance mirror, which hung between two windows.

It was only in such vagrant moments—when Rome was dressing for dinner, or in the brief half-hour after midnight which intervened between the poet's mundane diversions and his labour of literature—that the two friends, near neighbours as they were, now foregathered.

The London season was just then at its height, and Adrian Rome, with a little deft assistance, hardly perceptible, except to the initiated, from Mrs. Vesper, had almost mechanically been caught into its routine. Certain whispers, indefinable, yet authentic,—and no one could precisely state their origin,—had made him fashionable; and the first step being so compassed, his road from dinner to dinner, in the choicest of company, was smooth and inevitable. Certainly, the fact that he was his father's son—a sufficient testimony to his wealth and position—went far; but, beyond this, it was admitted, even by his enemies (and he was far too brilliant to be without these necessary appendages of a reputation), that Adrian Rome's vogue depended upon something more personal than the balance at his bank. With many, indeed, it was rather his striking disregard of those advantages, making him so desirable a guest to the mothers of marriageable daughters; his quite sincere desire to be accounted solely as a *débutant* of letters, as a serious recruit to the army of Art, which was the secret of his indisputable success. The imputation of being an amateur—he passionately resented that. It was, precisely, by clumsy persons who had, innocently enough, stumbled into this error, and revealed it to him in their talk, that Rome was voted, perhaps not without reason, insufferably rude. At least Corbyn could have testified that if he worked very hard at pleasure (at the social treadmill, as the impecunious barrister, who was, however, either too indolent or too philosophical to be envious, would have preferred to call it), it was a strained, almost feverish energy that he bestowed afterwards upon labour more legitimate; in long vigils, bounded only by sheer physical exhaustion, or the bitter reminder of dawn filtering in through the curtains with a light, even in summer, so deeply saddening and cold.

Corbyn, a born idler, clinging to his twelve hours of sleep, was amazed at this double, exhausting life of his friend, wondered how long it would endure, and which half of it would be the sacrifice, that, in the nature of things, a constitution not quite of iron must ultimately make.

It was only natural, he reflected, catching Adrian's image in the glass (the tie was just being adjusted to his satisfaction), that his friend's face should have changed since their Oxford days, though these were hardly remote. The lines about his mouth were emphasised; his pallor, always a little singular, was increased; altogether he was older, more mature, more a man of the world. The alteration, moreover, was not wholly external; Corbyn, finely observant, as many very indolent men are, found at least one quality which was novel—an immense restlessness in his friend's actions, a passion to be amused, to be occupied, even by trivial things, as though (and here the observer lost his way) he dreaded, beyond all things, solitude, with its accompanying tyranny of his own thoughts.

When he had finished dressing he lit a cigarette and passed over to his friend, stood leaning against the mantelshelf—an attitude habitual to him in his own rooms. Corbyn glanced at the clock, which wanted some minutes to seven.

"Turn me out when you want to go," he said, "or leave me here if you like. I must finish this pipe."

"Don't hurry," Rome answered carelessly. "I am to be picked up by a man. He won't be here just yet. Tell me what you have been doing all this time."

Corbyn protested that he never did anything which was worth chronicling; he would rather hear of the other's movements.

"How did you get through the—ceremony?" he asked. "How did you find Underwoods?"

Rome was silent for a moment, watching a perfect ring of smoke sail across the room. Then he said, rather moodily, not directly answering the question—

"I think it's a mistake ever to go back to places one has liked,—especially for funerals. They have a way of changing, which one resents, or of not changing, which one resents more."

"That is oracular," said Corbyn, observing him through his half-closed eyes, "but I partly understand. Which thing happened in your case?"

"I hardly know. In any case, it was a mistake: I shan't repeat it."

"You have a touch of the spleen," remarked Corbyn humorously. "I recommend repose, change of air: a week's cruise in the *Anonyma*.

A sudden light came into the other man's eyes.

"I wish I could, but I can't—just at present. I suppose I must see the season out. Then we will cut the whole thing—of course you are coming with me, Corbyn?—and sail away to the South Sea Islands, or the North Pole."

"I shall be charmed," said Corbyn. "In either of those localities I should think one would be pretty safe from one's duns. But perhaps the skipper might object."

"Seriously, I think he would like it," went on Rome, with a little laugh. "I didn't tell you, though, did I, about my new skipper,—the very prince and paragon of sailors,—or how I stumbled on him?"

Corbyn shook his head.

"So you have got rid of old Martin? Well! I hardly thought he would stay. Tell me of his successor."

"Martin was an amiable humbug, but an old woman," said Rome. "He was afraid of the wind, and he hated the Mediterranean: he was always making difficulties. Finally, during the last cruise, we got so hopelessly on each other's nerves, that Martin caught a convenient illness at Malta, and I sent him home. And at Malta I met Salvesen."

"Great heavens!" ejaculated Corbyn. "You don't mean to say you are skippered by a Swede?"

"A Norwegian," corrected Rome. "I admit it isn't quite orthodox, for a yacht. He hails from Kragero, a blonde, blue-eyed giant. When I found him in a drinking-shop in Valetta, he was out of a berth. He had been master of a trading brig, and had been sacked for drunkenness."

"On the strength of which recommendation you, no doubt, instantly engaged him."

Adrian laughed.

"It has a comical side to it, but I believe I did. The

fact is, I was taken with the man: he was perfectly frank about his vice, you know. He told me that he was liable to these—these attacks; but only when he went ashore. I said I would give him a trial, and he has stayed. I found he was precisely the man I wanted: he's a fine sailor, absolutely honest, without a particle of fear in him; and, to finish up with, he has become blindly devoted to me."

Corbyn took his pipe out of his mouth, examined its polished, dark bowl reflectively.

"Well!" he said at last, "I shall sail with you in future with considerably less confidence."

"Oh! I don't suppose we shall go to the bottom just yet," said Adrian lightly. Then he looked at his watch.

"My man is late. Will you dine with us—at some restaurant? We have to go to the opera afterwards."

"Who is your man, by the way?"

"Dalrymple Green. You know him, I think."

Corbyn exhaled a long volume of smoke, shook his head decisively.

"You don't like him; I forgot."

"Oh!" Corbyn began: but Rome interrupted him, with a deprecating gesture of one hand.

"You needn't be afraid to say so; neither do I . . . He amuses me, which is a different thing," he went on, answering the explicit interrogation of his friend's lifted eyebrows. "That is why we are so much together. Besides, he is an important type: what the French call '*strugforlifeur*';—with his feigned enthusiasms, his passion for success, his—"

But what further animadversions Adrian might have intended were cut short, at this moment, by the entrance of their subject, Dalrymple Green himself, correct, and smiling apologies for his lateness. He suggested a neighbouring old-fashioned tavern in Fleet Street as a place where a passable dinner could be obtained without much loss of time; and it was thither that the two presently adjourned, leaving Corbyn at the gate of the Temple to wander westward, in search of an ordinary less sturdily British.

Adrian cast a glance at him, which seemed half regretful, allowing his friend to believe that he would not have been sorry to take a night off, to dine with him vagrantly in some dubious, foreign place in Soho, and lounge away the evening afterwards, smoking, in a congenial *café*, or at the club.

Certainly, if Dalrymple was amusing, a type of edification, there were times when Adrian found his society a trifle tedious. To-night he made no pretence of listening to the journalist's fluent, if a little laboured, talk, when they had settled themselves in one of the small box-like compartments into which the dining-room of their hostel was divided. He ate his dinner in a moody silence, vaguely oppressed, disquieted, as he had been, intermittently, since that unfortunate pilgrimage (surely its origin in a funeral had really been by way of omen), with an irritation which rankled all the more, in that he could not, or would not, lay his finger on a tangible cause. His mind went feverishly chasing an idea, which still eluded him round tortuous corners: as a man racks his memory, quite vainly, for some lost phrase or word, conscious all the time that his search, when successful, will seem of a ludicrous simplicity. Possibly, a mere physical tiredness: so he justified his lassitude at last, with a stifled yawn; and agreed to Green's suggested remedy, a pint bottle of Perrier-Jouet. And Dalrymple, who always drank champagne (one of several Americanisms contracted during a lecturing tour in the States), and who was already half-way through his bottle, burst into praise of the wine, holding up his broad, flat glass to the light, watching admiringly the little, sparkling beads bubble to the surface.

"Ozone to men who live by their brains!" he dubbed it. "The nicest medicine! I have half a pint with my lunch, and drink it at dinner; another, when the wires come in, before I write my leader. You see it in my articles!"

Rome, a lover of still wines, whose palate was chiefly moved by the subtile charm of certain rare, old clarets, assented silently. His estimate of the dapper, elderly, young man, with his effervescent wit, his deft rhetoric, which made him really something of a power with a democratic, not too intelligent audience, his superficial cleverness, tallied well with the preference which he had just declared. These two, who had drifted, as men do in society, for no authentic reason, into the imitation of friendship, were certainly excellent contrasts, in more vital matters than their criticism of a wine-list. There was something, to a casual observer, almost meridional in Dalrymple Green's temperament; a suggestion of underlying passion, which his rather high, not too dignified voice, his lack of repose in society, of restraint in public speaking, corroborated. Under his air of the evergreen enthusiast, the devoted social reformer, there lay hidden (Adrian believed) a nature hard and keen as the blade of a knife; a never-sleeping, unscrupulous ambition. If he was not yet in the House (and it was certainly on the House that his eyes were fixed), it was hardly for lack of opportunity,—but rather because he played a waiting game, (whatever it might be, Adrian was sure that it was not lacking in profundity), and for the present a game, which he could play best outside the portals of St. Stephen's. The real Dalrymple might be more apparent later; at present, his interested observer could at least be certain that the Dalrymple of tradition very inadequately expressed him. Were most men of that pattern, all more or less masquerading beneath a manner? Adrian himself, with his aspect, a little cold perhaps, or languid, always reserved, and to many persons repellent, easily deceived the superficial, would hardly have betrayed his temperament, so nervous and passionate and, very conceivably, morbid. There was good in Green's recipe he owned, at last, when they had settled their bill and were adjourning. His mood was alleviated, at any rate for the time, and he was certainly more in the mood for rather frivolous musical sensations. For once, he could assent to his companion's explicit satisfaction that the opera of the night was Italian of the Italians; one of the lightest of Donizetti's compositions, fluently melodious; an occasion on which one was justified in making less of the music than of the company. He was inclined just then to cry truce with the larger emotions, and was aware that the storm and passion of *Tristan*, ordinarily his preferred masterpiece, would have been intolerable.

It was not a very brilliant house, the young men decided, when they had been ushered into their stalls, (the overture was just drawing to an end), and had devoted some minutes to a scrutiny, interrupted here and there by a smile, a bow, as one out of the sea of faces identified itself as that of an acquaintance. The Royal box was empty, and, Dalrymple Green protested with a contemptuous shrug, many others which were occupied were metaphorically as void, inhabited by nobodies, people whom he did not know even by sight. Adrian agreed it was no more than ordinarily fashionable; but he discerned faces which he recognised on all sides. Gerald Brooke's boyish figure inadequately filled a stall; in a box, Lady Lancaster's faded, elegant face wreathed itself into conventional smiles; she had brought her two pretty daughters with her, and the martial presence of General Verrinder loomed in the background; and further back, on the grand tier, Adrian found his attention drawn to another box, where two ladies were just then settling themselves; Miss Brabant, surely, under the wing of the Duchess of Turretshire?

"Yes; she is in town for a day or two," Dalrymple Green explained. "She was in the Ladies' Gallery this afternoon,—Minaret made a speech, was heckling the Home Secretary. What a handsome girl the niece is!"

Adrian's assent was lost in the final crash from the orchestra: the curtain went up, and for half an hour the murmur of voices was respectfully hushed. Adrian, however, uninterested in the music, and not a great admirer of the diva of the night, continued to devote most of his attention to the audience. Before the end of the act, Lord Henry Minaret had joined the party in his mother's box. He had come in late, and was standing; and Adrian could see his eyes moving round, in the restless fashion of a man in search of something, which, nevertheless, he hardly expects to find. Lord Henry also, it appeared, had not come there for music alone.

When the interval came, there was a general movement, a great vacating of seats: Adrian and his companion joined the flock of men in the corridors. Minaret was emerging from his box when they reached it, contemplating a visit to the ladies.

"My mother has just been asking about you," he said to Dalrymple. "Won't you go in?" And he laid a hand upon Adrian's arm, as he was about to follow, detaining him.

"Wait a bit, old fellow! Come and have a drink. I haven't seen you for an age."

They passed down into the bar, which was crowded with men, a medley of black and white smoking and talking. Adrian lit a cigarette, and threw himself on a divan, while his friend struggled for whisky-and-soda. Presently Lord Henry brought him a long tumbler, and stood looking down at him with rather a self-conscious smile. Then he said abruptly—

"The fact is,—I should be awfully obliged,—would you mind going to my people, and letting me have your stall?"

The other glanced at him with some amusement: after a moment he smiled.

"It's I who am obliged," he protested; "supposing your people will put up with me. But I warn you, my stall is not a very good one."

"Oh, I saw where you were sitting," put in Lord Henry, with assumed nonchalance. "I shall be very well there."

"Yes." Rome hesitated a moment: then, tentatively, "It commands an excellent view of—Lady Lancaster's box."

Lord Henry flushed a little, tugged rather nervously at his yellow moustache—

"Oh, I daresay!" Then he lowered his voice, continued, in a tone rather mournfully confidential.

"If you like to have it so! Yes, that is the only mortal thing I am here for—to have a look at her. It's very imbecile: I don't gain anything by it, but it's a sort of occupation. It doesn't do me any good, it's merely exasperating: I don't suppose I shall be able to stand more than an act of it,—but I'm bound to look at her. In a month or so, I shan't have the right to do even that."

Adrian simply handed him his voucher.

"I don't quite see where your right comes in now," he remarked rather drily.

The Duchess was in conversation with an elderly

foreigner, a person of distinction, no doubt, when Adrian entered,—a conversation which her smile of welcome, of reassurance, that seemed to acquit him of any share in Henry's eccentricities, was hardly allowed to interrupt. He succeeded to the chair at Marion Brabant's side, just then vacated by a tall youth who looked crestfallen and subdued, and seemed by no means reluctant to leave Adrian in possession of the field. It was a way with the girl's admirers, he could remind himself, to retire rather ingloriously: he had noticed that before. Her chilling urbanity, the hardly concealed contempt with which she bowed her handsome head to compliments, disarmed the most accomplished master of flirtation, and made her a veritable terror to young or sensitive men. This youth was quite unknown to Adrian, and a consciousness of a secret sympathy with him, spurring him on to accusations against this girl (whom, in a manner, he admired), of a discourtesy, of a stupid and unmaidenly pride, warned him unpleasantly of jangled nerves, of a temper suddenly thrown out of tune. He watched Lord Henry in his appropriated stall, blandly regardless of the scene, leaning forward a little, his head slightly on one side, resting on one hand. His friend's continued infatuation, in the face of obstacles quite insuperable, seemed to him again, as it had done when he listened to him, half impatiently in the smoking-room, an exasperating piece of folly; while an odd pang of something like envy mingling with this sentiment, led him to wonder whether, after all, he was not primarily angry with himself. Oneself! One's lack of will, and one's divided allegiance to incompatible gods: was not that more really the author of one's disasters than any things or persons or conditions one blindly reproached for them; and that prayer of Goethe's, the best to be prayed—"not to stand in one's own light"? Only, which was the ultimate light to hold by, in a world so full of multifarious and distracting gleams? Marion Brabant's voice, coming to him, as it seemed, from a great distance, brought him down from the clouds, unconscious of how much irritation and lassitude his expressive face had indicated for the preceding ten minutes.

"How this music bores you, Mr. Rome!"

"The music?" He gathered himself together hastily. "It is not inspiring; but I am afraid I have been very rude; it's a suitable accompaniment for conversation."

"Oh, I didn't want you to make it—for me," the girl protested. "Besides, you look tired."

He owned to the impeachment, adding—

"I have had a tiresome day."

"A busy day?" she queried.

"A very empty day," he answered.

She leaned back, fanning herself gently, meditatively; then she went on—

"In that case, I have no sympathy with you. There are so many things to do :—if one doesn't occupy oneself, one has no right to complain of being bored."

"Do you occupy yourself so much, Miss Brabant?"

"A girl cannot always do as she likes."

"But if—"

He stopped short, having had it on his lips to ask, "if you were married?" but an odd scruple, an unaccountable diffidence restrained him.

"If I were a man?" The girl continued quickly. "Well! If I were a man I should be occupied—"

"If you were a man, you would not waste your time in scribbling?"

His accent, a certain flash, half resentful, in his eyes, converted the question into a challenge : and it was as a challenge that the girl responded to it, after a moment's silence, during which she considered him deliberately, with her grave, cold scrutiny.

"No! I shouldn't write novels or plays, Mr. Rome. I am very ambitious; I should want to make myself felt—in a different way."

Adrian drew a quick, sharp breath, exclaiming with a certain acrimony, inconsequently, it seemed—

"How much you hate us, Miss Brabant!"

"Hate you?" She echoed him, rather mockingly, from behind her fan. "Why should I hate you? I thought we were reasonably good friends."

"Me, personally, perhaps not,—Heaven forbid! But all that we represent, I and my friends; our objects, our interests, our point of view,—the position of persons who live chiefly for Art. Can you deny that it's intolerable to you?"

She ignored his question, watched him for a moment with her steady, not unkindly eyes.

"How do you know that you represent all that to me, or any of it?"

"What else, pray, do I represent?"

"Yourself, surely," she suggested. "Things that I consider of importance. Why should you talk as if you were a nobody?"

He caught her up with a quick, impatient gesture, a laugh that sounded a little harsh.

"Now you've said it, Miss Brabant! No! don't try to explain it away, it's transparent, it's what I meant."

"I am sorry if I have said anything very dreadful," she remarked, "but I retract nothing."

"You make me wish that I were a pauper," he went on slowly, "an adventurer, with nothing but my ideas: it would be easier."

She smiled, as though she found the picture inconceivable—

"We like you better as you are, Mr Rome!"

He answered with a shrug; and their conversation lapsed, while they once more became sensible that an opera was in progress, turned their attention to the scene. The stall adjoining Dalrymple Green's was vacant now: it appeared that Lord Henry had been driven away. Adrian, also, was beginning to feel satiated; and he took the occasion which the next fall of the curtain allowed him, to retire.

As he wended his way homewards, his mind busied itself, unreasonably, with Marion Brabant, her cold, grave beauty, her perplexing character — with its almost masculine hardness of contour—her ambiguous quality. To-night was not the first occasion when a certain amount of friction, an undercurrent of acerbity, had attended their intercourse. There was something like, and yet antagonistic, in their two minds, which must needs produce exasperation, dividing them, even while it drew them together.

Into his feeling towards Miss Brabant, which was half admiration and half repulsion, an odd desire to subjugate her crept; to abase her pride, which at times clashed so stridently with his own; so that looking forward to their near meeting at Henley, it was rather an intellectual passion which goaded him, than the anticipation of any pleasurable emotion.

CHAPTER XIV

COMING out of his bedroom one morning towards the middle of July, Adrian Rome found amongst the little pile of letters on his breakfast-table,—invitations to dinner, tradesmen's circulars, and the like,—an envelope with the inscription of the Nondescript Theatre on its seal. It reminded him, that he was still in suspense as to the fate of his play: and he opened it, before he attended to his other correspondence, with a thrill of expectation. As he had supposed, the letter was from Cyrus Holmes; but it was with some surprise, that he proceeded to read a verdict in his favour. Yes! Holmes would produce the *Opportunists*; it would be in rehearsal as soon as earlier arrangements would permit: to so much, Rome gathered, the manager, who, however, requested an interview, was definitely pledged. His approval was tempered by certain criticisms; the title would never do; and a call for various alterations and modifications, chiefly in matters of practical stagecraft, which might easily be arranged. Adrian meditated over the letter, frowning at times thoughtfully, while he breakfasted. Actually, it required some such definite, practical reminder, to stir the slumbering ashes of his old fire of faith in the piece, in the Drama as a vehicle of Art. Other work was now engrossing him; and it was characteristic of his temperament always to be concentrated on the immediate, the present, so that what he had achieved became at once rather remote from him, and of quite secondary importance. And when he had lit his first cigarette, had drawn down the blind, modulating the intense glare, which the summer morning cast over his writing-table, already the faint, delightful thrill which Holmes' letter had stirred in him was subsiding. He settled himself for a long morning's work, writing laboriously, not very rapidly, but incessantly; until at one o'clock he could throw aside quite a number of long, white sheets, covered densely with his small and intricate handwriting, for that which was always with him the most arduous part of composition—revision, erasure, reconstruction. It was a novel, this time, which was absorbing him. Coming back from Henley,—it had been a delightful, though perhaps rather fatiguing, excursion,—he had been seized almost feverishly by a craving for work. And while the mood lasted, and his intimate satisfaction with his idea was still fresh enough to spur him on, he had abandoned all other occupations; refusing invitations, denying himself to people, living in a solitary security from interruption behind his sported oak; in order to make the most of his regained facility. More than one poignant experience of what the lack of this precisely right illumination meant—of an arid condition of brain and nerves when the mere thought of writing was hateful—warned him against neglecting to seize gratefully upon the moment, and endeavour to prolong it to the utmost. On this occasion, however, the inspiration had been of such duration that to-day, when at last he threw down his pen, and gathered his voluminous manuscript into a drawer, he felt only pleasantly refreshed, and not exasperated, at having worked it out. He drew up his blind, and stood for a moment, admiring the cool, green shade afforded by the Temple trees, inclined to lounge away the afternoon beneath them, luxuriously, with cigarettes and a volume of verse, crisp and dainty in its immaculate paper cover, newly arrived from Paris. But the necessity of lunching, and a desire, very rare with him, to lunch extravagantly and well, interfered with this half-formed intention. He dressed himself, and sauntered out, wandering westward by the Embankment, with a keen relish for the pleasant smell of summer, which, even in London, cannot entirely be suppressed. Opportunely, he met Corbyn near Charing Cross; and he carried him off to a favoured restaurant to be his guest. Corbyn smiled at his friend's elaborate criticism of the menu, and the exactness of his orders, finding his attitude, of a connoisseur in matters culinary, novel and unexpected. He protested humorously against an innovation, which, he declared, would completely ruin his afternoon.

"I was going to a *matinée*," he said, laughing. "But I see I must give it up. I have to lunch austerely, or I go to sleep."

He yielded, however, very readily, to the infection of Adrian's expansive mood; and when their extended luncheon was over, and they had arrived at the discussion of coffee and liqueurs, was only disposed to regret that the occasion could not be prolonged. He had never more admired his friend's brilliant capacity for making the most of an interlude of this kind. It was really a compensation for the many difficult and arid moments, which his intimacy involved, that, once in a way, it should offer an hour so frankly entertaining. Adrian's luminous wit, which flashed delightfully to-day round every topic they broached; his knowledge, his tastes, and more than all, perhaps, his relapse into that old manner of lighthearted pleasure in things,— in the summer sunshine, and the taste of good wine, in the mere noises, redolent of busy life, in the street below; the manner, which had first attracted Corbyn to him at Oxford, was all the more refreshing to-day because, recently, it had become so rare. He could account for it in a measure when Adrian somewhat tardily informed him,—it was just before they parted, of the acceptance of the *Opportunists*.

"That explains everything," he laughed. "My dear fellow, why didn't you say so at once? I didn't know what we were celebrating. I drink to the new dramatist —to the judicious manager."

"It's not that." Rome had suddenly grown serious; he threw away the end of his cigarette, spoke rather nervously, with a little hesitation.

"You mean, why I am taking my ease! It has very little to do with the play. But I have made a wonderful spurt,—found myself again, my vein; and I have been working furiously hard. To-day it came to an end; but it left me, I confess, exhilarated, I felt free and fresh— yes, free!"

He was silent for a moment, then he went on abruptly—

"So long as one can work, can write,—work that satisfies one,—the rest doesn't matter."

Corbyn laughed again, vaguely mystified.

"The rest can't matter much to you," he said.

The afternoon had waned sufficiently to render a call decorous, and when the young men parted, Rome turned his steps to Mrs. Vesper's house in Berkeley Square. He reminded himself that his late abstentions must have seemed a little strange, in view of the frequency with which, earlier in the season, he had knocked at her door. He was aware, too, of her interest in his fortunes as a playwright, and was by no means certain that the present result was not one for which thanks might be partly due to her efforts; at least, to her introduction.

He found her alone,—Marion had gone out to lunch, she explained,—sitting at a dainty Chippendale writing-table, while a little heap of square white notes, arranged at her side, testified to her diligence as a correspondent.

"No, you are not interrupting me at all!" she declared; "or if you are, it is a very welcome interruption! They will bring tea in a minute: I will just address this envelope—it is the last!"

"And where in the world have you been?" she asked, after a brief interval, coming towards him, and inviting him to draw his chair up to the tea-table. "On a honeymoon, I suppose, with your muse?"

Adrian shook his head, smiling, as he protested that he had been less ideally occupied: his muse had deserted him,—she had never compromised herself,—and he had been avenging himself by a vigorous flirtation with fiction. He explained, abandoning his humorous vein, how deeply this affair had engrossed him; and declared, finally, producing Cyrus Holmes' letter, that it was gratitude which had brought him, laden with excuses, to her door.

Mrs. Vesper heard his account in silence, tacitly ignoring his thanks, allowing him to assume that, if she had been of any service, her services were the last things which she would admit.

She sympathised with him on the subject of the alterations which his actor-manager demanded, vowing that if she were the author she would decline point-blank to alter a word; and she cast ridicule on the catch-penny title which Holmes had suggested for the play.

"But I am very pleased," she exclaimed at last, as he rose to take his leave, "though, of course, I expected it!" Then she gave a little laugh, and continued—

"Do you know, I imagined that you had something

special to say to me, and that that was why you were so long away. But it was hardly that—"

"My play! You mean—"

She laughed again at his air of bewilderment.

"Oh, it's of no importance; but it certainly wasn't about your play. Though, of course, I was on tenter-hooks about that."

Adrian had already cast a glance towards the door, but he seated himself again at this remark.

"My dear Mrs. Vesper!" he protested, "this is very tantalising of you. How can I go without hearing more, after this?"

Mrs. Vesper raised her eyebrows, glancing at him, and then dropping her gaze discreetly.

"You are very—fantastic," she said, with a smile.

"Fantastic?" he queried blankly.

"Certainly—in your treatment of your friends. Oh, I leave myself out of the question,—but, Marion; have you quarrelled? And at Henley you seemed to get on so well."

A gleam of intelligence began to dawn upon Adrian's puzzled mind, and in the light of it he slightly flushed.

"Quarrelled—with Miss Brabant? Never in the world. What put such an idea into your head?"

"I thought you admired her," said Mrs. Vesper softly, with a little sigh. "I mean, it has been suggested to me; silly people talk."

"Certainly, I admire her," Adrian murmured help-lessly,—"I admire her immensely; but she doesn't like me."

"Really?" said the lady, with an ambiguous smile, glancing at him meaningly. "Oh, don't misunderstand me!" she went on, after a moment, laying a detaining hand upon his arm, as he showed signs of departure. "I am not betraying any confidence: I know no secrets!

and, really, I am not a matchmaking person,—Heaven forbid!—even when it's so suitable. But I'm too interested; she is almost my daughter, and you are both so strange, so proud. She is like no other girl; I thought there must be a misunderstanding: forgive me if I have made a mistake!"

Adrian gazed at her for a moment silently, knitting his brow; then he uttered a little nervous laugh: he had succeeded in reaching the door.

"Oh, a mistake!" he cried; "perhaps it is I who have been making a mistake."

He found his way back to the Temple in a state of mind which bore very little resemblance to his serenity of the morning. The idea which Mrs. Vesper (hardly discreetly, perhaps, although he acquitted her of any conscious mediation) had suggested to him, really presented itself now, confronted him in definite shape, for the first time. He began to retrace in his mind the history of his acquaintance with this girl, whom, certainly, he had admired, and who now was suddenly placed before him as a woman who might be his wife. And he could recall no sign which she had ever given him of the preference which he was now allowed to believe that she entertained. If she had distinguished him in any way from other men who had equally sought her company, (and they were many), he would have said that the distinction had hardly been in his favour. She had been colder to him than to the rest; there had been at times a shade more of haughtiness in her manner to him than in her treatment, habitually disdainful as that was, of mankind in general. He endeavoured to deride the notion that, under it all, beneath this mask of calm indifference, a proud woman concealed a predilection;— no, he was not vain enough for that! And yet, against his reason, against his will, the conviction stole upon him that Mrs. Vesper was right. She was the last woman in the world to make a mistake of that nature, to convey to him such an inference unless she were quite sure that her premisses were sound. And he went on seriously, with a growing thoughtfulness, to consider the possibility of such a union. And as he considered, it began to appear not merely possible, but desirable; the thing which should be. Certainly, he was not in love with Miss Brabant; neither her memory nor her presence could perceptibly quicken the beating of his pulse: but she was a beautiful and accomplished woman, whom he admired, and an alliance with her contained at least the promise of an honourable security, which marriage on a more passionate basis might forbid. Gradually, he persuaded himself that this sentiment was sufficient, that he might do worse than ask her to be his wife.

Unknowingly, Mrs. Vesper had put forward her troublous suggestion at an extremely opportune season, at a time when it was most likely to bear fruit. Adrian was in a mood of reaction, from a perplexing passion which, he told himself repeatedly, had worn itself out. Whether, intimately, he was satisfied with this account of a relation that had once been so full of charm, one may be permitted to doubt; but it is certain that the image of Sylvia glanced at him now through a veil of misunderstanding. Imperceptibly, the breach had widened; and it was none the less real and separating because it was the result of no open difference. Ever since that afternoon at Underwoods, when Sylvia, stepping out of that singularly isolated position which she had always occupied in his mind, had presented herself in a new light, as a girl who could create scruples, difficulties; a person, moreover, with relations, encumbrances,—his pride and his love had furiously warred together. His recollection of the occasion had become increasingly unpleasant to dwell upon, until of late his one desire had been to bury it in oblivion. Even at the time, while he was under the charm of Sylvia's presence, he had rebelled against her attitude; since, he had accounted for it in a dozen ways, which were none the less intolerable, because they were, after all, inadequate, unconvincing. He would probably have resented strongly the suggestion that her association with her cousin, Montague Villiers (whose name so persistently intruded into his day-dreams), was a powerful factor—a prime cause of his irritation; but it may be doubted whether this was not, in fact, the case. And his exasperation was only heightened by a secret consciousness, deep down in his heart, that he was unreasonable, unjust. He steeled himself against the girl, even as she had armed herself against her heart; fought against his passion as if it were an evil thing; and was glad when, in the distraction afforded by society, or in the stress of his artistic labour, he had for a short hour succeeded in forgetting her. In the light of his newly-awakened enthusiasm, his art took the first place, chiefly filled his thoughts; everything else seemed more than ever secondary, unimportant; the idea of love, of marriage, the routine of life, more than ever troublesome.

To dispose of the harassing question once and for all: this seemed to him to be the solution, the desired consummation; he was anxious, mainly, to relieve himself of this perpetual necessity of balancing issues, of making a choice. That it was inevitable that he should commit himself, sooner or later, it did not occur to him to deny; and the sooner the plunge was made, he argued, the sooner would he be able to bring trivial affairs to a settlement, to possess his soul in peace. His art,—he pleaded fiercely that this was the first thing to be considered; that he was bound, as a matter of conscience, to so order his life as to prevent the intrusion of any element incompatible with a perfect devotion to this absorbing spiritual passion. If he must marry (and it seemed that it was expected of him), why, let him marry, in Heaven's name; marry, and have done with it. There was at least a certain security in this step; it promised to confer an immunity from the recurrence of dilemmas so embarrassing. He would marry, as he had taken his degree, in order to dispose of a troublesome formality.

CHAPTER XV

AND he fell back into the old routine, spent his days assiduously in haunting places where he met the same persons and said the same things; dedicated his evenings to the opera, when he was not at a fashionable first-night; concluded as often as not at a dance; and still found leisure, however late was his return to the Temple, to devote part of the night to his dearer labour, to the slow but steady elaboration of his book. His acquaintance increased enormously, became labyrinthine and immense; and at the same time, if he was always congregating with new persons, striking out, as it were, new roots, there was enough of the beaten track in his peregrinations to enable him to see more than ever of those with whom his acquaintance had begun.

Gerald Brooke and Dalrymple Green; Lady Lancaster and her pretty daughters; Mrs. Vesper and Marion Brabant, and the satellites of those inseparables; even Lord Henry Minaret, who, rather silent and *distrait*, but always very faultlessly dressed, had grown a more inveterate haunter of doorways and corridors through which Marjorie Lancaster, with her pretty impersonal smile, and her air of submission to the inevitable, was likely to pass, as the day approached which should finally install that young lady in possession of her elderly warrior and the famous Verrinder pearls: all these familiar figures seemed more perpetually to be crossing Adrian's path, appearing and disappearing with the fantastic effect of figurants in a complicated dance or ballet, as day by day his engagements clustered thicker upon him.

He cultivated Miss Brabant with a fresh interest and an increased regularity, after that day when Mrs. Vesper had exposed her for a moment in so unexpected a light. He had succeeded now, by the force of ceaseless consideration, in denuding that confidence of any direct purpose, in reducing it to, at most, the expression of a wish. At the same time, the impression which it had left upon him was vivid and enduring. He laid himself out, as he had never done before, to study Marion, to please her, was conciliatory and charming beyond his wont. And if at times his success was problematical, and the girl seemed to have grown more inaccessible than ever behind her barrier of reserve, there were, on the other hand, moments when she gave sudden signs of yielding—moods of extreme softness, in which she showed a desire that was almost touching to apprehend, to mould herself to his point of view. Then, victory seeming less desirable as it approached, Adrian himself would become half alarmed, would procrastinate and retreat. And, all the time, Mrs. Vesper looked on, complacent but remote; she had never shown any signs of recurring to the embarrassing topic, and had it not been for a certain subtile shade of understanding in her smile, he could have believed his awkward interval in her drawing-room to have been a feverish dream. As the season glided away, however, and to Adrian the precise *dénouement* became daily a thing more inevitable and clear, he was seized, even while he accepted the situation, with a desire to revisit Underwoods, to see once more that charming friend of his boyhood, if only for the last time. He did not yield to this impulse at once: in fact, he struggled against it with a vehemence which seemed a trifle uncalled for, in view of his repeated inward protests, that it was a very little matter which he contemplated, as it might have been a visit to a grave. But the impulse remained, impregnable to argument, stronger than his pride; it wore him out. He ended by shrugging his shoulders, and yielding, with a smile at his own fatuity that was devoid of mirth.

The day before, he had been one of the smart crowd which assembled in a West End church to witness the wedding of Marjorie Lancaster with General Verrinder. Most of the guests were known to Adrian, at least by sight, and they were all, with one exception, precisely the people whom he would have expected to see. The exception was his friend Lord Henry Minaret, who was standing twenty paces from him, and whose attitude he was consequently able to observe. There was certainly nothing notable in this, nothing which might lead the casual observer to guess that the occasion offered him any exceptional interest. He wore the white button-hole of convention in his coat, bore himself correctly and well; while his agreeable face was composed to the same expression of decorous, rather bored resignation, which predominated among the other guests. On the whole, Adrian was surprised that he should have come. Was it mere bravado, for the benefit of the bride? Or did his presence there imply at last a tardy acquiescence, a ratification of the essentially contradictory elements in the governing of human affairs?

They exchanged a few words in the porch, after the ceremony (neither of them was going on to the reception in Portman Square), but when they separated, Adrian's curiosity was not sensibly diminished. Yet there was a trace of acrimony, of lassitude in his friend's voice, ordinarily so frank and genial. It was finally with a feeling almost akin to envy, that Adrian parted from him. If his visible frustration was obvious, so also was the unwavering directness, the single-hearted sincerity of his desire. Well, there seemed satisfaction even in that, even in frustration which followed upon strenuous effort, to a man whose mind, never more than now, was in the condition of a house divided against itself.

By noon the following day he was at Underwoods. The journey down, in the tedious train, which stopped everywhere, had not seemed long to him: he was too intimately occupied. A revulsion had come over him; he no longer sought to stem the tide of his old tenderness, reproached himself only for procrastination, which had deferred the inevitable journey so long. And as imaginative men will, he busily invented a hundred charming modes and phrases, in which their meeting would be framed, tasting delightfully in anticipation the fruit of his humility, the gradual softening of the perverse maiden. And, all the time, he confessed to no definite aim or project in this pilgrimage: only, he had passed from the labour of introspection, was content simply to be guided by the accident of the moment. A meeting with Sylvia! His imagination played lazily around that, incapable of looking beyond.

There was no conveyance at the station, and he accomplished on foot the few miles which separated him from his goal. A walk irresponsible and happy; later he could remember that, and the thrill, not unattended by a certain sinking of heart, which accompanied his first glimpse of the village through the trees. Ostensibly, he was a stranger now, there was no longer the pretext of a call upon his old tutor. The sense of his isolation, of estrangement, smote him painfully when he passed the first cottages. A woman working in the garden of one of them glanced at him from under her white sunbonnet, with stolid eyes which betrayed no recognition, though he remembered her face well. And for the first time an odd diffidence overcame him, so that he had not the courage to take at once the familiar road to the little post-office. He wished now that he had written, had informed Sylvia of his coming. In his difficulty, he bethought him of the rustic who had the keys of his house, and directed his steps to a neighbouring cottage. It would seem natural enough to old Rudge, he reflected, that he should wish to look over this desirable mansion. And the next moment he laughed at the absurdity of supposing that his subtile, sentimental malady needed concealment from the most stolid of Berkshire peasants. He knocked with the head of his stick on the cottage door, and an apple-cheeked woman opened it. She recognised him after a moment, and grasped his purpose. Her master was in the fields, she explained, and he waited at the door while she sent a small tow-haired son to summon him. They stood by the door together, and the woman gossiped in the broad nasal dialect of Berkshire, which at times he found hard to follow. He listened, however, patiently to her flow of talk, knowing that sooner or later, if he put her no questions, she would touch of her own accord upon the history of the only household which interested him. After a while the name of Drew caught his ear, and was repeated in a conjunction which caused him to avert his head; what more she said was a mere vain sound passing through his ears. When she had finished, he looked vaguely at his watch. "After all, I shan't have time, Mrs. Rudge, to look over the house. I am sorry I troubled your husband. Tell him to do anything that is necessary." His quick change of purpose might seem an unreasonable peculiarity, but Adrian had suddenly ceased to care how his conduct might impress any of the inhabitants of Underwoods. He left the apple-cheeked woman still standing at her door, and wandered away up the village street. Mechanically he repeated to himself the few words which Mrs. Rudge had driven home to his understanding.

"Eh, dear, we be here to-day and gone to-morrow! Mrs. Drew—she died last month, and Miss Sylvia's gone to Birmingham, to her mother's folk." By dint of frequent repetition the jingle of mere words imaged to his mind grotesquely the definite, exasperating fact. He walked along rapidly, though his step had lost its buoyancy, as the proper aimlessness of his journey was borne in upon him. He passed the post-office without a halt, feeling no desire to assure himself that the name over the door was altered and strange. He was anxious only to leave the village behind him, to be free of observers, suspicious that his inner blankness might be printed on his face, so that even to rustic notice he must seem stupid and amazed. He did not pause until he had climbed the hill and stood on the bare down, which stretched to right and left of him, one fair, green expanse as far as his eye could reach. Then he flung himself down on the grass and rested. The village lay below him, partly hidden by trees, but suggested by the faint haze of smoke which curled up in thin, spiral lines through the quiet air. Presently he turned his face away from it with a fierce objurgation; and for a long time he lay there, looking up sullenly at the cloudless sky, a prey to the exceeding bitterness of his thoughts.

It was not so much the futility of his journey, so delicious in anticipation, which exercised him painfully, as the fact, that this departure of Sylvia, and her mother's death, should have come to his knowlege in a manner so indirect. That she should not have thought fit to write news so vital to him herself, enabled him, as he had never done before, to realise the full extent of their division, and he reproached himself passionately for having allowed estrangement to proceed so far. Now that Sylvia was gone out of his reach (it was characteristic of his temper and the curious views of fatalism which underlay his reason, that he accepted this severance as ultimate, where a man of more practical energy would have looked at the hundred ways of bridging it), it was to his pride alone, to his foolish half-heartedness, and not to any shortcoming in the girl, that he attributed her loss. He had been vaguely tender, lavish of adoring generalisations, but when had he ever explicitly sought her, as by countless indirect speeches he had given her the right to expect that he would? His distractions, his work, his need of contact with the great world, the pleasure of cultivating his personal popularity; he had allowed these things—vain enough they seemed to Adrian now, in his hour of solitary self-communion on the Berkshire downs—to come between him and his dearer, more intimate life. If he could acquit himself of absolute dishonour, he stood none the less confessed of culpable weakness, whereof now, in the fulness of time, he was reaping his reward.

He had forfeited opportunity, and let this girl, never desired more deeply than now, pass finally out of his life. In the season of her deepest need, she had made no sign to him: the mute reproach of this silence of hers seemed to put the seal of finality upon their separation; he read it like a sentence upon his own unworthiness; and if he would have protested against its severity, there was this against the presumption of his innocence, that he had allowed judgment to go against him by default. For two hours or more he lay there, motionless, on the brow of the hill, invaded by a rising lassitude, sick at the very thought of resuming, of reconstructing the disordered elements of his life. Grotesquely enough, it was the reminder of physical hunger—he had tasted no food since the early morning—which at last set him reluctantly moving. He felt dizzy as he rose; but, once on his feet, his desire to be away from Underwoods (the village, destitute of its old charm, moved him in the distance like a desecrated shrine), hurried him over the downs by a road longer, but more sequestered, than that which had brought him to the station. He embarked in the train with the feelings of a man who had said good-bye to his youth; that, and his love for Sylvia, so living in the morning, seemed all at once to have retreated irrevocably into the past.

At Reading he alighted for refreshment, and waited half an hour for an express which would carry him more commodiously to London. When it arrived, as he walked down the platform, selecting his carriage, a familiar voice fell on his ear, called him by name. He saw the unmistakable head of Gerald Brooke half protruded from the window of a first-class smoking carriage. Adrian, weary enough just then of the monotony of his own circuitous thoughts, hastened to join him.

Brooke welcomed him with the enthusiasm of a true conversationalist unexpectedly relieved from an unprofitable solitude, in which his gifts were quenched.

He smiled, however, with lofty pity when Rome asked him to account for himself.

"My dear Adrian! Why should you question a palpable gift of the gods? Let us assume that we have each dropped from the clouds."

He lit a cigarette, and handed his case to Adrian: the latter settled himself in the opposite corner. He could perceive that he was literally, as Brooke put it, "manna from heaven" to the gregarious poet pining for an audience, and resigned himself to the part.

"We moderns lack the sense of mystery," Brooke continued, as the train steamed out of the station, "that is why we are grown so tedious—some of us at least. For my part, I never go away on the most commonplace errand, but I invent some beautiful, romantic account of myself, for the benefit of my friends. To-day, I have been picking cowslips on the Cumnor hills."

Adrian smiled.

"Cowslips—in August? My dear Brooke!" he protested.

The other waved his hand with a gesture of benignant tolerance.

"Don't they flourish now? How wonderful of you to know, Adrian! I know nothing about them, except that they rhyme perfectly with 'lips.' If you insist on plain brutal facts, I have been up to Oxford on college business—trivial, stupid, impossible affairs: the place was deserted; it was very virtuous of me to go, and I was just reminding myself that virtue is always its own punishment, especially if it implies a railway journey, when you materialised yourself."

"I fell on you opportunely for myself," said Rome. "I was very blue."

"Yes!" Brooke went on impartially in the key of soliloquy. "Just then you came to me, from the clouds, or from Arcady. You see I am kinder than you: I don't seriously assume that you had business at Reading. You—"

He broke off suddenly, observing Adrian through the film of the smoke. He resumed with a sigh. "Ah, fortunate fellow! One doesn't need to invent for you. You have come from some strange and exquisite experience. You live the romances that we others often have not the courage to write. I can read it in your eyes—you have marvellous eyes, Adrian! lustrous, wine-dark, like old Homer's sea, capable of infinite changes. Just now, they have a sombre light in them, like the flame of the topaz in my ring. From what wonderful quest have you come?"

Adrian uttered a little, short laugh.

"A quest which carried me into a *cul de sac*—and so I came back."

A note in his voice, acrimonious, suggesting that the random shot had told, slightly disconcerted his fluent friend, who, hating confidences, deftly passed to less personal topics. In a breath, he gibbeted epigrammatically the head of his college, praised a poem of Adrian's in a current magazine, fathered unblushingly a witty cynicism of his own on a notoriously dull divine, and inquired whether they should meet that night at Lady Drumblaney's ball. Adrian half thought he would be there.

"Oh, you must come! One goes dutifully to see the last of persons: why not of the season? It dies to-night."

"Not soon enough for me," Adrian declared. "I shall be on the *Anonyma* in a week. I can do better work at sea. Hard work, after all, is one's cure for most things."

Brooke ignored the personal allusion, deprecated the word.

"Ah, we don't, can't work, you and I! Nobody works nowadays, but the lower middle classes."

"And the horny-handed son of toil?" suggested Adrian indifferently.

"A popular fallacy! He only represents us in Parliament, and organises strikes."

Adrian laughed.

"Who accompanies you?" Brooke asked.

"You, if you will? Minaret, if he can."

Brooke touched on the young Lord's presence at the Verrinder wedding, chronicled in the *Morning Post*.

"Rumour has it, that he would fain have assisted in another capacity."

"What doesn't rumour say?"

Brooke's low laugh, rippling out melodiously, seemed to point his assent with innuendo.

"It marries most of us, and divorces us when we are wed."

The word "marriage" enticed him once more to the path of generalisation. He mocked the popular superstition of elective affinity in the choice of a wife.

"There is only one woman in the world one ought not to marry—the woman one loves."

"In our practice at least we should please you; few of us do."

"Because she is generally married," Brooke cynically explained.

At Paddington they departed in separate cabs, to dress and dine, arranging to meet again later in the evening. Once more alone, Adrian became conscious that his chance meeting with Brooke had supplied him with the precise mental tonic which he desired; the difference between himself, at present, and the youth who had gone down to Underwoods that morning, no longer struck him as an inexplicable cruelty. To his passionate hour of self-reproach had succeeded a certain hard numbness; not of his intelligence, which remained singularly alert, but of his emotional life, which seemed dead, and, with it, all effective, personal desire. He looked at the youth of the morning with vague bewilderment, tending to become aversion: it was a person grown so strange. When he reached his chambers, he had the impression of having come back after a long absence.

CHAPTER XVI

WALKING along Piccadilly a few hours later, in the pleasant midsummer twilight, after dining fortuitously with Lord Hildebrand at a restaurant which they both frequented, Adrian found himself considering, in the desultory fashion which the distractions of a busy London thoroughfare are wont to impose upon a pedestrian's meditations, his Lordship's parting words —a confession somewhat strikingly at variance with that weary hedonist's mature cynicism, of which it was at the same time, in a way, a corroboration. They had been discussing, over their coffee, the eternal theme— woman, and her weakness, with reference to the supposed mastery of the superior man; and the old gentleman had admitted, with an incongruous air of candour, that he did not believe in what he chose to call a royal road to women's hearts. "I know fifty men," he declared whimsically, tapping his snuff-box, and gazing at the exquisite miniature of Madame Recamier which adorned its lid,—"fifty, at least, who are the proprietors—so they tell me—of infallible systems for breaking the bank at *trente et quarante*, and forty of them make no secret of their belief that there are methods equally sure of winning a woman's favour. *Eh bien*, not one of them has ever come back from Monaco with more than enough to pay his travelling expenses; not one of them has come out of an *affaire du cœur* with even so much credit!" Then he shrugged his shoulders, accentuating his point with an expressive grimace. "If I could be young again—young in body, with my not inconsiderable experience of life, it would be upon my youth, not my knowledge of the world, that I should pin my reliance. A man may watch the game for years, and not win so much in a lifetime as some careless plunger carries off at a single *coup*. And it is the same with women. It is all luck: the wise man leaves the tables when fortune frowns. Well, I hope you are wise; it's more than your father was before you!"

Adrian had found this dinner, face to face with the veteran of many experiences, a singularly appropriate sequel to the episodes (how remote they seemed!) of the long, unprofitable day. Even more than the hour which he had spent with Gerald Brooke, it had braced him, withdrawn him from the past, confirmed him in his new-born worldliness. Lord Hildebrand had unbent, growing almost genial, perversely, in recognition of the boy's moroseness: there was something in Adrian's mood which interested him, a challenge to his perspicacity in the expression which haunted the long, pale face, and leaped at times, momentarily, into the dark, restless eyes, in which the fire of some strenuous conflict seemed still to smoulder. But finally, he was obliged to acknowledge that he was baffled: the boy was in no humour for confidences, and it had never occurred to him to regard Lord Hildebrand in the light of a father-confessor.

While Adrian hesitated (he had stayed his steps instinctively on the threshold of his club), the great clock at Westminster boomed out the hour—ten; and he remembered his half-promise to Brooke, that he would keep him in countenance (a somewhat superfluous service) at Lady Drumblaney's ball. He recalled his wandering thoughts, plunged into the club to procure a buttonhole, and verify his memory of Lady Drumblaney's address, and in less than twenty minutes his hansom had pulled up at the tail of a long line of carriages outside a house in Eaton Square, which by its striped awning, red-carpeted steps, and the sounds of music that floated from its brilliant windows, eloquently betrayed the nature of the festivities that were already in full swing within.

It was not long before he encountered, in the interval between two dances, his disconsolate friend, Lord Henry Minaret, adorning a doorway, gazing stoically into the parti-coloured ocean of black coats and gay dresses, in which bright eyes, laughing lips, flushed cheeks, and daintily-curved, white arms seemed to eddy as in a somewhat deliberate whirlpool. They retreated, strategically, to a spot where the vigilant eyes of their hostess could not detect their breach of the rule which dictates, that in a ballroom no two persons of the same sex shall foregather, unless they have attained an invidiously privileged seniority; and congratulated each other on their approaching escape from the social routine, which had finally become so tedious.

"Well," said Adrian presently, "have you made up your mind? Which is it to be—Sanquhar, or the Isles of Greece? Sandy Macpherson and a moor suspected of harbouring grouse — or the *Anonyma* and my Viking skipper? Under which tyrant? Remember, I sail in a week, *ruat cœlum*."

"A—, any ladies on board?" queried the other, feigning a consuming interest in his programme.

Rome smiled. "That hadn't occurred to me. No, I think not, if you don't mind! I mean business; we're in for a cruise—none of your Solent picnics."

"All right," said Lord Henry softly, after a pause.

"I'm there! I shall be delighted to come. Bother the—the grouse!"

"Good man!" ejaculated the other, glancing at him shrewdly. "You and I, and Corbyn, and possibly Brooke: we will have a good time, and get the cobwebs blown out of our brains."

Lord Henry sighed. "It will have to blow pretty hard for some of us!"

The music had ceased, and they found themselves elbowed by a stream of refugees from the heat and brilliance of the ballroom. Miss Brabant passed, on the arm of Dalrymple Green, throwing them a smile and glance, which Adrian was obliged to share with his companion.

"I didn't know that your cousin was here," he remarked to Lord Henry.

The other glanced at him curiously, finding a strange quality in his voice.

"Oh, Marion? She hasn't been here long: she came with me and Mrs. Vesper. They had been to the Paderewski concert, and picked me up at the House—me and Dalrymple Green."

"The ubiquitous Dalrymple!" murmured Adrian absently, buttoning his gloves.

"He—well he's an awful bore, if you ask me!" said Lord Henry candidly. "I daresay he's a good sort, and all that, but he's so infernally clever, and he is always letting you know it. Do you happen to know if that is Miss Farndale? I've got to dance the next with Miss Farndale. No, I'm tired of Dalrymple: he gets on my nerves."

"Poor Dalrymple!" said Adrian, smiling vaguely. "But I like him: he makes such an admirable foil. A world composed entirely of charming people and nonentities, would be rather monotonous after all!"

Lord Henry laughed. "I won't ask under which category I come! But I wonder whether you have been selecting your yachting party on these principles; and if so, which of your guests represents the Dalrymple element. I assume, charitably, that the crew will be cast for the nonentities."

Rome glanced at him humorously. "My dear fellow, you are getting dangerous: one recognises the readiness of the old parliamentary hand! Brooke shall be our Dalrymple—for Heaven's sake don't breathe it! After all, they have something in common, only Brooke is an orchid, of the rarest, while the other represents some useful vegetable—let us say a cabbage! Ah, there is the music again, that delightful "Moonbeam" waltz. I wonder if your cousin has a dance left for me: I must ask her at once."

Lord Henry smiled. "Yes, you had better go—for my sake. I shall draw down upon my head the enmity of half the old ladies in London if I monopolise you any longer."

Then seeing that Rome looked at him with a puzzled expression, "My dear boy," he added, "surely you know that you are being stalked assiduously—that you are one of the *partis* of the season. Off with you, and give the guileless huntresses a chance."

Adrian laughed tolerantly, then a somewhat grave expression clouded his smile: he hesitated for a moment, colouring a little, and fingering uneasily the ragged edge of the broad leaf of a palm which stood in the corner near them.

"Do you," he said deliberately,—"do you consider that I am what is known as—what is the phrase?—an eligible *parti*? I—I don't care what the old ladies think, you see; they don't know me."

"Does anyone know you, you mysterious old beggar?"

rejoined Lord Henry, gazing at him curiously. "You really oughtn't to fish for compliments in such a bare-faced way. But, good heavens, man, of course you are—of course I think so! If I was a dowager with a pretty daughter, I should be on your track, you bet!"

"You might repent," said the other gravely, but with a faintly conscious smile, as he continued, "Well, I must try to find your cousin: perhaps I shall see you later. Don't forget—the *Anonyma* to-day week; we might run down to Southampton together."

Adrian found himself confronting Miss Brabant on the staircase, just when he had begun to wonder, with a strangely vehement feeling of anxiety, whether she was sitting out this dance with Dalrymple Green. In answer to his petition, she showed him her card, shaking her head doubtfully, explaining that it was full, "all except the last three dances, and I have been telling everyone that I shall not be here for them."

"May I take the first," he said quickly, "on the chance?"

She looked at him silently for a moment, then yielded her card to him, and waited while he scrawled illegible initials upon it.

"I have promised Mrs. Vesper not to keep her late," she added, glancing back over her shoulder as she passed forward on her partner's arm, leaving Adrian to wonder suspiciously why he had been so anxious to secure a dance with a girl with whom fortune had thrown him into contact almost daily for the last three months.

Flattening himself against the wall to allow the throng to pass, he glanced at his programme, and found that only two dances intervened between that which was now in progress and the waltz for which he hoped to induce Miss Brabant to remain, and that he had left himself without partners for either of them. After a moment's hesitation, he made his way to the recess where Mrs. Vesper was seated chatting with Gerald Brooke, and, watching his opportunity, showed her his programme.

"I'm going to be very selfish!" he murmured quickly. "I want you to promise to stay for No. 18!"

She raised her eyebrows, glancing at him and then down at the card, smiling with a nod of comprehension as she noticed Marion's name written opposite the number which he had indicated. He acknowledged her playful speech of assent with a few words of thanks, in which Mrs. Vesper looked in vain for any allusive meaning, and acting upon a sudden impulse, broke away in the middle of one of Brooke's most carefully studied impromptus, and, pausing for a moment to find his hat, passed out into the obscurity of the empty street. He had walked half-way down one side of the long rectangle, vaguely contemplating the dim vault of sky, into which the tall houses jutted steeply, the solitary lamps, and whispering trees, before he realised, in a flash, that his mind was made up, that he was at last face to face with the great question which had for so long haunted his meditations. It had all been settled, as it seemed to him, quite independently of his own volition, and in his weariness he was glad that it was so, content to acquiesce passively, almost without a protest. In less than half an hour he would return to the ballroom, to claim the promised dance; and before he emerged again into the pleasant darkness, in which he could walk with only the watchfulness of his own eyes to fear, words would have been spoken which he might then wish unsaid. He might repent—but the words should be spoken; his soul was weary of this long uncertainty; only one end seemed possible, and his restless nature called loudly upon him to hasten it.

When he re-entered the ballroom, a little late (the music of the eighteenth dance had already begun), and found Miss Brabant waiting for him, with a smile upon her lips which was like the breath of life to some peerless statue, he was struck with a quick thrill of admiration for her beauty, so elusive, and yet after all, for the initiated, so real—a quality which made itself felt almost as a rebuke, whelming his doubts in a flood of appreciation. She was tired, and her slight lassitude served to lend a certain charm of softness to her allure, bringing about, as it seemed to Adrian, more than a merely physical effacement of sharp contours: the delicate colour which her exertions had brought to her cheeks, the suggestion of disorder in her dark hair, all helped to complete the illusion, to make it difficult to believe that she could be cold, irresponsive, severe. For once she seemed a creature of generous flesh and blood, not a masterpiece of marble imagery; and the change, the added charm, enhanced her beauty marvellously.

"I have been very virtuous," she explained, as she surrendered herself languorously to his guidance. "I proposed to Mrs. Vesper that we should go, just now, but she actually declared that she preferred to stay! I am puzzled—but it was very nice of her. She is really too good to me!"

"Ah!"—began Rome. "Yes, she is positively too charming; I wonder she isn't afraid that it will become monotonous."

When they had accomplished a few circuits of the crowded room, Marion readily acceded to her partner's suggestion that they should leave the floor to more inveterate dancers, and seek the cool seclusion of a roomy balcony, where chairs were set under the glamour of Japanese lanterns, that hung overhead in festoons, nodding like great flowers on their stems. Through the tall French window they recognised Brooke in the darkness; he had just vacated a low basket-chair, the merits of which he lingered for a moment to recommend to Miss Brabant's attention.

"Mrs. Trevanion and I were only now regretting the absence of the moon," he added, turning towards them, as he held the curtain aside for his companion, a distinguished lady novelist, to pass: "the gods have taken the hint, and send Miss Brabant to supply the deficiency."

"I suspect he had already said that of Mrs. Trevanion!" declared Miss Brabant cynically, as Adrian seated himself on the cushioned ledge of the balcony wall, close by her side. "I, for one, don't regret the moon at all; it's so pleasant, the darkness: one can dream under cover of it without being afraid of betraying one's thoughts."

"Yes," replied Adrian appreciatively, "it's a great relief to be able to lay aside one's mask. In broad daylight everyone is obliged to pose, more or less."

Miss Brabant sighed gently, and for a time they were silent, listening vaguely to the curious medley of sounds which floated through the open windows of the ballroom—the strains, half plaintive, half rapturous, of the quaint Hungarian waltz, the rhythmic, multitudinous tread of feet, the light surge of silken skirts eddying over the polished floor.

"Forgive me if I am remiss!" murmured Rome presently. "I feel like a traveller, who, after walking for a long time between high walls, draws near suddenly to a corner which he hopes will bring him in sight of a fair country—his journey's end, the haven where he would be."

Miss Brabant opened her fan with a delicate feathery rustle, and then let it fall half closed at her side. "Why doesn't he hurry on, your traveller?" she asked lightly.

"He is afraid," said Adrian, with a curious sense of shame, blessing the friendly darkness, and yet wishing that he could see his companion's face, to read its presage. "There may be nothing but more high walls, or worse still, a dismal swamp, round the corner. Yes," he added, boldly throwing his scruples to the winds, " I am afraid; I am going to look round the corner, and it depends on you what I shall see."

"On me," she repeated almost inaudibly, half closing her eyes and sinking back into her low chair.

"Can't you guess?" he continued quickly. "You—you are my haven, my desire. I want you to come down from your pedestal, to say—to say that you care for me, that you will be my wife!"

The girl turned, opening her lips as if to interrupt him; when he paused she too was silent, but a faint rustle of the basket-chair betrayed her trembling.

"Are you offended?" he added, following his other words quickly, though the interval had seemed to him prolonged. "Have I spoken too soon? Do you wish for time?"

Marion sighed before she answered, still with downcast eyes, a trace of indecision marking almost imperceptibly the inflection of her voice.

"It would never do," she said slowly. "I don't understand you—your ideals. Remember how we have differed. Think of your art—how utterly I am outside it. I—" And her words were lost in another sigh.

"You—you don't hate me, then?" he put in quickly, perceiving her want of conviction. "Your fears—what are they? Do you think I haven't considered all that? I think I understand you—your sympathies, better than you do yourself. My ideals—why, you are one of them. You are too beautiful to be an alien to Art—to all that is most beautiful in the world. Ah, Marion, say that you will—that you will; all the rest is nothing."

Miss Brabant clasped the arms of her chair, leaning forward a little: she uttered no word, but he was so close that he could hear her breath come fast, detect the rapid rise and fall of the spray of white flowers which lay upon her bosom. Then she turned her beautiful head towards him slowly, with downcast eyes.

"Are you sure?" she murmured. "Are you very sure?"

CHAPTER XVII

NEARLY a year later, upon a particularly sultry evening in May, an interested little party had foregathered in the manager's room, in Cyrus Holmes' theatre—the "parlour," as he preferred to call it, with allusion to a larger and more famous apartment in the classic house of Molière, whose traditions, so sanely artistic, he wished it to be supposed he was popularising, on the less congenial banks of the Thames. The heat was excessive, in spite of a certain studied nudity in the room's arrangement, which suggested coolness,—it had a bare, brilliantly polished parquet, very sparely relieved with pale India matting; but upon the faces of everyone present there was imprinted, besides the discomfort of the weather, augmented for most of them by a superfluity of grease paint, the expectant anxiety, with its accompaniment of suppressed irritability, of persons embarking on an adventure. An adventure, indeed, was pressing upon them very nearly. For the last fortnight the bills of *Compromise: a new and original Comedy, by Adrian Rome*, had been abroad; and the company, all the leading members of which were here assembled, was now within an hour of its production. Cyrus Holmes, already dressed for his part,—he was cast for the prodigal husband,—sat at a little table, impatiently smoking a cigarette, while from time to time he glanced nervously, frowning a little, at the clock on the chimney-piece. Archie Longdale, the

Captain Romilly of the piece, whose appropriate soldier-like aspect was justified by his history (he had never regretted exchanging from a marching regiment, while his military fame was still as insignificant as his pay, into the histrionic ranks), ladled out claret cup to various ladies in pretty, summer costumes, who sat fanning themselves uneasily in different parts of the room. Presently he paused in this occupation, to nod enquiringly to a man in evening dress who had just strolled round from the front. It was Peter Corbyn, who, as a particular friend of the author who had assisted almost more assiduously than the author himself at rehearsals, and a dramatic critic for an evening paper of some esteem, was by this time quite an intimate of the "Nondescript" family.

"It's filling," he remarked, in answer to the actor's impatient query. "The stalls are just beginning to come. You will have a crack house."

Cyrus Holmes broke in impatiently.

"I'm not afraid of that: a *première* is always a *première* here; there isn't a seat to be had. It's the tone they will take, the tone! I am afraid of the first act, and still more of the last. There are audacities; and I can't forget the dress rehearsal, it went all wrong."

Corbyn smiled with all the assurance of his years, giving a sanguine twist to his moustache.

"Everything always goes wrong at dress rehearsals: and the worse it goes, the better for the first night. You told me that yourself, Mr. Holmes. Oh, I haven't a qualm. Besides, there's not a dull line in the piece."

"I hope you are right," answered the actor shortly.

He walked over to the buffet, and helped himself to a glass of wine.

"Where is Rome?" he asked, after a while. "It's

very odd: he hasn't turned up at all to-day. Have his nerves given way?"

"Not in the least. Rome is never nervous when you expect him to be. I should think he would be round soon. I saw him in a box five minutes ago, with his wife and some other ladies . . . Hasn't he been to see you yet, Miss Lucerne?"

The actress whom he addressed shook her head at him over her big palm fan. She was a slight, fragile woman, with bright, dark eyes and a small, whimsical mouth. Her age was an enigma which no one, save perhaps the schoolboy in the pit, ever cared to solve; that she was young was obvious (for women of her type, youth is an elastic period); that she was not endowed with the gifts that are usually regarded as constituting beauty, was perhaps hardly so manifest, for something indefinable about her mobile face seemed to most people an efficient substitute for these qualities. Corbyn was her warm admirer, and considered his friend fortunate in having such an exponent for his heroine: an actress so subtile and so sure, whose force appealed so uniquely to the intelligence, who cared so little for physical effects.

"You are not nervous, for one," he remarked, glancing at her approvingly.

"I am only impatient," she said quickly. "Besides, I am in love with my part—with Cynthia; I don't know when any part has pleased me more. Do you know?" she went on confidentially, lowering her voice, "I have adopted some of your suggestions, since last night. Some of them were very clever; I didn't know how clever, till I tried them."

"It is you that are clever," he deprecated. "But what have you changed?"

"It is not so much the details, as the general scheme.

I've altered the key. I don't make the transition—after she finds out. I take it very lightly, as light as air, all through. It was something you said which gave me the notion."

Corbyn laughed.

"You give me a horrid sense of responsibility. Please don't tell Holmes, or the author. But at least if I said anything good, you might have the kindness to remind me of it."

"It was very good; it was about tragedy generally. You said that to get an intensely tragical effect out of modern situations, one must take them in the tone of comedy."

Corbyn considered her for a moment, pulling thoughtfully at his moustache.

"I am sure you can do whatever you try," he said at last.

Miss Lucerne gave a little, petulant laugh.

"What a pity the author doesn't agree with you!"

"Oh, he does, he does," protested Corbyn; "give him time."

"He doesn't believe in me," went on the actress, with a note of regret in her soft, rich voice. "He thinks I haven't—haven't the physical capacity. I am not his idea of Cynthia Mallory. Very true! but I can impose my idea upon other people. Besides, he gives me no help; all the hints I have had, have come from you. I can't be his idea, if he doesn't tell me what he has in his mind."

"Oh, what Rome has in his mind!" Corbyn exclaimed vaguely. Then he went on with an air burlesquely paternal.

"My dear girl! I am sure you will be perfect, and so, believe me, is Rome. But he is a poet, remember, essentially—though he happens to have written a good play. He knows nothing about the theatre: that is why he leaves it all to you."

The actress ignored his interpolation, continued in her previous vein.

"I thought it might be useful if I saw his wife. I got a glimpse of her in the Park last Sunday, she was with a lot of people; one of them was a Duke. But it was a failure. She is handsome enough and a real swell, but she is not 'Cynthia Mallory.' Poor Mr. Rome," she went on, with what seemed to Corbyn the height of inconsequence, "what a pity he writes plays!"

"When they are so good?"

"Especially—if they are good."

"You mean—you mean—" He broke off with a gesture of bewilderment. "No, I give it up. You may understand each other, but you are dark enigmas to me."

"I don't understand him," protested Miss Lucerne, "but sometimes I pity him."

Corbyn's eyebrows were raised suggestively.

"In the name of wonder, why? It isn't the emotion he most frequently excites."

Miss Lucerne was silent for a moment, while she consulted a little, jewelled watch.

"He hasn't much time, if he means to come behind at all." Then she resumed, "I mean that he seems unhappily placed. He cares too much about Art to be simply a swell—he might be such a big one; and he is too thick with the smart people to be a good Bohemian. And yet, at heart, I believe he prefers the *coulisses* to Mayfair. My dear fellow, you have only to look at his friends!"

"Yes, they are Dukes," put in Corbyn laughingly. "But do him justice; he has others—ourselves, for instance."

"Oh, for all I count!" ejaculated Miss Lucerne, whose unimportant tones, however, betrayed no accent of pique. Her eyes had wandered away to the door, which was open for the sake of the pleasant draught from the stage. "Here he comes!" she exclaimed, "and he is bringing somebody with him. Is this another of the Dukes?"

Corbyn followed the direction of her gaze, nodding to his friend, who had stopped for a moment, apparently to explain to his companion some internal economy of the theatre.

"Precisely!" he replied, smiling. "If he isn't a Duke, at any rate he may be; he's the son of one—that's Lord Henry Minaret."

The new-comers joined them, and introductions followed, while the general movement, and an exodus of visitors, gave notice that the business of the evening was about to begin.

And after a moment Corbyn and Lord Henry Minaret found themselves isolated, while Adrian moved across to spend the few minutes that remained in a review of his forces.

"Perhaps we had better go in front," Corbyn suggested, as a wave of melody from the orchestra surged in upon them. The other silently acquiesced, and they made their way together to the stalls, which were already densely filled, and dotted with familiar faces.

Corbyn, for one, followed the progress of the piece with an interest that was almost passionate in its intensity. If he had not the pardonable pride of authorship to sustain him, his exertions at rehearsal, where Rome had really been tremendously lax, at least entitled him to view it, in its present development, as a foster-child who did him credit. Long before the play was over, he had admitted the value of Miss Lucerne's innovations; while the appreciation with which he noted certain of her instant, exquisite touches, was not diminished by his consciousness that not a dozen of the audience were capable of following him there, of perceiving with what essential rectitude, just such and such an effect had been made. When the curtain fell, however, it was plain that the sense of a fastidious house was with Corbyn, that Miss Lucerne had secured another triumph, and that Adrian Rome's first dramatic venture was successfully launched. The players were summoned before the curtain, and separately applauded; a bouquet was handed up to the heroine of the evening. Cyrus Holmes, in answer to the inevitable call of a first-night, regretted blandly that the author was not in the house.

"And now," cried Corbyn, drawing a sigh of relief, preparing to fall into line with the outflowing audience, "to find Rome and pay him our compliments."

Lord Henry, who had spent half the evening in Mrs. Rome's box, followed him in silence; and gradually and with difficulty they made their way into the small, crowded lobby (everything in Cyrus Holmes' theatre was neat and compact as a bandbox), which was radiant with pretty women, in a gay diversity of opera cloaks, who stopped to exchange fragmentary farewells, and stray bits of criticism, while they shrouded their heads delicately in lace and gossamer, before they stepped into the street. Corbyn stood on one side, while his companion saluted here and there an acquaintance, and conversed for a moment with Mrs. Rome, one of a little group of ladies, who waited, cloaked and hooded, for their carriages. Presently Lord Henry joined him, with an apology, and they passed out together into the comparatively empty corridor which led to the stage, where supper was prepared, and where Adrian presently joined them. Even his extreme pallor—his face was like a mask of ivory—hardly seemed to contradict the nonchalant calmness with which the author received his friends' congratulations. It was rather the effect of physical weariness, than a testimony against the perfect steadiness of his nerve; though on the face of his unaccountable absence from the theatre during the progress of the piece, Corbyn had begun to distrust this. He explained it naturally enough, in answer to Corbyn's playful expostulation: an arrangement with Miss Lucerne. She had taken the notion into her head, that she would play with more facility if he did not confront her from a box; she wished not to see him until it was all over, and she could assure him of a substantial success. Personally, he had been very glad to oblige her, especially as the poor little woman had appeared not to have been particularly pleased with his attitude towards the rehearsals (after all, he had missed very few). However, he had made his peace with her, he had sent her an enormous bouquet, and had hurried round immediately after the descent of the curtain to assure her that her "Cynthia" was exquisite. Yes, he had seen a good deal of the second act—quite enough to form an opinion—from the back of his wife's box.

He broke off to introduce Lord Henry to Cyrus Holmes, who had just entered, having now exchanged his stage costume for correct evening dress, and whose bland, hospitable smile announced, palpably, that with the professional raiment he had put off the *rôle* of the irritable actor-manager for that of the charming host.

"Yes, it went very well," Corbyn heard him observe; " it will carry us through the season, you know. That is all we want."

The room began to fill; a couple of dramatic critics drew Corbyn into a corner, to discuss the piece with him with animation, referring at times to notes scrawled on a programme or a cuff. A babel of voices ensued, as, one by one, actors and actresses of the company, reinforced at times by a guest from another theatre, strolled in from their dressing-rooms. Gerald Brooke's mellow laugh sounded a deep note to the fluted accompaniment of chattering women; every now and then a champagne cork popped. Everyone wore an air of good-humoured relief, which Corbyn found an assurance, more substantial than any approving phrases could be, of the success which his friend had made. And the excitement carried infection with it, so that even the disinterested, who had not the excuse of previous tension for their geniality, took their key from Cyrus Holmes, and were frankly hungry, boisterous, and amused. It was not until they had seated themselves that Corbyn, welcoming a happy juxtaposition, was able to have a word with Viola Lucerne. She looked at him silently, for a moment, with bright, expressive eyes, while he helped her to *mayonnaise*. Then she asked abruptly—

"Well, what will you say of me?"

"Wait till to-morrow afternoon," he said, in an undertone, which the clatter of tongues all around them permitted. "It will take me till breakfast time to put it all into shape."

"You needn't tell me," she went on after a while; "I saw you, I played to you. Ah, my dear fellow, if everyone who comes to the theatre were like you—what a perfect audience!—what great things we might do!"

Corbyn's laugh betrayed a little confusion.

"You have surprised my secret," he said humorously. "Yes, I have a ridiculous, a puerile passion for the theatre, for good acting—acting like yours: it's my object in life, the one thing which makes it worth living."

"Why don't you go on the stage?"

Corbyn made a gesture of deprecation.

"Not for the world! Oh, I'm not stage-struck in that sense: besides, it would destroy the illusion, the glamour;—that's what I want, the illusion! To-night it was complete,—yes, at one moment I had an impulse, a perfectly insane impulse, to rush round and tell you that—that you were adorable, and that I adored you."

He had reduced his voice to a whisper: the actress gave a little forced laugh. Then she said quickly, but her fine voice contained a suggestion of bitterness—

"That you adored 'Mrs. Mallory,' you mean. Well, that's all right—what I wanted. But I'm afraid that you must wait to tell her so, Mr. Corbyn, until you play 'Captain Romilly'; you'd do it quite as well as Archie."

Corbyn was silent for a moment; then he said quickly—

"I rather think I meant Viola Lucerne."

The actress looked at him gravely, he could see that she was flushing through her rouge: presently she laid her hand, with an intimate gesture, which pleased him oddly, on his coat-sleeve.

"Don't you fall in love with me, Mr. Corbyn! Not that I think there is any serious danger—champagne and midnight, you know! But I can't afford to lose you as a friend. I suppose I may call you one, or are we not to see any more of you now that the ship is afloat? I was going to ask you to come and see me—"

"Ah, don't put it in the past tense," he broke in.

"Well, in the present, then. Come and see me sometimes, Mr. Corbyn,—when—when your legal duties allow you." She laughed with gay malice. "I'll seal a compact of comradeship with you: you're one of the best fellows I know."

Corbyn filled his glass, and raised it to his lips.

"Consider it sealed—our compact," he said, with the miniature of a bow.

At the other end of the table, in the immediate circle of Cyrus Holmes, the increasing merriment testified perhaps as much to the excellence of the "Nondescript" champagne, as to the agility of Gerald Brooke's wit. Minaret, too, Corbyn noticed, seemed at his ease, devoting himself to a florid lady at his elbow, and adding every now and then his quiet, self-contained laugh to the fund of general mirth. Adrian's long, pale face also bore signs of unwonted animation, as though he too had at last determined not to be behind-hand in his recognition of the expansive moment. Corbyn's eyes rested upon him more than once with stealthy curiosity, and turned away at last dissatisfied. He could not have accounted for the impression which he had received, but it was not the less disquieting, that, after all, his friend's share in the festivity was a superficial one: he was genial with an effort, and forcing himself to be brilliant, but his heart was signally out of it. Corbyn's mind wandered off on to the paths of vague conjecture, from which he was only aroused by the light touch of Miss Lucerne's extended hand.

"Good-night, Mr. Corbyn!"

He rose quickly, returned the greeting, retaining her hand for a moment longer than was necessary.

"You are really going? And our compact—when does that begin?"

She glanced at the clock, laughing gently.

"At this present, abandoned hour, Mr. Corbyn, if it's not dragging you away—and you will come and find me a cab?"

Corbyn's simple response was to follow her. When he returned, twenty minutes later, to say good-night to

Adrian, he found in the pressure of his friend's hand a reassurance for which he was vaguely grateful; if Adrian was silent, his grasp at least was expressive, and Corbyn, before he turned away, found time to murmur that he would have given more money than he could count to look back on such an achievement.

CHAPTER XVIII

SOME days afterwards, Corbyn, who had failed in several attempts to find his friend at his club, made a pilgrimage west of Pall Mall, and knocked at a house on the north side of Eaton Place, in which, upon their return to London, after a prolonged sojourn on the Continent, Mr. and Mrs. Rome had installed themselves.

The footman, who received his card, ushered him into a little library on the ground floor, just then empty; and for ten or more minutes the visitor occupied himself in an interested survey of the apartment. It was full of books and pictures; and besides the many quaint and rare *bibelots*, which had adorned the old Temple chambers, he could discern additions,—a censer, and a pair of handsome candlesticks, the work of some Renaissance silversmith, that spoke of researches on the Lung' Arno; a quantity of faience, and pieces of old furniture, redolent of Breton interiors (part of the honeymoon had been spent in a château in Finistère), which assured him that Adrian's passion for collecting had not been quenched by matrimony. The table was littered, with familiar untidiness; and the odour of tobacco smoke, which hung about the fantastically bright curtains of thin Genoese linen, if not so ingrained as of old, still testified to his friend's persistent occupation. A writing-table by the window faced directly upon a small but pleasant garden, from which a vague perfume of summer floated in. Corbyn seated himself by this table absently, finding the situation almost ideal for a literary man; and he had ample leisure, before he was interrupted by his host's entrance, to let his mind wander away on the paths of conjecture. His meetings with Rome recently had been so much in public, concerned so exclusively with his theatrical fortune, he had seen so little of him in his married character (it is true that he had received a card for Mrs. Rome's day, and had not forgotten his feeling of isolation—Rome himself being absent—upon the one occasion when he had responded to it in person), that he was sensible of an explicit curiosity at this his first approach to a more intimate point of view. Outward symbols and effects of the marriage state apart, was Adrian intrinsically altered? From his standpoint of the unmarried, if not unmarriageable person, the formidable tie, with all its implication of change, appeared stupendous, seemed to render his claim, even upon the old Rome, shadowy and unreal. He recalled the element of surprise, almost of incredulity, which had attended his reception of the news of this engagement—a surprise which had been diminished, indeed, by the discovery that amongst Adrian's closer acquaintance (for a long time their paths had been diverging) the engagement seemed an inevitably simple consummation of the expected. Simplicity, however, was a quality which Corbyn would so little have expected to attend his friend's choice of a wife, that its very presence here was a ground for suspicion. That this marriage was admitted on all sides to be excellent, unimpeachable, conventionally just, seemed to Corbyn, approaching it nevertheless in by no means a hypercritical mood, one mystification the more. It was so reasonable an arrangement, that it left nothing to be supplied by the imagination; and imagination being a faculty to which, both by precept and example, Adrian had always allowed such exorbitant claims, he would have had his friend plead guilty at last to inconsequence, if not to an intellectual lapse.

Charitably, one might assume, however (the assumption was rendered easier by Corbyn's almost complete ignorance of the lady except by current report), that for the persons most concerned, the felicitously paired themselves, the essential quality existed. If that were so, he was prepared with that intelligent acceptance of the situation which is the benediction of an unmarried friend. In the meantime he was reduced to a suspense of judgment tempered by curiosity—a curiosity which he hoped his friend might, if only unconsciously, help to dispel.

When Adrian, however, at last put in his appearance, apologising for the delay, the other found him no more than of old inclined to transparency.

"It's an age since I have seen you," he remarked conventionally, after he had installed the visitor in a more luxurious chair—"seen you properly, I mean. I don't count rehearsals, or a chance word in the street."

"A middle state between interview and correspondence," suggested Corbyn, "with the advantages of neither. Well, it is not I who am to blame. I have looked for you; you are never at the club. I don't wonder, now I see how charming your house is."

"One house is very much like another, I am afraid," Adrian interpolated. "No, I have been very little to the club. Of course, one's time is not quite one's own. Marriage, whatever else one may say about it, is certainly an occupation."

Corbyn tacitly acquiesced: he continued with an enquiry as to how the time abroad had been spent; the general scheme of travel had been imparted to him; pictorial, expressive detail was lacking. Adrian sketched a pilgrimage not deficient in variety. The Tyrol, Italy, the Breton coast, had successively been visited. There was a note of enthusiasm in his voice, previously a little languid, as he spoke of this last experience; the charm of that sea-washed village, the old château, ruinously dilapidated, but in parts habitable enough, with its great neglected garden, and the grass growing rank and luxuriant from between the paving-stones of its courtyard.

"I took the place for a year," he went on, "at a fabulously low rent. We stayed a month. I could have lived there for the rest of my life, but my wife grew restless. However, we shall go back there. I have had the Horatian inscription over the door restored, 'O rus, quando te aspiciam!'—a prayer I pray daily," he went on with a fretful accent. "It was a place to work in, besides, with no society, and out of the way of the tourist; with no noise except the wind and the waves—a grey, silent limbo of a place."

Corbyn smoked his cigarette in silence, watching him with interest. Presently the other continued—

"Yes, one might do good work there. Here, in the thick of this bustling, pushing rabble, if one can put pen to paper at all, it is a miracle. The result is—what one would expect."

"Oh, come now," Corbyn protested, "and I am fresh from the 'Nondescript' triumph!"

Rome stopped him with a deprecating gesture.

"Spare me, my dear fellow. If that play has bored the poor gallery people as it has bored me! . . . Let us talk of something newer and truer."

In the course of the few minutes for which Corbyn was alone, his roving eye had lingered, with a momentary curiosity, upon an object which struck him as a somewhat singular ornament of his friend's otherwise strictly workmanlike writing-table. It was a parcel-gilt silver figure, some eight inches in height, of a woman arrayed in the hooped skirts of a bygone age, elaborately and fantastically wrought, with an attention to detail which corroborated the impression of antiquity which the aspect of the material itself conveyed. Now, as the first flow of conversation exhausted itself, and the two men relapsed into a lazy enjoyment of their easy-chairs, his wandering eyes once more halted upon this work of art, and he asked his host indifferently where he had picked it up.

Rome, turning in his chair, allowed his eyes to rest on the object for an instant with an expression which the other, still observing him, found a little mysterious; then he stretched a long arm towards the figure and handed it to Corbyn.

"A Norwegian bride-cup," he explained, with a somewhat unaccountable smile hovering on his lips. "Yes, it is really a cup—or rather two cups, though you might not suspect it. You see, the figure is hollow; the woman's skirts form one cup, a tolerably capacious one, and the basket which she is holding over her head forms another—a kind of liqueur glass. I am told that it played an important part at Norwegian wedding feasts."

"Did they stick it on the cake?" asked the other, interrupting him. "Is it ornamental, or useful?"

"I was going to tell you," continued Rome, still smiling gravely. "Both cups were filled with wine, and at a certain stage in the proceedings the machine was handed to the bridegroom, who was required to pledge the company, disposing of the contents of the larger cup without spilling a drop from the smaller one."

"Lord, what an ordeal!" interposed Corbyn; "and the bridesmaids no doubt trying to be funny at the poor beggar's expense. And what became of the wine in the smaller cup? and how could you possibly fill both at the same time?"

"The wine in the smaller cup was the bride's perquisite. The performance was not quite so arduous as at first sight you might imagine: although the requirements of the design make it necessary that the cups, when the figure is standing in its normal condition, should be end to end, you will see that there is a kind of swivel arrangement which makes it possible to reverse the smaller cup. So it ought to be easy enough to fill them both. I haven't tried!"

"It didn't figure, then, at your wedding?" said Corbyn humorously. "I don't remember to have noticed it on that festive occasion."

"No; you might have seen it, though, for it was one of the wedding presents."

While Rome was speaking the same curious expression flitted over his face more than once, and when he went on to reveal the donor of the gift as Gerald Brooke, his friend, though he was still mystified, imagined for a moment that he had found the key which would enable him to interpret this ambiguous mood.

Corbyn made no immediate comment; he was silent, handling the figure and inspecting closely the quaint chasing and elaborate repoussé work. When he spoke, it was to ask whether Norwegian tradition attached any peculiar symbolical meaning to the ceremony which Adrian had described; it had been on the tip of his tongue to enquire whether Brooke had endowed his gift with any such reference, but something in his friend's attitude, a shadow of some deeper feeling underlying the humour of his smile, implicitly compelled him to a discretion which, in any case, he would hardly have ventured to violate.

Adrian threw the end of his cigarette out of the open window, first lighting a fresh one with it, before he replied.

"I am not acquainted with the legend," he said briefly; "no doubt there is one. Brooke ought to have sent some account of it with the figure. I should like to know what happened when the bridegroom spilt the wine in the smaller cup. I daresay Brooke doesn't know anything about it; he probably picked it up somewhere, and thought it had a certain charm of quaintness. Or perhaps—" After a pause he continued, "Perhaps he thought the allusion, if there is one, might seem a little . . ."

Corbyn laughed, dismissing his scruples.

"After all, the allegory is sufficiently obvious—the disproportion, the dependence—"

"My dear fellow," Adrian broke in, with just an echo of his friend's laugh, "isn't that a little too cynical? For the Norwegians, I mean, not, of course, for Brooke!"

At this point an interruption occurred. The door opened, and Corbyn, looking up, caught a glimpse, reflected in the mirror which hung on the opposite wall, of the face of his friend's wife. Before he turned, rising quickly from his low chair, he had time to notice in the reflected image a slight expression of a surprise which struck him as by no means distinctly pleasurable, so that the smile which Mrs. Rome wore when she advanced to greet him, while it hardly convinced him that he had been mistaken, carried with it the charm of the unexpected.

The lady's toilet, which was rather elaborate, suggestive of an occasion of social importance, betrayed the fact that she had either just come in or was on the point of going out; an unbuttoned glove over which

she was busying herself, daintily adjusting the fit of the
slim fingers, turned the scale in the favour of the latter
assumption. Her greeting of Corbyn was extremely
gracious. It was the first time that he had seen her
so privately; on other occasions he had been obliged
to interpret her attitude in reference to the world in
general, as represented at the wedding, a comprehensive
dinner party, and an extremely catholic reception. It
had already been made manifest to him (inclined though
he was to exercise a certain caution in his appreciation
of his friend's choice of a wife) that Mrs. Rome was a
beautiful woman, with a manner that, under the unsatisfactory title of the "grand air," he had often seen
inadequately imitated on the stage; it struck him now
that the removal of the outward apparel of coldness
which was, perhaps necessarily, associated with these
qualities, might reveal the woman as mistress of
fascinations of which he had been prepared to pronounce
her incapable.

"You were looking at Mr. Brooke's ridiculous cup?"
said Mrs. Rome presently. "My dear Adrian, why don't
you relegate it to a more appropriate place? One
would think you regarded it as a kind of talisman, a
source of inspiration."

Her tone slipped from mild resentment to an amused
contempt, while Corbyn eyed her furtively, wondering
whether his scrutiny would detect in her face a shadow
of the curious expression which contemplation of Gerald
Brooke's wedding present seemed to have called into
her husband's. He had gathered up his hat and gloves,
with a few words of apology for the protracted nature
of his visit; there could be no doubt that Mrs. Rome's
entry in bonnet and cloak had given the cue for his
departure, but she politely echoed her husband's protest
against this desertion, and he lingered, mentally bemoan-

ing the social inexperience which rendered him incapable of making a graceful exit.

"But you were going out, Mrs. Rome. I'm afraid——"

Adrian interrupted him. "Not until this evening surely, Marion? I have an idea that we are dining somewhere—but this afternoon?"

"Lady Lightmark's garden party," murmured Mrs. Rome, half apologetically; "but the carriage can wait, it is really quite early . . ."

"Oh!" protested her husband petulantly. "And I wanted Corbyn to read the first act of my new play before I send it to the typewriting people. It has been waiting for weeks," he explained, turning to Corbyn for sympathy. "Something always turns up! People ought not to be allowed to give garden parties in London. Even if it doesn't rain (and it always rains), the trees 'come off black,' and the lawn is generally just big enough to make a sort of setting for the tea-table. No, London gardens certainly have a charm of their own, for people who are tied to London; but the happy proprietors ought to luxuriate in them privately."

"I like London gardens," said Corbyn, desperately, edging towards the door. "London would be quite inhabitable at any time if every house had one. I should like to make it penal to build a house without a garden. I—I really believe the want of gardens is a fertile source of crime!"

Mrs. Rome smiled indulgently. "That seems a very reasonable theory, Mr. Corbyn. I don't think I ever heard of a gardener who was a great criminal."

"They are generally Scotchmen," put in her husband, with doubtful relevancy.

"That is hardly a crime, after all," suggested Corbyn. "But I must release you now so that you may go to your garden party, Mrs. Rome, otherwise I should feel that I was doing violence to my own theory. Good-bye."

"Good-bye, my dear fellow," said Rome, offering his friend a cigarette; "but I don't think that you ought to have suggested that a newly-married couple like ourselves stand in need of your antidote! You must come and dine with us quietly one day soon,—I really want you to help me,—and then you will be able to—to judge whether we exhibit any criminal tendencies."

CHAPTER XIX

THE Ascot race meeting would have been voted singularly incomplete without General Verrinder to dispense liberal hospitality in the sacred enclosure, and to provide a favourite for his guests to lose their money over on the day devoted to the Cup. His somewhat old-fashioned, precise attire was no less familiar to inveterate haunters of lawn and paddock than the uniform of the Master of the Buckhounds or the colours of the senior steward of the Jockey Club; his coach had become almost as much a feature of the landscape as the judge's box or the Grand Stand. Lady Verrinder, in the scheme of whose early education a course of race-going had not been included, found the occasion—her induction, as it were, into the mysteries of the Turf—a little trying; accustomed though she was to being stared at,—her prettiness was of the kind which provokes criticism,—she had never before figured as the cynosure of so many pairs of knowing eyes. It was obvious that the men—there seemed no end to them—who saluted her husband, with raised hat or brandished whip, as they made their way slowly along the heath, were considerably puzzled as to her identity. She imagined, with mingled feelings of amusement and indignation, that they were making bets among themselves, and that the odds ruled slightly in favour of the assumption that she and her sister Phyllis were the elderly warrior's newly-emancipated granddaughters.

She declared presently, when her husband had departed to interview his trainer in the paddock, that she had never seen so many smart frocks, so many pretty faces; and one of her companions, glancing askance at Miss Phyllis Lancaster, protested, with a fine youthful blush, that he was entirely of her opinion.

"I was really quite afraid of my gown," she confessed, "when we started, but I understand now what my maid meant when she said that it was impossible to be too smart for Ascot. One really might wear anything—all the colours of a paint-box—without being conspicuous here. Phyllis and I are comparatively dowdy, after all. Oh, I assure you I hate compliments, Mr. Lascelles; don't be ridiculous, but tell me who everybody is, and particularly, show me a bookmaker."

Mr. Lascelles proceeded to point out the celebrities—the latest plunger, the owner of the winner of the Derby, the popular jockey.

"But I must see the horses, I must have a bet!" exclaimed the lady. "Is it correct to bet, Mrs. Dollond? I love horses, and I adore betting. How do you do, Lord Henry? Do come and take care of Phyllis while I am gone. Mr. Lascelles insists on taking me to see Wingfoot in the—the paddock, don't you call it? You know, Mr. Lascelles, I have never seen one of my husband's horses yet!"

"Gracious!" said Mr. Lascelles naïvely, as he unstrapped his race-glasses, glancing back regretfully at the seat he had just vacated, upon which Lord Henry Minaret was leisurely depositing himself. "I wish I hadn't! They invariably lose—when I back them."

"Oh!" said Lady Verrinder reflectively. "Then you shall back Wingfoot to-day,—only for a little, you know,—and I will bet against him. How would that do?"

Mr. Lascelles laughed, shaking his head a little doubtfully.

"And this is really your first race meeting," he murmured vaguely. "For a beginner, you show great promise—it's clear that you have a natural gift for it. You ought to make a book, by Jove!"

"Now you're laughing at me, Mr. Lascelles; it's really quite unkind of you. I know I am very ignorant, but it is not my fault. Mamma always was—well, rigid. She thinks racing is immoral. I don't believe she would have let Phyllis come to-day if she had known."

Mr. Lascelles studied his race card intently.

"Is—ah—is Miss Lancaster fond of racing?"

"This is my sister's first experience of it," replied the lady sweetly. "Rather early to form an opinion, isn't it? Besides, Mr. Lascelles, surely you know that ladies are *never* fond of racing; the *sportwoman Anglaise* only exists in the French journalist's imagination. Women go racing because—well, because they are taken."

"To look after their husbands?" suggested Mr. Lascelles.

"To look after husbands!" put in Lady Verrinder. "Precisely! I'm afraid that you are very cynical, Mr. Lascelles. What does that bell mean? And what are they all talking about so loudly in this enclosure? What a dreadful noise—it sounds as if they were quarrelling. And do you really mean to say that those little long-tailed creatures are racehorses? What wretched little animals to make such a fuss about!"

Miss Lancaster had blushed a little, very faintly and becomingly, when Lord Henry Minaret greeted her, and after a moment's hesitation took possession of the seat at her side. Mrs. Dollond, who was seated close behind, remarked maliciously to her companion, Sir Richard Lightmark, the handsome Academician, who was also of the party, that the girl couldn't have coloured more prettily if she had done it on purpose. Sir Richard replied that he quite thought she had,—the woman of to-day was *capable de tout*.

After delivering himself of the few polite phrases which the occasion seemed to demand, Lord Henry relapsed into silence. His eyes followed for a moment the retreating figures of Lady Verrinder and Mr. Lascelles; then, instead of admiring his extremely pretty companion, he seemed buried in a conscientious perusal of the list of the horses that were to contest the next race, the event of the day; but Miss Lancaster, glancing askance at him, detected, with some inward wonder and amusement, that the card at which he was gazing with so intent a frown was upside down. She presently challenged him, giving expression to her merriment in a charming ripple of laughter; taxed him with his evident abstraction, enquiring whether he was pondering over his next speech. He confessed, apologetically, that he had not even the pretext of his parliamentary duties to offer in palliation of his remissness.

"Then you must have a guilty conscience—you must have been losing money, Lord Henry; confess that you have been making a plunge. Isn't that what you call it?"

Lord Henry shook his head. "No, I haven't been betting. My brother represents the family in that department."

"Oh, but you ought to back Wingfoot. At least that is what General Verrinder has been telling all his friends —of course I don't know anything about it. He has done something wonderful—given a stone to Pelican in a trial, whatever that means."

Lord Henry smiled; his good-humoured face, with its unemotional cast of features, discreetly disguising the great weariness which he felt.

"What do you stand to win, Miss Lancaster? Gloves enough to last you till Christmas, I suppose?"

The girl laughed, showing him her programme, and pointing, with a taper finger neatly cased in russet suède, to a few words scrawled in pencil on the margin.

"That is my only bet—I made Mr. Lascelles write it down for me. See, Mr. Lascelles lays me six pairs of gloves against the winner."

Lord Henry raised his eyebrows, with an inward chuckle at the girl's innocence.

"I congratulate you," he said gravely. "That looks like good business for you. I won't ask you if you want to hedge a little of it. May I write my own name and ditto under Mr.—Mr. Lascelles' note? There, now, that is my only bet. I daresay Mr. Lascelles will wish presently that he could say as much. I haven't been thinking at all about the racing. To tell the truth, I have been rather taken up with a new departure which I am contemplating. In fact, I am going to—to make a plunge, though not in the sense which you meant just now."

Miss Lancaster glanced at him quickly, and then across the lawn at the gallows-like erection on which the numbers of the runners and the names of the jockeys were being displayed. He wore a mysterious air, she thought, and she wondered with a little thrill whether he was going to . . . It need hardly be said that this young lady was no stranger to the history of Lord Henry's infatuation for her sister. The episode was running its course just at the time of her emancipation from the schoolroom, and her youthful sympathies had been entirely on the disappointed lover's side. It had occurred to her, more than once, in the secrecy of her virginal day-dreams, that the task of consoling this unhappy mortal was one which it would not require any extraordinary degree of pressure to induce her to undertake; and, moreover, it was one which she was eminently fitted to perform. She was not Marjorie, it was true, but, after all, she was absurdly like her; they had the same tastes, they even wore the same dresses.

So far, in spite of the havoc wrought by her blue eyes and exquisite complexion, Phyllis had only received one offer of marriage; the only scalp which adorned her maidenly girdle was that of a young gentleman of extremely tender years, who was now completing his first summer term at Oxford. She was charming, but she was also portionless; and the after-dinner conferences of far-seeing matrons of Lady Lancaster's stamp had pronounced the matrimonial market as suffering from an untoward depression. Eligible men were at a premium: they had never been so scarce or so shy. All things considered, Lord Henry, with his chance of surviving a childless elder brother and an octogenarian father, was a quarry by no means to be despised. It is only fair to add that Phyllis herself was far from being the designing young woman which, from this brief statement of the situation, she may have been made to appear. Indeed, her sister's marriage, with a man old enough to be their grandfather, had not been accomplished without her vehement protests. It has been said that she sided with the disappointed lover; and at the wedding ceremony she had presented the rare anomaly of a genuinely tearful bridesmaid. If Lord Henry Minaret was the object of deep-laid matrimonial schemes, Miss Lancaster, at least, was no active party to them. If she had allowed herself for an instant to wonder whether his embarrassment portended a declaration, it was because she was too frank to disguise from herself that, worldly reasons apart, such an offer would be extremely attractive.

Her vague anticipation was not, however, to be

realised; for her companion went on presently to explain that his parliamentary career was, for the time being at least, to be suspended. He was going abroad almost immediately—to Canada, with Lord Camelford. He spoke vaguely of diplomatic possibilities.

"Oh!" exclaimed Miss Lancaster, with exactly the right degree of surprise in her clear voice—it was a voice of a quality which lent to her most trivial utterances an importance which some people found disproportionate, and even irritating: "What will your constituents say to that?" Then she added hastily, as he began, with an air which was eloquent of the value at which he rated the opinion of the electors of Lowmouth, to explain the circumstances of his withdrawal, "Please don't; I know you are going to say something about the Chiltern Hundreds, a mystery with which my feeble intellect utterly declines to grapple. I've no doubt you can explain it in two words, but I had really rather you didn't. Don't you hate being told things— things which one ought to know? Like the date of the French Revolution, and—and about Bimetallism, and Local Option. Though perhaps you don't have to be told! How long shall you be away? After all, that is the question which has most interest for m—us!"

Mrs. Dollond, who, quite involuntarily and without any desire to play the eavesdropper, had overheard these last few words, wondered, with a tincture of contempt for the probable density of a mere man, whether Lord Henry (whose less penetrating tones did not reach her) had appreciated the little betrayal which they involved. Just then an interruption occurred; the confused medley of voices, ranging from the discreet undertones and silvery laughter of ladies to the boisterous cries and raucous utterances of the less aristocratic mob who crowded the heath, culminated in a staccato shout, dropping like a volley fired by raw recruits, of "They're off!" Lord Henry rose, like his neighbours, unbuckling the case of his field-glasses, which he adjusted and offered to Miss Lancaster.

"I do hope Wingfoot will win!" murmured the young lady. "Isn't that him" (her grammar suffered from the excitement of the moment) "in a pink jacket with striped sleeves,—the jockey, I mean,—and he's such a long way behind?"

Mr. Lascelles, who had returned with Lady Verrinder to the coach just in time to witness the race from this point of vantage, reassured her.

"They have got to go round again, you know. And Billy Gunn (that's the General's jockey) has waiting orders. You will see him come through all right presently."

"Waiting orders—come through?" echoed Miss Lancaster, turning to Lord Henry. "What does he mean?"

But Lord Henry was discreetly silent: the task of enlightening feminine ignorance as to terms technical was one which experience, pleasantly culled at Henley and Lord's, warned him to shun.

The cries, which had lulled while the earlier and less interesting part of the race was being run, were tumultuously renewed as it neared its close. Shouts of "Wingfoot, Wingfoot!" vied with counter-cries of "Privateer!" as these two horses, favourite and outsider, were seen by the experienced to be fighting a desperate finish; the clamour reached its climax; a few triumphant cheers sounded above the hubbub, and then comparative quiet was restored.

"It was a near thing, by Jove!" exclaimed Mr. Lascelles, his eyes fixed on the board upon which the winner's number was being hoisted. "A short head, I should—"

Then he closed his race-glass with a vicious snap, smiling ruefully. "Number 3,—just my luck,—that's Privateer—a twenty to one chance!"

"What! is it over?" said Miss Lancaster. "And hasn't poor Wingfoot won?"

"No," Lord Henry admitted, "I'm afraid he hasn't. Lucky you didn't back him, Miss Lancaster."

"Dear, dear!" murmured Lady Verrinder. "How savage the General will be!"

"You have won your bets, Miss Lancaster," continued Lord Henry gravely. "Five and three-quarters, and four buttons, I suppose? I will send them to you as soon as I get back to town. I think I ought to say good-bye now: I am obliged to go to Towers to-morrow, and I sail in about a week's time."

Miss Lancaster dropped her eyes, digging the point of her parasol into the soft turf, while her companion glanced askance, with some hesitation in his bearing, at Lady Verrinder, who was now dispensing tea, the centre of a small throng. The achievement of the object which had brought him to Ascot—to say good-bye to Marjorie— no longer appeared to be a matter of extreme simplicity.

It was Miss Lancaster who broke the silence, after an interval during which a gleam of intuition revealed to her the doubt that occupied Lord Henry's mind. She handed him her empty teacup, smiling brightly, but with a curious feeling of disappointment, of frustration, heavy at her heart.

"Didn't you say you were staying with the Heatherfields, at Ashley? They are very old friends of ours, you know, and Marjorie has asked them to come over this evening—it's only a short drive—to join in a sort of impromptu dance. They will want to bring you, of course: as a dancing man you will be invaluable." Then she added archly, in an undertone, "You know, so many of the General's friends are old fogies whose dancing days are over. They will come and look at us, and distribute a few broadside compliments, and then they will beat a retreat to the billiard-room, or get up a game of poker."

Lord Henry's face brightened for an instant, "Ah, that will be awfully jolly! You must keep at least three dances for me, Miss Lancaster — else I may be tempted to join the poker-players! Well, then, I needn't say good-bye just yet—but *au revoir*. I must try to find the Heatherfields, or they will be driving off without me: they won't stay long after the big race."

He turned away, raising his hat, but drew near to the girl again, to add, in an indifferent undertone which, apart from the slight blush which clouded his persistently cheerful countenance, would hardly have deceived her newly-awakened vigilance, "Oh, by the way, you might—if you don't mind—you might ask your sister to keep a waltz or two for me—I may be late."

To which request Miss Lancaster's reply was a little nod, and the faintest of smiles, thrown at him over her shoulder, as she turned to speak to Mr. Lascelles.

A dinner somewhat protracted (Lord Henry, nervously expectant, would have employed a stronger epithet) had drawn approximately to an end, and the ladies were already marshalling themselves for their retreat to the drawing-room, when their hostess, Mrs. Heatherfield, uttered a little cry of self-reproach, clasping her hands tragically as she paused near the door of the dining-room, which it had fallen to Lord Henry's lot to open. The lady, a tall, graceful person, with a reputation for beauty based solely, yet securely, on a pair of brilliant eyes, a youthful complexion, and a charming manner; who affected dresses à la Watteau, and indulged an enthusiasm for the art of fence, of which she was a mistress, and for small dinner parties, invariably brilliant and select;—this lady proceeded, in duly contrite tones, to explain that her present distress was due to her unpardonable omission to inform her guests (they were a small party, barely a dozen, all staying in the house), to whom she apologised severally and collectively, that she had accepted on their behalf an invitation to a "scratch dance" at the Verrinders'. "This very evening," she added, turning to her husband—"she was Marjorie Lancaster, you know: they are staying at Guisebury House for the week. I only heard from Lady Verrinder this morning," she continued, "but, of course, I ought to have told you before. I think such of us as are going had better start almost at once: I ordered carriages for nine o'clock. Thank goodness I remembered that!"

Mr. Heatherfield, a devoted husband, who was of great importance somewhere in the City, but merely an amiable adjunct at home, protested loudly, declaring that nothing should induce him to go: and he appealed humorously to his guests to abet him in his rebellion. In the end, however, dancing shoes were called into requisition, buttonholes and bouquets hastily improvised, and the party arrived at Guisebury House in time to take part in the third dance.

Lord Henry, detaching himself, not without some difficulty, from the ladies of his party, hastened to claim the dance which he hoped that Marjorie had set apart for him: he found her busily endeavouring, with Sir Richard Lightmark's assistance, to organise charades, or a cotillon—she really didn't know which; and she declared, laughingly, that she could not make any rash promises. Finally, however, she relented, and as the result of his persistence, Lord Henry found himself waltzing with her, about an hour later, when her duties as hostess had become less exacting.

"Phyllis gave me your message," she said lightly, when they paused near an open bay-window, into the curtained recess of which they presently withdrew. "She said that you were going abroad for a long time: is it true? And why do I never see you now?"

He glanced at her quickly, wondering whether her indifference was as complete as her words and her manner seemed to imply: he was slightly provoked, in spite of his devotion and his wish to spare her.

"You can ask me that!" he murmured, in a voice according ill with the speaker's boyish face, so eloquently expressive of an easy conscience, a heart unravaged, debonair. "Good Lord, are women so heartless?"

Marjorie uttered a little lingering cry, a sound half sigh, half protest, rebuking his bitterness.

"Are you going to scold me—again?" she whispered, slowly opening a great fan of white ostrich feathers, over which she looked at him with an expression at once apprehensive and pitiful.

"I am very sorry, for — everything!" she added quickly. "But what can I do? I don't think I ought to let you scold me! Why can't you be sensible? Why can't you accept things as they are? It's the only way, in this wicked world! If I am heartless, well, you ought to consider yourself lucky ..."

"Lucky!" he echoed.

"Yes, in—in having escaped me," she added petulantly.

He was silent for a moment, considering her with plaintive, sullen eyes—her delicate prettiness which no emotion seemed to ruffle; her smooth, candid brow; her placid bosom, which rose and fell so quietly under her necklet of sapphires, scarcely lifting the spray of orchids which nestled at one side, each flower daintily poised, like a hovering butterfly, among the maidenhair.

"Do you mean," she continued hurriedly, fearing, in spite of the superficial calmness which deceived her companion, what the silence might bring forth,—"do you mean that you are giving up your seat, that you are going into exile, simply because . . ."

"Because I can't help loving you, Marjorie," he put in quickly as she hesitated. "Yes, I may as well say it now, once for all; I am running away. I may be a coward, but after all . . ."

He turned, and gazed out into the garden, where the trees stood mysterious in the moonless night.

"For Heaven's sake, don't think I am appealing to your pity!" he added abruptly. "I don't care a rap for Parliament—who does, nowadays? I'm not trying to get you to ask me to stay; I have not fallen so low as that! If—if you did ask me, I should simply go further!" He broke off, with a miserable laugh. "What an idiot I am—to make a scene like this, when I only wanted to say good-bye to you quietly, and—and to tell you that if ever you want a friend . . ."

"He will be in Canada!" put in the girl, echoing his laugh. Then she sighed.

"I don't want you to go away thinking me utterly heartless! Go—go—if you must. Yes, you must— And—if I asked you to stay, you would simply go further?"

He came closer to her, stooping over her, holding out his hands.

"I can't bear it!" he said hoarsely. "Let us say good-bye here, where no one can see us; the music is beginning for the next dance, they will be looking for you."

She let him take her hand: when he relinquished it,

she began to move forward into the room, but struck by a sudden impulse, paused for a moment to select a flower from her bouquet—a delicate orchid, the counterpart of the spray which she wore in her bosom. "I don't know whether they grow in Canada," she exclaimed whimsically, with a break in her clear voice. "The General took a prize for these at the last Horticultural show."

Lord Henry accepted the flower silently, with a glance in which gratitude struggled with perplexity, and they passed together into the ballroom.

CHAPTER XX

At number ninety-nine Eaton Place an informal little dinner had been in progress, and the men, after a shorter interval than usual over their wine, had just joined the ladies in the drawing-room. The occasion was the immediate departure of Lord Henry Minaret,—he was to embark on the next day at Liverpool,—and, in spite of the presence of Mrs. Vesper and Dalrymple Green (the latter included at Minaret's request as succeeding to the reversion of his seat, which in spite of Reform Acts remained always very much at the disposal of the Turretshire interests), the gathering had no less the air of an intimate family party. The master of the house, who had been the last to enter, hesitated for a moment on his passage across the large room, struck trenchantly by this aspect, by the familiar grouping into which the others had already fallen. He took up a dainty cup from off the high oak mantelpiece, crowded with such frail ware, and examined it thoughtfully, from time to time allowing his gaze to stray disinterestedly to the company, from which he seemed just then to be separated by more than a measurable space of carpet. The Duchess of Turretshire—in town for a few days to superintend her favourite son's departure—had bestowed herself in a large arm-chair, and, as was natural, the young man had subsided into an adjacent seat. The others formed a little group—Marion, her long, white hands, on which the rings glistened in the

delicate candlelight, resting on a piece of interrupted
embroidery in her lap; Dalrymple Green, standing, his
face wreathed in political smiles, bending forward
deferentially to the Duchess, for whose benefit he
discharged himself of the latest lobby anecdote of the
Prime Minister; while Mrs. Vesper, turning her back for
a moment to the piano,—it was not the least of this
amiable woman's qualities that she was always ready to
fill up the interstices of conversation with admirably
discoursed fragments of music,—seemed to complete the
circle. The anecdote provoked a chorus of modulated
laughter, and thence the conversation grew more general;
always the talk of Turretshire, it seemed to Adrian,
listening remotely as he caught here and there a name,
an affair, an instance, local or personal; allusions, which
escaped him, being readily caught up by each one of the
quartet. It became apparent to him, after a while, that
they had fallen into a relation, the spontaneous ease of
which his participation would only dispel; and he drew a
short breath of relief, as he assured himself that the nicest
notion of what was dutiful in a host required nothing
more difficult of him than simply to leave them to themselves. It was a hot and windless night: the flame of
the candles did not flicker, nor were the flimsy silk
curtains perceptibly stirred by any air which entered
through the open windows. Adrian stepped out un-
noticed on the balcony. Below him stretched the
silent square: the dark, motionless boughs of the trees,
blotting out the opposite houses, were defined rigidly
beneath a canopy of starry sky. Under a gas-lamp at
the corner a policeman had come to a pause in his beat,
and his figure, the only one visible, seemed to Adrian to
intensify the solitude. Once a coach and four flashed
by, with a stupendous clatter, then, as the noise of its
wheels died away, the square resumed its natural quiet,

while, through the silence, without to a sensitive ear diminishing it, there penetrated continuously the muffled rumour, like distant thunder, of busier thoroughfares, the noise of greater London. It was a night and place for contemplation, but Adrian, leaning against the parapet, for a long time relished only the effect of solitude, of darkness, upon his harassed nerves. Presently the subdued hum of voices from the drawing-room ceased, and was succeeded by harmonious sounds from the piano: he recognised one of Bach's most exquisite Preludes, and the polished execution of Mrs. Vesper. He listened with appreciation, and after a time his consideration passed from the melody to the performer, to his introduction to her—it had closely followed his first encounter with his wife—in the drawing-room at Towers. From that had ensued their closer intimacy, with its many results of more or less importance; his whole mundane education, —no doubt at the beginning of their acquaintance she had found him lamentably crude;—his social importance, and indirectly, of course, his marriage.

Retrospect, or indeed much inward questioning of any kind, was a luxury which, of late, for no very intelligible reason, he had denied himself; and when he went on now to reflect, on how few occasions since his marriage Mrs. Vesper had crossed his path, the notion had sufficient novelty to move him with the force of a discovery. It impressed him oddly, was a proof of the desuetude into which his fine faculty of observation had fallen, that this accident, if accident it were, had not struck him before. Such a simple fact, of course, might admit of a very simple explanation: if he had not seen Mrs. Vesper, it was merely because he had not chosen to call at her house. That was an oversight, no doubt, since he had been to a score of houses where he amused himself less: yet was it not ample proof of a change in their relation, that she had allowed such an oversight to become habitual? There was a discrepancy, moreover, in her abstention, which seemed to remove it from the realm of accident: her presence with them to-night was only one of many signs to remind him that, whatever subtile shade of difference might mark her attitude towards himself, she was none the less unalterably concerned with his wife. She had been invisible, but she had been felt: her hand was always there; the very house was full of her; and Adrian could only set it down to his obtuseness that, when she seemed to have receded most, he had not observed her conspicuous presence prominent in the background. He faced this problem with a certain confusion of emotions, which might seem disproportionate, were it not to be remembered that his attitude towards his fellow-creatures had always been that of interpretation; that he viewed mystification as an insult; and was now suddenly confronted with an uncomfortable misgiving that for once, and in the case of a lady with whom he was intimate, he had been simple as a child. This brilliant, discreet, impenetrable woman of the world, to whom he was surely grateful for much, but who made no claims—had he never sufficiently accounted her? Had she more to do with his life than he believed, more perhaps than he could wish? He left the question unanswered, finding it a grotesque one, after all—dismissed the subject. It was merely his tiredness, his idleness (for some time past the time which he devoted ostensibly to literature had been fruitful only of irritation and ennui), that permitted him to indulge in such a train of thought. Deep down in his heart, he was aware that he let the question pass, simply because he was afraid. The accidents of one's life—even to himself he would not call them errors—occurred through one's own fault, or that of

Providence. The backs of the gods are broad, and are to be flagellated occasionally without too much injury to one's pride; but he revolted from the idea, and shunned the temptation of accusing another of any unhappiness which might be his. A man's fortune, or misfortune, is simply the sum of his mistakes; if Adrian had made any, he had made them with his eyes open, a free agent if ever man had been; he would not lose sight of that fact, nor believe for a moment that because one was unhappy there lay in that any reason why one should also be unjust. Yet his impression had been too startling, and was too recent, to be quite dissipated, when presently, under cover of the music, he took up his position again in the room, and found himself regarding Mrs. Vesper's inexpressive back with something of that bewilderment with which one discovers a familiar object, through some unexpected illumination, suddenly to have grown strange. He could reassure himself, had he needed reassurance, that the lady had not altered in cordiality, when, soon afterwards, the breaking up of the little party left them together for a moment.

Mrs. Vesper had risen, was standing indecisively in the middle of the room, but, in response to Adrian's tacit invitation, she sat down again; her smile was rich with benevolence.

"It is true, I am not in a hurry; I will wait until the leave-takings are over; and I have not spoken two words to you to-night."

"Ah, well!" said Adrian; "if you have been talking to Harry — I haven't the heart to grudge him any satisfaction. He will have so few in Canada."

Mrs. Vesper gave a discreet little sigh; a vague tribute to the general sadness of a situation which could not adequately be rendered in speech. She continued, her eyes fixed upon the carpet—

"Poor, dear Duchess! She feels it so much, after all her other troubles." (She alluded to the settlement in England of the reprobate heir with his unmentionable wife.) "And she has always depended so much on Henry. Perhaps politically, though, he was not a great success."

"No," Adrian admitted. "But there is at least one person who views his eclipse with singular complacency—Dalrymple Green."

Mrs. Vesper had opened her fan, and over its gentle vibrations she now gave him a brief, brilliant glance.

"That reminds me—I have a quarrel with you. Marion has told me—she is immensely disappointed—you are very provoking. If you had seen the matter differently, there could have been no question of Mr. Dalrymple Green. Perhaps even now your decision is not unalterable?"

Adrian was silent for a moment; he was conscious of a quickening of his pulse, of a certain intimate excitement, and again, as half an hour previously, he seemed to tremble on the brink of a revelation, which once more he deliberately postponed. He resumed, in a tone of forced lightness—

"I discussed the question exhaustively with Marion this morning; I don't think she is disappointed. I think we agreed to consider the notion as an excellent joke." He laughed. "If Lord Henry was not precisely a political beacon, pray, what should I be like in the House? A farthing rushlight?" Then he added, as if by an afterthought, "I am obliged to you for the suggestion; it did not strike me before that it was you I had to thank."

Mrs. Vesper swept the suggestion aside, glancing at him strangely.

"Oh, my notions! Who am I to indulge in such things? It was Marion's idea, to mention no one else. Why shouldn't I say that I have reason to believe that it would have greatly pleased the Duke?"

Adrian arched his eyebrows impatiently. Presently he went on—

"It begins to take the aspect of a conspiracy—against Dalrymple Green. By the way, if he knew the extent of his obligation to me, how he would hate me!" Then he added abruptly, "The Duke, he is an excellent old gentleman, but I do not see why I am bound to consider the Duke so much. I would prefer to consider you."

"Consider only yourself," pleaded the lady, with the conciliatory voice of a person who declined to recognise irritation. "Or, if you consider me, consider me as a woman who takes the deepest interest in you, in your welfare."

"Believe me, I have never doubted that," said Adrian quickly. Then he hesitated, went on with a little laugh, a perceptible flush: "Only—only don't let it carry you too far—your interest."

Mrs. Vesper regarded him obliquely with her fine, imperturbable smile.

"You mean that you might come to resent it? My friend, you are very difficult."

"Ah, no!" he protested. "I mean, your expectations are very great—I may disappoint you."

She was silent for a brief space. She had again risen and was adjusting the clasp of a bracelet which had entangled itself in the lace that edged her sleeve. When she had finished, she observed quietly—

"Yes, my expectations are very great. But I think

too highly of you—of your intelligence? No, I am not afraid of that."

He looked at her for a moment with a puzzled expression, to which she presented the same blandly impenetrable countenance; and it was on his lips to ask, with some impatience, what in Heaven's name her expectations were, when the entrance of his wife restrained him.

"Have I been very long?" she apologised. "Harry is in the smoking-room. I told him that I would send Adrian down."

Her husband glanced at Mrs. Vesper irresolutely. With a prompt interpretation of his attitude, she smilingly extended her hand.

"Then don't let me detain you. Besides, I am on the point of departure."

"Ah, well!" he answered. "Then I will go and smoke with the exile. Good-night."

Lord Henry had already equipped himself with a cigar, at which he was pulling meditatively, and a tall tumbler of brandy-and-soda, when his host joined him. His attitude suggested a search after physical comfort; but if he had found that, it was no less apparent that he still chewed the cud of bitter reflection. Adrian filled a pipe, and smoked it for some time in silence—a silence, the awkwardness of which was perhaps hardly felt by the other, but seemed inexcusable to himself. It embodied so great an implication of the lack of vitality which had come to characterise their old habits of friendship. There had been days when, under similar conditions, on the eve of a substantial parting, confidences on either side would have flowed more readily. It was not without regret that Adrian made this admission, and his regret was rendered more acute by the knowledge that, if this were true—if they could no longer broach intimate topics with any approach to ease—the initiative in reserve had been his own. Certainly, he had long ago ceased to be confidential, even with himself; and if Lord Henry preferred to throw the thin veil of a decent reserve over his feelings and motives, Adrian, interested though he might be, had not the right to expose them. And, indeed, if the other had been more communicative, Adrian was not sure that he could have made any adequate response. When one's friend is transparently in love with a married woman, the situation has its reticences; and perhaps, after all, the better part of confidence is reserve. Nevertheless, if the occasion had presented itself, Adrian believed that he could have preferred a salutary word—a cut and dried homily, in the manner of Lord Hildebrand, on the absurdity of permitting a woman seriously to deflect one's life. They were important, certainly, but by no means so important as that. And he had a moment of pitying, half-impatient superiority towards his friend, who had so many moral leagues to travel before he reached that secure pinnacle of indifference which, he prided himself, was his own. When they spoke, whatever may have lurked in the background of their speech, it was only the material travels in store for one of them upon which they touched.

"You will be glad to be rid of the House?" Adrian had remarked abruptly, when, after some desultory discussion of dates and distances, silence had once more threatened them.

"Oh, I don't know," said Minaret vaguely. "I don't dislike it as much as you would." Then he went on after a pause, with a smile: "I can't exactly see you standing for Lowmouth. I told Marion it wouldn't hold water. Besides, you have your work, your writing. When is that novel coming out? And a literary man is mostly rather out of it when he takes to politics."

"My work!" repeated Rome shortly. "The less said of that the better. But, as you say, I am not cut out for politics. Besides, I believe I am a Tory,—a reactionary,—and, so far as I can make out, we are running a Whig *salon*." He stopped to knock the ashes out of his briar, before he continued, with a certain restraint—

"Did I tell you that the lease of Brackenmuir had fallen in?"

"Your place in Perthshire? The family moated grange?"

"A barrack in the desert—yes! It was let for a long term in my father's time to M'Crosky,—the distiller, you know,—and he is anxious for the arrangement to be prolonged."

"Of course, you won't be so accommodating?"

Rome shrugged his shoulders.

"I suppose not; at least, I shall let Marion decide."

"Then it is decided. Marion will like it very much."

"It is a good thing that somebody should like it," observed Rome drily.

Lord Henry sighed audibly, finished his glass, which he tacitly allowed the other to replenish. Then he continued, with a smile—

"I like it also, but I am disinterested. I shall be in Canada. In three years you will certainly have it let again; I shall have no benefit of your grouse."

"In three years?" Adrian repeated the phrase in the tone of enquiry, but without personal application, as though he consulted an oracle. "Besides, you will come back before."

"Barring accidents, I am going, as I said before, for three years."

"The accidental is what always occurs."

"Accidents?" Lord Henry dwelt on the word as if he would thrash some curious meaning out of it. "I should have said, great changes."

"That is different. Nothing ever changes, except one's point of view."

"Oh, my point of view! No," he added, after a moment, "my point of view is stationary."

"Well," said Adrian at last, "there is shooting in Canada, I believe, to say nothing of the salmon."

The other glanced at him gravely through the blue smoke of his cigar.

"Oh, damn the shooting!" he said deliberately; and, after a moment, he added, with equal deliberation, "And damn the salmon too!"

Adrian laughed, but rather mirthlessly. Decidedly, conversation did not flourish to-night. He glanced at the clock; it wanted a few minutes to midnight; but Minaret was lighting another cigar—a large one, that would last an hour. A barely suppressed yawn, perhaps, warned the guest of his indiscretion, for he began to protest that his host should not stand on ceremony; they had known each other long enough to dispense with that. Adrian needed little persuasion to take him at his word, and leave him to a vigil which he probably preferred to fulfil in solitude, and was certainly determined to prolong.

CHAPTER XXI

A LIGHT shining through the half-opened door of the drawing-room crossed his vision unexpectedly, and, entering the room to repair the supposed negligence of a servant, he was surprised to find his wife still in occupation. The noise of his entrance disturbed her, and she glanced round from the little writing-table at which she sat, before she resumed the task upon which she was engaged. Adrian subsided into a low chair not far from her: he took up a novel, began cutting the crisp leaves listlessly with an ivory paper-knife: after a while he abandoned this pretext of an employment and closed his eyes. A Louis XV. timepiece marked the seconds persistently, and equally audible was the passage of Marion's rapid pen: but for these sounds, the house seemed steeped in the silence appropriate to the hour. He did not know how long he had dozed, when he looked up presently to find his wife standing over him.

Earlier in the evening, doubtless, many of the lights had been extinguished, and the room was now sparely illuminated by a shaded lamp, a place of dim alcoves in which Marion's contour, if it had lost some of its brilliancy, was figured to her husband by compensation with a certain rich softness, which ordinarily it lacked.

"I apologise, Marion," he said, with a smile responsive to her own, "if I was asleep—was I? I left Harry to his own society—I fancy he preferred it. It's tremendously late — or early. I didn't think to find you up."

"Yes, you were asleep; I have been watching you," she went on, after a moment, and her smile was complicated by an expression half wistful, a look which puzzled him. "It's strange to catch someone asleep; you look quite different, Adrian—someone else, as if—as if there were two persons in you, and one only came out in sleep. And I was wondering which was the real you—perhaps that one?"

"An improvement on the other, let us hope . . . What a number of notes! You've been busy." He spoke quickly, parrying her attention; the personal note was struck by her so seldom, in spite of their material intimacy, their most private speech being most often characterised by a tone of almost punctilious reserve, that he had come to dread the least sign of any inconvenient exception. She glanced absently at the pile of square envelopes in her hand.

"Three—four—six—they had to be written."

He was silent for a moment, knitting his brow thoughtfully, while he felt in the breast-pocket of his coat, from which, after some search, he produced a letter.

"You remind me that I have something to show you. It's about Brackenmuir; I was keeping it for to-morrow, but as we are here, you may as well read it now."

She took the letter from its oblong legal envelope, turning a little towards the lamp, while she perused it. He had risen to his feet, and stood with his hands clasped behind his back, watching her with his restless eyes.

"Yes?" she said at last tentatively; and then as he persisted in his silence, "Have you answered it?"

"My dear Marion! Without consulting you? What do you think of me?"

"I should have thought it only admitted of one answer."

"I had an idea you would find it so," he went on inconsequently, considering her with his fine smile.

"A desirable property,—at least they tell me so,—infinite acres, with a commodious dungeon in the middle of them. For part of the year, at least, we should have to live there. I suppose I should be the laird,—I am sure you would be an admirably efficient laird's lady. Perhaps I should have to wear a kilt. In the summer, it would not be intolerable . . . My dear Marion, I will do whatever you wish."

"What I wish!" She repeated the phrase impatiently, and for a moment it seemed to him that her eyes were placidly resentful. But she continued, with an even voice which betrayed no sign of exasperation (he was conscious that he had been exasperating), in a tone calmly explanatory, such as one might use to an unreasonable child—

"It is not a question of what I want, it is what you should do—what is reasonable, in the fitness of things. Surely one is not arbitrary in considering that? I consider it a good deal, I am not ashamed to confess it. May I ask what it is that *you* want?"

"Generally, to please you, Marion," he said quickly; "and in this matter of Brackenmuir in particular. Let us consider it settled."

She half averted her face with a quick movement, and her pallor was suddenly invaded by a flush of anger.

"I will not have it put upon me," she cried inconsequently, "it is not fair, it is unjust." Then she added abruptly, "How you hate responsibility—importance—

a decision! But this time I am not going to help you. You must do as you like."

Adrian regarded her with imperturbable good-humour.

"I like whatever you like, Marion. Haven't I proved it abundantly? In this case—"

She interrupted him frigidly,

"In this case I have no predilection. You must really excuse me. It is a matter of complete indifference to me whether or no you renew the lease."

She had gathered up her extensive drapery in preface of departure, and for a moment they stood confronting each other, with eyes that were suave and yet hostile.

"Come, Marion," he said at last gravely, "this is an important matter. I should advise you to consider it —to sleep on it. I confess I don't understand your attitude. It seems to me childish. To-morrow I will— take your instructions."

She made no response; and if he would have interpreted her silence as consent, he was warned by the hard iridescence of her eyes, which gave no signs of yielding.

"Let me take your letters," he said urbanely, in a tone which closed the discussion.

"These notes? They are not so urgent as all that— they can go in the morning."

"They will give me a pretext for a stroll—it is too insufferably hot to sleep."

And when he had dropped his budget into the nearest pillar-box, he walked for half an hour round the deserted square, in a state of disgusted reaction which was not solely due to the temperature. He regarded the scene which had just taken place—quiet as it had been, it marked an epoch—with a vague trouble which changed presently into a very poignant regret. Surely the mockery of good intentions had never been more hideously displayed? For, in handing his wife the letter from Mr. Featherstone, he had been merely prefacing a piece of generosity, a graceful waiving of preferences of his own. He had not really intended to let Brackenmuir; his objection to it was in the abstract; it represented another impediment, one more of those inevitable growths which seemed to him to hinder the liberty of action, and above all the liberty of feeling, for which of old he had pleaded so passionately. It was the disadvantage of real property, as he had once declared with perverse humour, that it was the proprietor who was owned. But when one was already so entangled, what did one entanglement more or less matter? It had not been without pleasure that he had calculated on giving this satisfaction to his wife, which he knew she craved. Unhappily, he had not been able to resist the temptation to be ironical, and a sentence which the perverse ingenuity of woman had interpreted as a sneer, had frustrated everything. It was no longer the question of the lease which was at issue: that was dwarfed by the vital difference which had displayed itself between his wife's conception of things and his own. That Marion had been so—so strange—he could come no nearer to the precise qualification of her attitude—was of more importance than any dispute as to the desirability of retaining possession of a Scotch estate. It spoke much of his discomfiture that in seeking some explanation of her aberration, vaguely irritated against her as he was, he would have given a good deal if he could have assured himself that she was heartless, that he had no place in her regard. If he could have accused her of that, his conscience—ah no, his mind, would have been easier. But he could not conquer the belief—and he resented it, because it was in the face of evidence, and seemed to put him in the wrong—that he would always be more to this cold, proud woman who was his wife, than she had ever been to him.

CHAPTER XXII

BEFORE many months had elapsed from the date of his probationary enrolment in the army of dramatic journalists, Peter Corbyn, weighing probabilities with the careless providence of his youth, found that his duties were sufficiently exacting, and his prospects on the whole roseate enough, to furnish, at least to his own satisfaction, the pretext, which he had long been seeking, for abandoning the increasingly distasteful study of the law. As he had anticipated, the step was regarded as a species of moral suicide by his relations in Wales. His aunt wrote an inordinately lengthy epistle from Haverfordwest, commenting in no measured terms on the flagrant iniquity of his act. He was given to understand, that if he maintained for three months his lamentable attitude of apostasy, the end of that period would inevitably be signalised by the complete and permanent withdrawal of all pecuniary assistance. This ultimatum, in spite of his anticipations, proved for the moment staggering; but an elastic temperament enabled him to harden his heart, and before he had exhausted the proceeds of the last parental cheque, he was fortunate enough to find himself attached to the paid staff of a fairly respectable evening paper, as critic of the Drama; and a few weeks later he was engaged, on the recommendation of his friend Adrian Rome, to contribute a column of gossip on Art, in its broader aspects, to one of the omnivorous weeklies. His income was extremely small, and his editors by no means the most regular of paymasters, but he enjoyed the satisfaction, than which none could be keener, of earning money by the pursuit of a vocation so congenial that, if he had been a rich man, he would willingly have paid for the privilege of following it.

The novelty of the thing was already somewhat threadbare, but the charm remained. In his eyes, professed cynic though he was, every actor was a charming, brilliant fellow; every actress the embodiment of wit and beauty. He had not ceased to lend an almost reverent attention to the talk, trivial enough, of the smooth-shaven masters of unlimited leisure who decorated of afternoons the bar of the Golden Cage, so appropriately theatrical, with its acres of marble and mirrors and gilded mouldings, so conveniently situate in the very High Street of Stageland; to escort actresses to rehearsals, to chat with them in discreet undertones at *matinées*, or in the seclusion of their surburban fastnesses, was still a privilege with which he wondered secretly to find himself endowed. He was happy, grateful to Fortune in that she had proved so complaisant, but his ambition was at the same time far from being satisfied. It was true that he had set foot within the charmed circle, but what he longed for now was to dominate it, to enrol himself among the little group which glittered at its centre. To be a critic was, after all, not enough; the very name implied exclusion, an outside standpoint; the profession, viewed strictly and conscientiously, involved the maintenance, if not of hostility, at least of an armed neutrality. In the dreams of his boyhood he had seen himself swaying an eager audience with an inflection of his voice, a movement of his hand; wresting in one triumphant season their laurels from an Irving or a Booth; now, when experience and the wisdom of his fifth lustre had taught him that such visions were desperately futile, it was as an impresario, manager, that he dreamed of grasping a golden fame. To rule a theatre was his ambition, to found a new epoch, to inaugurate a Renaissance in dramatic history, his modest aim.

"All I want," he said one day to Viola Lucerne—they were snatching a few minutes in the sunshine of St. James's Park, after the *matinée* at the Nondescript,—"all I want is a popular theatre, and a few good plays."

"Really?" smiled the lady, arching her delicate eyebrows, and turning a little in her chair. "Do have wings, while you are about it, and Aladdin's lamp! And a million or two—you would want all that, if you mean to run a theatre!"

"The theatre," continued the other gravely, ignoring her interruption, "that would not be a very difficult matter. But the plays,—the soul of the bricks and mortar,—there's the rub!"

Miss Lucerne tapped the ground impatiently with her foot. "Ah," she protested, "you get your theatre, my dear boy, and I'll find you plays by the vanload! In London you can't throw a stone without hitting someone who has written a play, or wants to write one."

"Good plays, I said," put in Corbyn patiently. "Otherwise I should prefer to write my own."

"Well, isn't there your grand friend, Mr. Rome? Doesn't he write the very best; so good that there is nothing for the actors to do, except make up and show themselves? I declare you make me tired!"

"For Heaven's sake, don't try to be American!" murmured the other, leaning back in his chair and stretching out his legs. "I admit that Rome has written one play, and a thundering good one, but do you suppose that he will ever write another?"

Miss Lucerne threw a quick, sidelong glance at him. "You mean that she won't let him?"

Corbyn whistled softly. "My dear child," he said quaintly. "She? You musn't let your ideas run away with you. For all we know, Mrs. Rome may be holding Adrian's inkpot for him at this very moment."

"I can see her doing it!" said his companion, in her best comedy manner, lamentably wasted on a flock of water-fowl and two privates of the Grenadiers.

"He's too monstrously rich," put in Corbyn inconsequently. "The whole thing is absurd. He ought to be running the theatre, don't you see, and I ought to write the plays. I shouldn't care how rich he was, so long as I had—the genius; or how clever he was, so long as I had—the guineas. But as it is, well, I admit it, I'm perfectly green with envy!"

Miss Lucerne rose abruptly. "Let us cross the bridge, and then you can put me into a cab. This is all very well, but I can't get through the evening without dining, and it's past six. What a nuisance it is being one of the 'beginners' in the first act! Just you remember that, when I'm your leading lady."

Corbyn got up more deliberately, flicking a drift of cigarette ash off his coat-sleeve. "Ah," he said, looking at her with attention, as she stood pluming herself, a little after the manner of one of those dainty water-birds which in her alertness and trimness of figure she so closely resembled, "aren't you that already?"

Miss Lucerne turned her back on him, with a little impatient flirt of her skirts, which would have suggested to an observer that the situation was wanting in novelty. Then she glanced back at him with a tolerant smile. "I'm going to lead you out of the Park anyway, you envious creature! And you might have dined with me, if you had been good."

"Lord!" said Corbyn hypocritically, with a surreptitious finger on the few coins which lurked in the seclusion of his waistcoat pocket—two or three stray shillings, and a half-crown which felt uncomfortably like a florin—"I thought you said you were going to dine with some people at the Cosmopolitan?"

"Well, you might have come too! You don't want an invitation to be able to dine at a restaurant, I suppose?"

The other sighed. "No; well, the fact is, I'm busy. I shan't have time to dine. I've got to meet a man presently, and then, there's that new show at the Gaiety."

"Busy!" echoed Miss Lucerne scornfully. "I suppose you are still hunting for the paragon who is to play that Dutch girl in your precious play. You won't get anyone to do it better than I should."

"Perhaps not: of course you would do it charmingly, as you do everything. But—"

"Ah, take care, you are ruining your compliment!"

"It doesn't suit you," said Corbyn briefly. "Yes, I admit that she is still in the clouds; and Vanderfelt has promised to put the piece in rehearsal for the next Unconventional performance, as soon as we can get our company together."

"Well, I wish you joy of it! I don't think you'll translate any more Dutch pieces in a hurry, that's all! If you find your 'Geërtje' this side of Christmas, I shall be surprised. But perhaps that will be quite soon enough for the Unconventional show?"

"The season of the Unconventional Theatre will begin early in October," said Corbyn gravely. "I ignore your distinctly flippant suggestion, Miss Lucerne; considering that you are on the permanent free-list, you ought to be more respectful."

Miss Lucerne laughed derisively, quickening her step

as they crossed the little suspension bridge which spans the charming, unappreciated lake. "Is not the entire audience on the free-list? I think we ought to be paid for coming; you always give one the blues with your pieces! You don't pay your actors, the least you can do is to remunerate your public!"

"I find the levity of your tone deplorable!" protested Corbyn, shaking his head. "You really ought to exhibit more reverence towards a society whose single aim is the encouragement of literary and dramatic talent. It is to be hoped that Adrian's play won't run much longer, if this is its effect on its exponents."

"Mr. Rome wouldn't care much," suggested the lady. "He—he never comes near the theatre now; I haven't seen him for ages."

Corbyn regarded her enquiringly for a moment, struck by her tone.

"Oh, he had his triumph—on the first night. That's all he cares about. Shall we get into this hansom? It looks rather like a property horse, but I daresay it's all right."

Miss Lucerne settled herself in her corner of the cab, casting a quick glance at the reflection of her face, pale, and quaintly demure, in the little cracked mirror which confronted her. Then she fingered for a moment the tassel of the dark-blue silk blind, which hung, like a heavy eyelid, half-way down the window at her side.

"So Mrs. Rome doesn't approve of her husband writing plays?" she murmured carelessly, when the rubber-tyred wheels of their vehicle began to run silently on the wooden pavement of Whitehall.

Corbyn frowned a little, his eyes intent on the cigarette which he was carefully rolling, and they had passed the Horse Guards before he answered.

"That's a problem which I leave to you, Miss Lucerne.

I don't understand women, and I don't know Mrs. Rome. So what can I say?"

The girl regarded him with a fine air of amused indifference.

"Gracious—a problem! My dear Peter, how serious you are! What does it matter? That Dutch play of yours is spoiling you. Turn it into a farce, or it will turn you into a—I had better not say what! That's a compliment," she added hurriedly, as their cab pulled up in the Strand at the portals of the Cosmopolitan; "you see, I admit that you are rather nice as you are!"

Five minutes later, Corbyn had left Miss Lucerne seated with her friends at one of the little tables which dotted, mushroom-like, the floor of the vast restaurant, and was walking briskly eastward along the crowded thoroughfare, dodging the current of traffic with all the deftness of a practised Londoner. The crowd was denser just outside one of the theatres, where a new melodrama had convoked a patient swarm of patrons of pit and gallery, and while he paused for an instant, with intuitive curiosity, he found himself confronted by no less a personage than Mr. Montague Villiers, who hailed him effusively as "Good old Uncle Peter," and, linking his arm in Corbyn's, drew him, in spite of a faint show of reluctance, into the portals of the Golden Cage.

"I was just on a gin-crawl myself, dear boy," Mr. Villiers announced, as they drew near to the long bar, the summit of which presented an expanse of polished marble, so dazzling in its smoothness that it was easy to lend a credulous ear to the story of the gifted barmaid, who had been wont to send a full tumbler sliding from one end to the other without shipwreck, or the jettison of so much as a single drop.

The place was full, as was usual at that hour of a Saturday; a few men were dining at the tables which

were ranged along one side of the room, and three or
four little groups gave almost constant employment to
the nimble damsels who officiated behind the bar. While
Corbyn's arrival was hailed with demonstrative approval
by the members of the little cluster to which he and
his companion attached themselves, it was evident from
their greeting of Villiers that this gentleman's absence
had been of but brief duration.

There was a chorus of "It's just about time for
another," quoted appropriately from a popular song;
and one humorist enquired anxiously whether Mr.
Villiers had forgotten his umbrella, or his change.

Montie (so they styled him, while "Uncle Peter" appeared to be Corbyn's recognised sobriquet) encountered
their chaff with a serene indifference, born of long practice.
He stayed long enough to consume a Hollands and An-
gostura at Corbyn's expense, and to pay for a second
round himself; after which Corbyn discovered that he
would only just have time to dress and discuss a frugal
chop before the hour fixed for the rising of the Gaiety
curtain.

"I'm going to the Gaiety show, too," said Villiers, as
they emerged into the Strand. "I shan't have time to
dress; we might dine together?"

"Good," said Corbyn, with tempered enthusiasm.
"Do you mind coming round to my chambers, while I
change my clothes?"

The other nodded his acquiescence. "How's your
Dutch piece going, by the way? Have you called a
rehearsal yet?"

Corbyn sighed. "It's turning my hair grey. I can't
find my leading lady."

"Lord!" said the other. "That ought to be easy
enough; or do you want such a blazing star?"

"I don't want a star at all. That's just the difficulty.

I want a girl with more talent than experience, someone who will take people by surprise—make them talk."

"The devil you do!" said Villiers reflectively. "A star in the pip, I suppose you mean. I wonder . . ."

Then he was silent for a few minutes, and Corbyn changed the subject, with a reference to the new burlesque, shortly to be set before them at the theatre which they were passing.

Later, while Corbyn was plunging desperately into his well-worn dress clothes, his guest neglected the cigarette and copy of the *Era* which had been offered to him to beguile his solitary waiting in the sitting-room, and devoted himself to a course of meditation.

"I suppose it's all right, your Dutch play?" he said, when his host rejoined him, with a pair of patent leather shoes in one hand and a clothes-brush in the other. "Not too low in the neck, I mean—the sort of piece a lady could play in without feeling queer?"

Corbyn looked at him for a moment enquiringly before he answered.

"Oh, it's all right. The kind of piece a girl could take her mother to see, as they say in Paris. We don't want to make Mrs. Grundy sit up this time."

The other rose, plunging his hands into his pockets, and whistling the air of the latest music-hall ditty, while he contemplated absently the array of programmes which ornamented the frame of the mirror over the mantelpiece.

"If you like to lend me the play," he said presently, "I think I know a girl who might do. I want to bring her out in something—something recherchy, don't you know. Let me take the play home to her,—she's living with me and my old woman down Brixton way,—and

I'll get her to study it up. It'll be good practice for her, anyhow, and then you can come down and hear her do it. It's take it or leave it, dear boy! But, you know, I wouldn't make the offer to everyone."

Corbyn expressed his thanks somewhat awkwardly while he struggled into his Inverness cape. The idea struck him as an almost ludicrously forlorn hope: he found it difficult to imagine that his ideal Geërtje would be found in the shape of an unknown damsel living at Brixton under the same roof with Mr. Montague Villiers and his "old woman"—better known as Miss Flossie Faraday, the Favourite Serio-comique Nightingale of the London Halls. But he was disposed to clutch at straws; the realms of the probable seemed to have been exhausted, and there was always a chance that quarters apparently unlikely might harbour the rare bird. A search of a few minutes among the papers which littered the one large table in the centre of his room brought to light—the delicate radiance of a London summer evening—a disreputable type-written copy of *The Lady of the Moon*, still encircled by the wisp of pale green ribbon which had confined its vagrant pages during its passage to the Temple from Miss Lucerne's house at Hampstead.

Corbyn handled the packet for a moment with something of the deprecating tenderness of an author for an oft-rejected manuscript; then he crammed it into the pocket of his overcoat.

"It's rather bulky," he said briefly. "I'll give it to you after the show this evening. I hope Miss—your friend won't object to the dog's-ears," he added, when he had sported the oak and had overtaken his friend at the foot of the staircase. "Miss Lucerne rather lost her temper over it, I fancy: it looks as if she had chucked it out of the window two or three times."

"Violent Lucerne, we used to call her when we were on tour with the *Silver King*," said the other. "Nice little girl, devilish nice; but she hasn't the physique for a great actress. Just you wait, Uncle Peter—wait till you see my client, Juliet Arden!"

CHAPTER XXIII

"I DINED with Montie Villiers on Saturday night," said Corbyn, casting a humorous glance at Rome, whom he had encountered fortuitously in Lincoln's Inn Fields. "He was in great form. Quite an old friend of yours, by the way, isn't he?"

Adrian looked up quickly, with an expression which, for the moment, checked his friend. He seemed about to speak, but he only frowned; and the other continued light-heartedly: to see Adrian frown was neither novel nor portentous.

"He was in wonderful form—eloquent upon the sanctity of Art, and maintaining in the same breath his laudable theory that the public is the only infallible judge, the final court of appeal on all questions connected with it. What an impossible creature it is!—but I delight in him, he amuses me—"

"The public!" broke in Rome savagely. "Damn the public! One ought not to use the word, even in mockery. Forgive me—you don't know how sick I am of that many-headed, muddy-minded bogey; I would almost rather hear you open up the interminable discussion of politics."

"Heaven forfend!" ejaculated the other devoutly. "You're safe, *mon vieux*; my knowledge doesn't extend beyond the name of the Prime Minister; I don't know enough to write a gallery verse for a topical song. Well, suppose we talk about ourselves, then; that will be much more interesting. Tell me about your novel. Does it progress? When may I ask for it—at all the libraries?"

"I write about a page a month, now," said Adrian tersely. "I had written about half the book when I married. The calculation is easy!"

Corbyn was silent for a minute, gazing reflectively at a workman who was painting the low railings surrounding Leicester Square.

"What a discontented idiot you must think me!" added the other, with a sufficiently mirthless laugh. "I feel that I am an idiot all the time. I ought to be happy enough, n'est-ce-pas? I have plenty of money, a charming wife, and the newspapers say the kindest things about everything I write. And yet — How unsatisfactory one is! I suppose I want change of air. That is generally regarded as a panacea, isn't it?"

Corbyn shrugged his shoulders. "It's the easiest thing to change," he said. "Except one's clothes—even that is a considerable relief, sometimes — or one's mind, which, after all, one can't change, worse luck; one only rakes up the surface, and it's confoundedly hard to smooth it over again. I should not object to a change of air—but I should want to take London with me. Well, I suppose you will be on the wing very soon? Don't forget to send me some grouse!"

Adrian smiled. "I will, if I see any. But they are not very common in the Channel. We are going for a cruise off the coast of Brittany, I think. My wife has to pay a visit first—at Lady Verrinder's; she goes to-day. I've just been to see my solicitor to tell him that I shall not be accessible for a couple of months. The *Anonyma* is getting her stores on board. There will be a berth at your disposal whenever you like to join. Brooke has definitely declined to join us at St. Malo—so he is sure to be with us."

"Are you taking a party?" enquired Corbyn diplomatically, with a nod expressive of his thanks.

Rome hesitated for a moment. "I hardly know; I believe my wife has asked some friends—the Verrinders, I believe—they will pick up their own yacht at Brest; Mrs Vesper, probably, and Miss Lancaster—the charming Phyllis, you ought to know her."

"I remember," said Corbyn. "I have met her at your house—a pretty, fair-haired damsel, with a discouraging mamma."

"Precisely,—though the attitude of the mamma is not invariable; it depends! Are you in a hurry, or will you come to the 'Nondescript' for an hour or so? There is to be a rehearsal of my play: Holmes is sending a company off to the provinces, and I half promised to look in."

The other nodded a cheerful assent. "By all means —I have an especial weakness for the provincial mummer; he doesn't, as a rule, try to disguise himself as a respectable member of society, like his metropolitan brethren. I expect it will be rather a lark."

"Doubtless—for everybody, except the author!"

"Oh, you can afford to laugh, too. You needn't care about the provinces; you have made your hit."

They turned up a side street, passed quickly through a swing-door, with a nod to the custodian, who was reading a sporting paper in a kind of sentry-box inside, and picked their way down a steep and tortuous staircase to the wings, where a few figures loomed in the obscurity which a rapid transit from the brilliant sunshine outside rendered the more bewildering. They paused for a few minutes, after exchanging a brief greeting with the stage-manager,—a bustling tyrant with a very shiny silk hat, precariously perched on the back of his head,—listening to the voices which came from the dimly-lighted stage, and accustoming their eyes to the darkness.

Presently Rome tapped his companion on the shoulder.

"Let us go in front," he suggested. "There are a few people in the stalls; it's so confoundedly draughty here."

They passed through a fire-proof iron door, stumbled down a dark passage, and pushing aside a heavy curtain, found themselves in a region to which the daylight faintly penetrated—the corridor outside the stalls, which they entered. Among the little cluster of people who occupied seats in the middle row, they presently recognised Mrs. Holmes—a pretty, vivacious, little woman, dressed like a fashion-plate, whom Corbyn remembered to have encountered at a hundred private views—and the rococo figure of Miss Lucerne.

"No," murmured Mrs. Holmes, in reply to Adrian's whispered enquiry. "Cyrus isn't here; he has gone to the East End to make a speech for some charity. Why, I can't think. I can't begin to suspect him of philanthropy."

Adrian smiled. "Oh, it's the sort of thing that's expected of actors and bishops and that kind of person nowadays."

"Did you hear that?" said Corbyn, leaning forward to address Miss Lucerne, who occupied the seat immediately in front of his own. "Decidedly, I shall never have the courage to get married if that is what one may expect one's wife to say about one."

Miss Lucerne laughed softly. "I didn't know that men ever condescended to think that it required courage. I thought it was only the preliminaries that were supposed to present difficulties."

"Oh, the mere plunge has terrors of its own, of course! But the waters are so deep, so full of hidden rocks—and it's such a long way to the other side!"

"Heavens!" put in Mrs. Holmes. "He is thinking about the other side already! Don't be such a coward, Mr. Corbyn; remember that the Humane Society's drag is kept in—in the Divorce Court."

Just then an interruption occurred; the comparatively uninteresting education of two minor characters came to an end, and the stage-manager crossed the stage quickly, calling the "beginners" for the second act.

"And mind your p's and q's, ladies and gentlemen," he added humorously, as they gathered on the stage. "Especially your cues: the author's in front, and if he hears any fluffing, he'll let you know of it."

Mrs. Holmes had made her escape, on the pretext of talking to someone about the dresses, and Adrian, finding it difficult, as the first spark of curiosity died out, to rivet his attention on the actors, abandoned the effort and allowed his thoughts to wander unchecked, in swift bat-like flights, through the stimulating darkness of the empty auditorium. An appreciation of his surroundings, absent and intermittent, perhaps, but instinctively accurate, betraying the trained observer, formed the resting-place to which his vagrant imagination at intervals returned. He had attended many rehearsals since the first of his play (how remote that moment of fruition seemed!), but the occasion never failed to strike him as curious and interesting. As he sat alone in his stall (Miss Lucerne, after vainly endeavouring to lure him from his silence, had migrated, with Corbyn, unobtrusively, to the stage-box), he felt, at times, like a disembodied spirit, watching from some shadowy limbo the tragical humours of the little comedy of life. More than once he was obliged to brace himself, in order to dispel the illusion—to grasp at such realities as the white waistcoat and radiant hat of the hovering stage-manager; the gas flaring from the tall T-light in the centre of the stage; the broom and flapping duster of the charwoman, who prowled ghoul-like among the shrouded seats of the dress-circle, with a fine disdain for the goings-on below. At intervals came interruptions: the re-echoing tap of a hammer, and the raucous voice of the stage-carpenter who wielded it; vague cries, and a heavy rumble of traffic from the street; even these sounds seemed infinitely remote, mere echoes from another world, wrapped and muffled in the pall of clinging darkness. The boxes, except those next the stage, to which the gaslight faintly radiated, touching Viola Lucerne's pale face and Corbyn's hands, seemed abysmal gulfs of blackness; the pit, one might imagine, stretched to infinity. A small uncurtained window, high up at the back of the gallery, gave entrance to a ghostly ray of sunlight, which seemed to faint upon the threshold of the impenetrable gloom, recognising the futility of its effort to join the centre of artificial brilliance upon the stage so far below. It was hard to realise that the passing of a few hours would fill this vault with radiance, laughter, and life; that it would seem an appropriate setting for beautiful women, flashing jewels, the music of voices, and the rustle of pretty dresses.

Adrian emerged from the soporific waves of his reverie with a start, to find himself called upon by name to decide some technical difficulty which had presented itself to the busy people on the stage; he left his seat, and drew as near to his tormentors as the intervention of the seats of the orchestra would permit. One query led to another; the representation of the piece in the provinces demanded certain small alterations, which, in spite of their triviality, could not, it appeared, be effected without considerable discussion, in which he was content to take the smallest part, his indifference recoiling upon himself in the shape of the futile suggestions which it provoked. When at last he was released, he found himself deserted by his friends. Corbyn and Miss Lucerne had vanished; the afternoon was far advanced, and, glancing at his watch, he reminded himself that he had promised to meet his wife at the railway station, from which she was to depart on her visit to Lady Verrinder.

A certain nervous fear of seeing the little rift, which he already sometimes imagined lay between them, widen, as well as a feverish desire for solitude, as the occasion for work, had prompted Adrian to proffer a shallow pretext for remaining in town—to attend to rehearsals and legal business—while his wife fulfilled her engagement to Lady Verrinder. The separation of a few days, he argued, not very hopefully, might serve to restore the moral and mental equilibrium which the ravages of a busy season had not unnaturally impaired. It was to nerves unstrung, to weariness and want of change, that he preferred to ascribe their recent dissension, which, unimportant as it might be in itself, his foresight marked as ominous. If Marion had betrayed some surprise at his suggestion, she had acceded with a readiness—a sweet reasonableness, he acknowledged—which would have done credit to a woman possessed of more tact than she could lay claim to. Acute as his mental vision was, it had not occurred to Adrian to suspect that pride might be in some degree answerable for his wife's attitude, for the reticence which he had admired; he had allowed himself to conclude, with a flush of gratitude for her sympathy, that she, too, recognised the occasion as a convenient opportunity for relaxing, for a while, a state of tension for which outward circumstances were entirely to blame.

"At last!" she exclaimed lightly, when he met her on the platform at Waterloo. "Do you know that I have been waiting nearly ten minutes? If time-tables go for anything, the train ought to have started long ago."

"I'm sorry," he began apologetically. "I—"

"Oh, it isn't your fault that I'm so ridiculously early. It was absurd of me to think that any railway company could be punctual in such weather. It's too hot to do things in a hurry, isn't it?"

Adrian assented, declaring that in August one ought to stroll through life with an eye to short cuts and shady paths. Then he added quickly, rather disconcerted by her smile. "You know, it's a mystery to me how you manage to catch trains. I never do. I was quite convinced that you would miss this, and go by the next. I had made up my mind for half an hour's solitary contemplation of the bookstall. It's very nice of you not to scold me; I appreciate your forbearance. I suppose punctuality is a virtue—it's such a bore that I feel sure it must be. Is your luggage all right—and the invaluable Elise?"

Marion nodded. "Yes, and the carriage is waiting to take you back—and that is more than you deserve. I have secured a comfortable corner, and I have *La Peau de Chagrin* to read."

They paused for a minute at the door of the compartment, while a tired inspector interrupted their conversation with his mechanical demand for a display of tickets; and Adrian had leisure to wonder, for the hundredth time, at the rare, distinctive quality of his wife's beauty—a beauty so elusive that on first acquaintance one would hardly recognise it as such; so real, nevertheless, that, for the few who knew Marion well enough to be numbered among the initiated, there seemed to be no limit to its gradual revelation. The fulfilment of the exacting routine of a long season had left its traces, in the shape of a certain refinement of contour, a slight weariness, that had its compensation in an increased charm of delicacy, in the softened lines of lips inclined to stiffness, the more unveiled expression of calm, disdainful eyes.

When she had settled herself in her seat, leaning forward a little, with one arm resting lightly on the ledge of the open window, her eyes encountered his, and a slight flush answering the expression which no woman could have failed to read in them, lent an additional charm to her allure. She turned her head sharply, recognising and repelling his admiration, although she appreciated it, with a movement which, like the instinct that prompted it, was rather wanting in grace.

"Elise might as well have come in here with me," she said brusquely, glancing askance at the old lady who occupied a corner seat at the other end of the compartment, with a touch of the suspicious intolerance which marks the courtesy of an English traveller towards a chance companion. "Even her society would be better than none!"

Adrian smiled. "My dear Marion," he protested, "surely you have had enough society! And haven't you Balzac—the very best? Shall I find Elise for you? She is probably reading Gyp's latest, or the *Queen*, in a second-class carriage, with a packet of bonbons to season the fashion-plates; she would feel flattered, no doubt."

Marion looked at him absently, frowning a little, before she replied. "No—no, never mind; the train is just going to start." Then she glanced past him at the bookstall, beating a tattoo on the window-sill with her finger-tips.

"I—I wish I was coming with you," said her husband urbanely; "it would be very charming."

Marion flushed quickly. "Why"—she began, and then paused, biting her lip. "You—you might have come." She breathed quickly.

Adrian dropped his eyes, with a shadow of a frown, feeling his insincerity punished, then he looked down the long platform irresolutely.

"Oh, it's too late now," added his wife. "The Verrinders don't expect you."

A minute later, the train began to glide out of the station, slowly, with laborious ease. To Marion, sinking back in her seat, the face of her husband, with an expression in which she tried to imagine that regret was the dominant element, still seemed framed in the square of the open window. It haunted her, with its dark, inscrutable eyes, with a smile of farewell overriding its faint perplexity, long after the express had carried her into the midst of the parched fields of Berkshire; and even the witty pages of her author failed at first to banish its persistent presence.

CHAPTER XXIV

ADRIAN stood on the still crowded platform, and watched the tail of the receding train until it passed out of sight. Afterwards, as he slowly wended his way homewards (he had preferred to walk, dismissing his carriage, in the first flush of his contentment at being once more the master of his own time), he could remind himself, without too much anxiety, that this was really the first appreciable separation—and such are salutary, after all, between the most appropriately mated—which had occurred in his married life. His way took him past the Embankment, and presently he stopped, leaned on the wide parapet, looking down idly into the broad river, which, like live things, seemed to be rendered more sluggish by an August sun; watched a penny steamer plying; noted the innumerable little shafts of gold which flecked the surface of the broad, slack stream, like bright feathers sprinkling the brown plumage of a bird. Actually, he was nicely mapping out, like a schoolboy surprised by a holiday, the disposition of his few days of liberty, which expanded indefinitely, in his forecast of their full laborious hours. His work,—his neglected, forgotten work,—yes, it was with a view to that, the opportunity of that, his work, the perpetual need of artistic creation, which, however intermittent, was, after all, the sharpest stimulus of his life, for ever restlessly urging him, that his enforced loneliness seemed so rich an occasion. To pass a certain span of time without interruption in the company of those dear and immaterial people of his imagination, must always be in the last degree the holiday of the artist. And Adrian embraced his opportunity with more enthusiasm than he had believed nowadays to be within his capacity, enjoying the emptiness of the large house (a character which it shared with many of its neighbours, for habitable London was already putting up its shutters), and even deriving a certain perverse relish from the precarious and unpunctual nature of his meals. But after a day or two spent almost entirely in the library, he was obliged to confess, with a sinking heart, that, if the effort had been considerable and the occasion unexampled, the result was barren in the extreme.

It was in the evening that he came to this conclusion: he was still sitting at his writing-table before the open window, through which fresh garden smells, invigorated by a transitory shower, penetrated agreeably; and the light had waned so gradually, or his preoccupation had been so great, that he found himself, before he was aware, in an obscurity, which exposed the hollowness of his laborious pretext. He dropped his useless pen with a gesture of impotence, shut the window hastily,—for the darkness had brought an unseasonable chill in its train, —and threw himself wearily into a chair by the swept and garnished hearth. It seemed to him, just then, that he had reached the end of his tether, of his facility, his genius, his talent—call it what you will; of that, nothing seemed left but a memory, and he mourned for it, and all its unfulfilled promise, as for a dead child. He had been patient, had chosen his season, and built his altar, but for all his waiting the fire from heaven had not descended; his hieratic studiousness had brought forth no inspiration; and nothing seemed left but to beat a spleenful retreat, demolishing the unachieved, unsanctified pile. And he abandoned himself to the depression of the hour, to the tide of self-pity which surged over him, and which was not without its element of self-reproach. He was driven irresistibly upon that pitiable summing-up of experience, which at seasons the least introspective man cannot escape; and, face to face with his verdict, he found it no more tolerable because the failure which confronted him was as inexplicable as it was vague.

Certainly, there remained a tangible result of his labour, in work, not quite imperfect, by no means unappreciated, of not too remote a past, to which he might point; but that seemed an inconsiderable set-off to his state of mind. Therein, essentially, and not in any positive or popular achievement, was to be sought, to his fancy, the true measure of an artist's success. And his outward, enviable state only seemed to accentuate the wretched poverty which was his inward portion. He reminded himself how, years ago,—although these were not so many,—he had looked forward to his inheritance with a pleasure that contained an element of awe. Riches were so generally the compensation of the dull, that when, once in a while, they fell into the right hands, there seemed a priceless opportunity to more and others than their bright-witted possessor. Yes! he had been glad, unfeignedly glad, of his great fortune; and there was no grossness in the idea—he would start neither a racing-stable nor a harem; it meant to him simply the union of great liberty with the power of turning it to the best account—in life, in knowledge, in creative art. And now, after all, he was asking himself whether his opportunities had not been his destruction, and his money veritably a lion in his path? So difficult is it to ride up Parnassus in a carriage and pair. Certainly, there were moments when he could envy Corbyn—his poverty and his enthusiasms, his pervading belief in the free drama that was to be—the Theatre of Art. Adrian could send his Theatre of Art a cheque for fifty guineas with the best will in the world, but a draft upon his conviction, his effective sympathy,—that was another affair; he feared it might be dishonoured.

He dressed, summoned a hansom, and for the first time for many months dined at his club. It was like a revival of his bachelor days—the days of his liberty: he found himself at the same table, and the company, too, had scarcely altered. Even the waiter had not forgotten that he drank Pontet-Canet, and had a weakness for olives. Only, a new poet had sprung up, had entered the circle; and the quatrain had succeeded the triolet, and the triolet was voted *vieux jeu*. And, as of old, Brooke's clean-cut conversation at once suggested and dominated the stream of rapid, paradoxical talk; as of old, Dalrymple Green, who, since he had taken his seat, wore spectacles, and studiously endeavoured to look older than his age, added a note political, or political-scandalous, to the æsthetic harmony. Had not the master of elaborate conversation laid it down, that, in talk, as in cookery, the ingredients mattered nothing so that the service was fine? So they discussed political measures as if they were pictures, and gave to the turn of a verse the importance of an affair of State. Presently the name of Corbyn cropped up in conjunction with his scheme, which came in for its share of ridicule.

"The poor old theatre," said Brooke, "is dead—" He interrupted himself with intention, waved a bland finger, smiling at Rome. "I beg your pardon, it's dying. To-morrow is the last night of your play. Even that could not keep it alive; after that, let us decently bury it. Let Corbyn galvanise its corpse, if he can."

"Why should he?" protested Sebastian Smith, the languid poet. "Besides, Corbyn is really too antiquated.

The Theatre of Art is in existence. It has two temples in Leicester Square."

"Ah, the ballet!" said Brooke, with unction. "Yes, the world is not wholly bad. Let us give thanks for the ballet. It is music, and a picture, and a poem all in one. It has all the fascination without any of the vulgarity of the opera. It is a Whistler put into song, a dream made flesh. Sebastian, how unkind of you to remind me that I might be in a stall at the Alhambra, when I am going to Mrs. Vesper's crush!"

"I am weary of the ballet," sighed Sebastian Smith. "It resembles an epic, and everything bores me which is longer than an epigram. That is why I am so tired of life. But I am going to a hall to-night. Who will come with me? I am going to see Little Tich."

Rome shook his head.

"I don't care for the music hall, and — I have an engagement."

The languid youth protested.

"How strange of you! The music hall is the last refuge of Art. There is nothing between 'Götterdämmerung' and Little Tich. Have you seen the charming quatrain I wrote round the brothers Pietrosanto—those adorable acrobats? I published it in the *Horizon*."

Brooke interpolated an explanation: "It is Sebastian's review: upon everything on which somebody has said the last word he says one word more. It comes out twice in thirteen months, the edition is strictly limited, and each copy costs a hundred francs."

"Why francs?" queried Dalrymple Green.

"It gives an exotic touch," explained the proprietor complacently. "Besides, it is printed in Bruxelles, and Toulouse Lautrec is going to design a cover."

He had risen, was arranging the strange orchid in his buttonhole. Dalrymple Green pushed back his chair, announcing that he too was a patron of the Variety Stage.

"The County Council has monopolised these places too long; it is time that the House of Commons looked in."

"Have you really an engagement, Adrian?" Gerald Brooke asked, when they were left alone. "Or did you invent one, to put off that foolish boy? I call him foolish, though he is charming: he actually believes more than half of what he says. He has just come down—he is the new generation."

"I prefer the old generation," said Adrian shortly. "At least their affectations were amusing."

Brooke smiled, as he lighted a final cigarette. "The affectation of the younger generation is always the antithesis of the last. Formerly, to be a poet, one had to dress badly and carry extravagant hair. Nowadays —observe dear Sebastian—one is shaven and shorn— one is close-shaved by Charles, and buys one's coat of Poole . . . Come with me to Mrs. Vesper's crush!"

"The old generation!" Adrian repeated absently. "No, I am going to pay it a visit. I can't come with you to Mrs. Vesper—convey my excuses."

A moment or two later, as they came down the steps of the broad portico, he added, more definitely—

"I am going to see Lord Hildebrand, my ancient guardian." Brooke received the name with a soft laugh.

"I met him once in Paris; we were dining at Cubat's —he reminded me of Talleyrand." He paused for a moment, with one foot already on the step of his cab.

"He sketched me, in a line; if you will promise to repeat it everywhere, I will tell you what it was he called me—"An Elzevir edition of Rabelais."

Gerald Brooke flung the citation, Parthian-like, at his

friend, and disappeared with a rich laugh, while Adrian directed his steps towards South Audley Street, meditating vaguely. He had contemplated no such visit when he came out, but he was suddenly conscious of a wish to see Lord Hildebrand, who had been for some time, and with an air of permanence (he had sold his Parisian Penates), established in London, but whom, for one cause or another, he had neglected. That Marion disliked him, distrusted him profoundly, or rather the tradition which he represented (for she had never set eyes on the scandalous old man), was no doubt a reason of a kind, but it seemed to him now hardly a reason that should have weighed. He was becoming aware, with a growing sense of dissidence, which was more than the issue of an egoistic impulse, which might by and by have the sanction of his clearest reason, that the list of Marion's disapprovals was an onerous one, too heavy to be borne; and that concession must some day or other be exhausted. And Marion's conscience (if it had been a religious conscience, seeking expression in mystical pieties, he could have respected it, but it seemed to him purely social) struck him with a cold terror. And he wondered idly, but with a genuine dismay, whether one day he might have to face it, and fight with Marion and that shadow of something awful and unknown, an incarnate respectability, which loomed behind her, for dear life, for his very soul's salvation. To have, for an adviser in such a case, a man like his whilom guardian was perhaps a benefit to be contrived.

Adrian was shown directly into the little dining-room, where he found the old man sitting over his coffee; he greeted him as though they had parted the day before, and called for another cup. In answer to Adrian's enquiry, he remarked that his health was excellent, saving a touch of gout—he glanced sardonically at his foot, which was swathed in a formidable bundle, and reposed stiffly on a low stool.

"A respectable malady," he commented; "it should make even my sister esteem me. But she suffers from it herself."

He put in a polite, indifferent question or two, as to his young friend's doings and intentions, when the man had left the room. The waxen, cadaverous mask of his countenance was composed to an expression of urbane interest; but his keen, cynical eyes seemed to penetrate through Adrian's brief and evasive answers, giving him an unaccountable sense of discomfiture.

"And you have a *salon*, I hear? as it was understood in my young days. A *salon*, and a beautiful and accomplished wife? . . . Where did I hear it?" he went on. "How does one hear such things? I suppose my man heard it from somebody's maid—your wife's maid, most likely."

Adrian smiled deprecatingly.

"She's very respectable, a paragon, my wife tells me," he murmured.

"And you mean that my poor Achille is not? Well, he got it from somebody else's maid. I suppose it is true. They know so much more about us than ourselves, and they have their reward—from the editors of the Society papers."

"The *salon*! I think that is more Marion's than mine."

Lord Hildebrand took snuff; tapping his box, he resumed after a moment—

"You must allow me to congratulate you on your success. I am told—Achille tells me—that your name is always in the papers. Once upon a time, a long time ago, my name used to be constantly in the papers, but that was another affair; they spoke of me in terms—"

He broke off abruptly, asked blandly—

"And your wife?"

"She is very well," said Adrian quickly; "she is staying with Lady Verrinder, in the country."

"Verrinder!" The old man arched his eyebrows reflectively, seemed to be drawing on his recollections. "Cuthbert Verrinder? And he's married? well, he had not much time to lose. Everything is behind him; and the lady?"

"She, on the contrary, had time. She is very young—and foolish. Everything is before her."

He got up to leave. Lord Hildebrand looked at him for a moment, with his fine, inscrutable smile. "After all, you disappoint me," he remarked humorously. "You've settled down so promptly—and so well. You've done everything that you ought to do, and left undone all that you shouldn't do. In short, you're unimpeachable correctness."

"And, *après*?" Adrian forced a little laugh, with one hand on the door.

"*Après*—you look as if it didn't agree with you. You look ill."

"I'm tired—of London, and the people in it. I shall run over to France in the yacht, as soon as my wife comes back. Good-night."

He went off languidly, and Lord Hildebrand was left in vague meditation over some elusive, inexplicable quality in his young friend's manner. And solitary as he was, his meditation was accompanied by a faint, ironical smile. He rose painfully, and, leaning with one hand on the table, took down from the wall a dainty miniature. It was the dark and debonair face of Adrian's father — handsome Rupert Rome, portrayed when he was near the age of thirty. With certain essential differences, such as the long beaked nose, and that typical air of a gay, moral recklessness which characterised the days when the century was yet young, it presented striking resemblances to Adrian, especially in the eyes and lips. Lord Hildebrand's smile was accentuated, as he gazed at the portrait of that passionate lover of woman, as though it exhaled an aroma of long-forgotten scandals. The son, too, unless physiognomy was at fault, and heredity belied, had in his blood, with other tempestuous qualities, that dominant tendency of the race, more often than not disastrous, to be swayed overwhelmingly by the fairer half of humanity. And yet, to all seeming, he had already found a safe anchorage in calm and decorous waters.

Lord Hildebrand shrugged his shoulders sceptically, with the air of a person who was not deceived by appearances, however plausible, who foresaw breakers ahead, cataclysms merely postponed.

"*Nous verrons*," he said to himself. "At any rate, if there isn't a woman, there will be, and it is certainly not his wife."

CHAPTER XXV

AFTER all, it was a small party which a fortnight later sailed down the Solent in the *Anonyma*. At the last moment the Verrinders had refused; although this refusal did not extend to Phyllis Lancaster,—and, indeed, this young lady's mother had welcomed the opportunity of committing her, in Marion's safe custody, out of reach of a detrimental flirtation, to the security of the high seas. Gerald Brooke was in Paris, ostensibly for the Salon; he might join later, as Corbyn also proposed to do; of other expected guests, Mrs. Vesper alone duly embarked, but then this lady was, as everyone agreed, a host in herself, and amply filled all gaps.

It was, perhaps, her presence which made Adrian reflect, one morning (they had left Guernsey the night before, and he was up betimes to watch for the first, faint outline of the Breton coast)—question himself, as to whether even the immemorial delight of the sea might not, under certain conditions, fail of its effect. Was there not, perhaps, something inseparable from Mrs. Vesper's company (it was, no doubt, part of her charm, her cleverness), which seemed, even on the free decks of a yacht, to burden the salt breezes of the Channel with an odour of London *salons*, exotic, aromatic of the world—of that world precisely which Adrian was most anxious to forget? At least, it required a wind of more than ordinary volume to dissipate the feeling of restraint which, more and more, the knowledge of her presence imposed on him.

Such a wind had risen during the night, gathering strength with daybreak, and the graceful cutter was scudding before it, heeling over beneath the weight of her snowy canvas, as Adrian came forward to smoke his first pipe. Salvesen, the skipper, was there before him—a tawny giant, with blue eyes, and a vast yellow beard, which flew out in the wind like a flag; he gazed through his glass straight ahead, where the horizon was as yet a blank communion of sea and sky.

Eastward of them, several miles off, but clearly defined in the rare air, was the low line of the Cherbourg peninsula, which the cutter widely skirted. Over it, just where Coutances might be, the sun had now risen in a nebulous red rotundity, presaging a hot day. At present, there was that freshness in the air, which, in its perfection, only attends the opening hours of a summer morning out at sea.

"Shall we catch the tide at St. Malo?" Adrian asked presently.

The skipper deliberated.

"We shall just do it, if the wind holds."

It freshened sensibly as he spoke, with a sudden gust which made the cutter plunge violently; her sharp bows just grazed the crest of a curling wave, and the white spray that was scattered over the deck glistened in the sunlight like coloured fire.

Adriad laughed, and shook himself.

"Unless you can resign yourself to getting in that topsail, it will take French leave in a minute."

Salvesen looked aloft doubtfully. He took a peculiar pride in sailing the yacht under a perilous abundance of canvas, and it was grief and pain to him, when he had to climb down and confess himself defeated. He was still hesitating, when a second and fiercer squall caught them; there was a sound of straining cordage, and the yacht shivered.

"Damn the wind!" he said. "She will always blow too much or not at all—damn her!"

He gave regretfully the order which prudence dictated, and went aft to take the helm; and a moment later two men swarmed up the rigging and struggled with the refractory sail, which they gradually hauled in, to a rending noise like stage thunder. The cutter was brought up to the wind again, and, sensibly lightened, resumed her course, taking each green wave, and surmounting it, with the free, unfettered motion of a bird.

A little peal of laughter made Adrian look round. Out of the companion hatchway a face had just appeared —the face of Phyllis Lancaster, matutinal, fresh, rosy. She clung to the balustrade, and glanced out doubtfully, appealingly, distrustful of her power to cross the deck in safety.

"You're up early, Miss Lancaster. Wait a bit—let me help you. We're rather boisterous this morning."

She extended her hand laughingly, and he came aft and assisted her dexterously into a seat in the stern; then he stood, leaning against the taffrail, looking down at her.

"Well, this is courage! I was afraid we should see none of you now until we were snug at anchor in harbour."

"Oh, I'm a splendid sailor!" Miss Lancaster demurred. "Only, I can't walk about quite easily yet."

"That will come," said Adrian. "In the meantime, let me get you a cup of tea."

"Will you? And a biscuit, please; I'm desperately hungry."

He disappeared down the companion to interview the steward; returned almost immediately, followed by this functionary with a tray. He leaned against the taffrail, with one arm passed round a stay to steady himself, and they ate their hard ship's biscuit in silence. From time to time Adrian let his eyes rest on the girl, absently. He found her charming, in her little serge frock, her yachting cap, from which her rough, brown hair blew out; with a charm which was, after all, no more than that of youth and health, yet seemed harmonious with the hour and the occasion—that young morning, the salt breeze, the buoyancy of waves. When he had seen her before, at his own house, or at her mother's, he had thought of her as a faint impression of her sister, or at least of her sister in her younger, virginal days, before she became Lady Verrinder and an unchallenged beauty. The resemblance was facile, unmistakable as far as it went, but he saw now that it did not go very far. She was not so pretty as Marjorie, or she was prettier; but it was not that alone which struck him; it was an essential difference of expression, of temperament. She could knit her brows; her charming eyes were capable of resolution, did not, like her sister's, contain that constant note of wistfulness, as it were an appeal to all the authorities to let her off easily, to respect her frailty, to treat her kindly, and, above all, not too seriously. Poor Marjorie had been very pliable, but Phyllis seemed to him built more sturdily; she might develop a will of her own. Adrian was the more impressed by this trait, when he became aware that the girl was already the heroine of a little drama. During the last few days, which they had passed in Guernsey harbour, or cruising round the islands, a sort of intimacy had sprung up between them. The girl had met his advances at the outset with a queer reluctance, an ill-concealed hostility, which had somewhat startled him, until he had discovered from Marion that her presence with them was not so much of her own seeking, as a rebuke, a punishment meted out by maternal solicitude to a rebellious chit. Marion spoke in cold tones of a Mr. Lascelles, a most ineligible subaltern in a cavalry regiment. She had been glad to take the child out of his way. Yes, no doubt she had encouraged him, it had gone a certain distance. But when a thing is plainly impossible, a girl of discretion submits. Her chill dismissal of the subject sounded to Adrian ominously towards the lovers' hopes, and, unreasonably enough, for he knew next to nothing of the circumstances, aroused in him a sense of antagonism.

"I shall certainly let her know that I, at any rate, am not in the conspiracy," he said, with humour.

"I beg you will do nothing indiscreet."

"For what do you take me? I am thinking of my own comfort. If the girl is to be on my hands, if it is necessary to sacrifice Lady Lancaster—conversationally—well, you mustn't count on me."

His wife hesitated for a moment; then, looking askance at him, with that faint flush, that odd expression, to which he had grown accustomed, although it had not ceased to puzzle him, she remarked in a tone which practically dismissed the subject—

"We can always count on your indifference."

Marion was unaware as to how far he had fulfilled his threat; but certainly it was not long before the first restraint with which Miss Lancaster had met him was comfortably relaxed. As she had said, she was a good sailor, taking only a frank and healthy pleasure in that occasional vehemence of the waves which drove the other two ladies to the sanctuary of the saloon.

To Adrian her company was often refreshing, like

that of some engaging child. She was vivid and bright, and her mother's system of education, which had come so perilously near success with poor Marjorie, had failed to extinguish all the nature in her. He began to entertain a covert longing for Mr. Lascelles—his name was sometimes mentioned—to succeed in his nefarious designs. At least, he believed the young lady to be quite capable of showing fight.

They had finished their fragmentary breakfast when Salvesen came up; he lifted his cap, with a foreign gesture, to the young girl.

"You will be able to see the land, if you come forward, Miss."

She rose and walked to the bows, steadying herself with one hand upon Adrian's arm.

They looked out over the heaving waters. Straight ahead they could discern easily the little archipelago of islands, mere barren rocks, which are dotted round the entrance to the harbour of St. Malo; Chateaubriand's tomb; and the extremity of the mole, with its undistinguished lighthouse glistening in the sun. The girl gave a regretful sigh.

"Why, we're nearly there," she said. "I'm almost sorry; this has been so delightful."

"I'm afraid you would not find it so delightful if we lost the tide, and had to hang outside. We shall be in by ten. If you are not very hungry, we will breakfast on shore—at some hotel."

"Yes, that will be charming. Poor Mrs. Vesper, how glad she will be! She is not going to get up till we are actually at anchor. When I came on deck, her maid was bathing her forehead with eau de Cologne."

Adrian smiled rather grimly.

"She had better keep her eau de Cologne until we are in the harbour. She will want it then."

"Gracious!" cried the young girl. "It won't be rough inside?"

"Not rough, but, you see, St. Malo, or, at least, the harbour, is the most notoriously evil-smelling place in Europe."

"And it looks so delightful! How long shall we be there?"

"We are entirely at your orders." He hesitated, then went on, "However, I believe Marion wants to wait for letters; perhaps a day or two."

She reflected for a moment; then she resumed, "Well, we needn't be always on board."

"No, we will go up the Rance to Dinan, by the steamer. We will run over to Dol—it has the most enchanting cathedral. We will go to the theatre, supposing the piece happens to be—*convenable*. We will even go and dance at the Casino, if you like. Besides, we may have an addition—two additions—to our party."

"Whom do you expect?" she asked quickly.

"My friend Corbyn—I don't think you know him? And, possibly, Gerald Brooke."

"Mr. Brooke—he's too terribly clever," she protested. "I'm afraid to say a word to him."

"That isn't necessary, so long as you are able to listen."

The girl smiled.

"I don't quite like that either. There's a mean." Inconsequently, she went on, watching the waves, "It is easier to talk to people like you, who know how to be silent sometimes."

"I'm afraid that implies I have often been very dull."

"No, not dull," she said quietly, but purposely withheld any explanation.

One of those sudden silences of his to which she alluded, and which are natural enough, after all, at sea,

—as though the wind had a property of blowing through all those trivial and irrelevant matters which are the staple element of most manufactured talk,—succeeded, and she watched him curiously. She had noticed that he had two manners, and this one she took—quaintly, for it implied a complete indifference to her presence—as a tacit compliment, the more valid as it was unconscious, and he believed her to be quite unobservant, a supposition which made the quick-witted girl smile. Had this not been so, she felt assured that with her, too, he would have maintained his other aspect—that perfectly well-equipped and urbane manner which had struck her when she had seen him in company with Mrs. Vesper, or with his wife, which she could almost believe he maintained with the latter in their closest intimacy—a manner so excellent, and yet so factitious. She preferred his remissness to his punctilio, and was amazed at the difference between them at each transition, discerning, when he was off his guard, as now (and coming perhaps nearer the mark than most critics), how really remote he must be, when he seemed most present, most prepared; and suspecting that his social relations had come to be a sort of elaborate and grotesque etiquette, from which he must be glad to escape even into mere blankness. And her amusement and her insight were never keener than when she realised his consternation if he should ever grasp the knowledge of how she judged him.

It was not a very cheerful little party that breakfasted at St. Malo an hour after the *Anonyma's* arrival in the insalubrious port. Corbyn had boarded the yacht almost before she had dropped her anchor (he had passed her, he explained, just after daybreak, on board the packet from Southampton), with news which, conventionally sad in itself, had the further effect of breaking up an expedition, the members of which discovered now, if for the first time, that it was not altogether lacking the elements of enjoyment. The Duke of Turretshire had been dead for twenty-four hours. This was Corbyn's budget, to deliver which he had expedited his departure from London; and a couple of telegrams were presently brought to the yacht confirming the news, and summoning Mrs. Rome to Towers, to the bedside of the bereaved Duchess, whose health had proved unequal to the shock. That all the ladies of the party should return to England with their hostess, by the steamer leaving St. Malo in the afternoon, was almost inevitable; and, in the eyes of Mrs. Rome, at least, it seemed only decorous that Adrian should accompany them. It was arranged hastily that Corbyn should be left in charge of the yacht, which was to proceed more leisurely to Southampton, to be rejoined by her owner so soon after the funeral as circumstances would permit.

"Sorry, old chap," said Adrian, as he parted from his friend. "You would have liked Miss Lancaster, I feel sure, and— However, you will find Salvesen good enough company for a day or two, and perhaps, after all—"

He paused, glancing up at the grey town, huddled steeply behind the mediæval menace of its embattled walls, with an expression half humorous, half wistful.

Corbyn laughed a little nervously, "Oh, you know, so far as I am concerned, I am not a carpet knight. Candidly, I think I was rather afraid of the ladies."

Adrian nodded gravely. "Lady Lancaster would have been rather afraid of you," he suggested presently. "I was promising myself some amusement!"

Corbyn looked puzzled for a moment. "Thanks, very nice of you!"

"Oh, everyone goes through that sort of thing,"

murmured the other, with a rather elaborate air of carelessness. " You—well, it's only fair, you have been a spectator long enough. Remember, there are people " —he shrugged his shoulders—" who can't get on without something to talk about. Scandal, if you like ; but, after all, it's very human."

" Ah," Corbyn protested, with a shrewd glance at the other, " you forget, my friend, that is one of the penalties of greatness. I am insignificant, *moi*; leave me at least the immunities of my otherwise hardly covetable position."

Adrian shaded his eyes with one sunburnt hand, watching absently the struggles of the vociferous Breton dock-hands, who were filling the steamer's hold with an endless stream of boxes and hampers, that suggested, vaguely, eggs and butter.

" Immunities ! " he repeated. " You will be lucky if you find them. Don't lean on that reed ! "

A bell rang clamorously, in warning of the packet's departure. Corbyn turned, raising his straw hat in salutation of the ladies, who had installed themselves, in a little intimate group, upon the bridge. " After all, I am light, you know. Perhaps, if I don't lean too confidently ? Well, *au revoir*; I wish you well through the next few days."

" I don't like light people," declared Mrs. Rome, who had overheard part of Corbyn's last utterance. " It means that—that one can't depend on them."

" My dear Marion," protested Mrs. Vesper, "you know, I always thought you so independent. Now, I don't want to depend on anyone, except my doctor and my dressmaker."

" And your cook ? " suggested Adrian lightly. Then he added, with a furtive glance at his wife, " Don't be hard on poor Corbyn : where should we be—we others

—without our butterflies? He will marry one of these days, and then—"

"Ah," murmured his wife, getting up and glancing over her shoulder at the receding quay; "do people cease to be light—when they marry?"

Adrian gave a sigh, half petulant, half tender. "Some people—don't cease—to be serious!"

CHAPTER XXVI

"You know," Lady Verrinder had remarked, flippantly, one afternoon, as she handed her empty teacup to her host,—" you know, when I see you in your wife's drawing-room, Mr. Rome, I always think of you as a visitor—and a not very intimate one; I am always expecting you to pick up your hat and gloves, and retreat—in a kind of surreptitious way, like people always do,—particularly men,—as if they were afraid of being prevented—towards the door. Of course," she added hastily, wondering a little whether she had not transgressed, by an inch or two, the elastic limits of that not too rigid discretion which formed, vaguely, one of the articles of her belief,—" of course, you are perfectly right; it is not—oh, one could say it so much better in French,—not correct for a man to assist at the *fiveocloques* of his own wife ... You don't mind, do you, Mr. Rome? I don't see why you should, in the least,—but then you're so deep,—I don't suppose you can understand a trivial person like me. Not that there's anything to understand, you know; I hardly ever mean anything. One just—talks!"

And Rome had protested that he was only too delighted to find himself corroborated, reinforced in his position (had she not implied, with admirable delicacy, that he was a model of the correct?), by so undeniable an authority as Lady Verrinder. And although he would never have confessed that he regarded the mundane little woman's opinion as anything but a negligeable quantity, he still derived a certain comfort from her suggestion, that the tendency which he had been inclined to stigmatise as symptomatic of a growing remissness, possessed, in the eyes of the worldly, its redeeming qualities, was perhaps not altogether to be reprehended.

As time went on, his domestic relations had arrived at a certain superficial settlement. Mrs. Rome no longer habitually invaded her husband's study, early in the afternoons when she was "at home," to enquire, with that air of submissive tolerance which was still uncomfortably suggestive of a sense of injury, whether he would not, later, abandon his pen and ink in favour of her tea-table: he had attained the semblance, at least, of a privileged immunity, and if his ideas sometimes declined to flow, it was not because they were checked by any haunting fear of interruption or reproaches.

It was seldom, indeed, that the rustle of petticoats made itself heard in the region which lay behind the door which Mrs. Rome, on occasion, pointed out to a parting guest as belonging to "the room where my husband does his scribbling—he writes, you know." Mrs. Vesper had been known to penetrate to Adrian's fastness, but this had happened far less frequently than the intimacy which had existed between them before his marriage would have made it natural to expect. Indeed, the room might have been said to maintain a certain tradition of its master's lost bachelorhood. Of his old associates, Corbyn was no stranger to the place; he had spent many long evenings there, when Mrs. Rome was out of town; and Gerald Brooke, perhaps, ran him closest in the assiduity of his attendance. The room contained a low easy-chair of extraordinary depth

and luxury of cushions, and, on the wall facing it, a
"Portrait of a Lady," ascribed to Botticelli; and their
combined attraction was one to which Brooke was
always ready to succumb.

"The physical and the spiritual; comfort and beauty,"
he protested, late one afternoon, when, after encountering
Adrian on his doorstep, he had been easily induced
to re-enter the house. "How dear of you, Adrian, to
provide for one so completely! I should like to sit
here, indefinitely, and gaze at your fair lady, until she
stepped from her frame, to tell us how Sandro beguiled
the hours when she sat to him, the history of that
wonderful collet of silver and pearls (Ghirlandajo's
handiwork for a ducat!); and why, ah, why did he give
us only her head and shoulders? And what is she
thinking about, that makes her smile so gravely, so
obscurely and delightfully? Think what a simper it
would be, how impossible to live with, if one of our
portrait painters of the Royal Academy had mistranslated
her! What a pity—for Botticelli—that I didn't
live in the fifteenth century!"

"So that you might have sat to him?" hazarded
Rome, with a smile hovering on his grave lips.

"Oh, that of course! But I meant—so that he might
have heard me talk about his pictures. Think how it
would have encouraged him!"

"Poor Sandro!" murmured the other ambiguously.
"Were there many people upstairs when you left?"

Brooke shrugged his narrow shoulders. "Oh, it
was one of Mrs. Rome's usual Fridays; there were—
people," he said vaguely. "Mrs. Vesper, I seem to
remember, and Dalrymple Green, I think. Oh yes,
he was talking House of Commons with your wife.
Really, Adrian, I didn't expect you to run a political
salon!"

Adrian smiled a little bitterly, holding out his right hand and surveying minutely the ink stain on its middle finger. "Do I—run it?" he protested. "My wife is responsible, and the amiable, inevitable Dalrymple—" He paused for a moment, then added with increased bitterness, "You know how I hate it!"

Brooke raised his eyebrows a little, shooting an enquiring glance at the Botticelli.

"Politics, I mean," the other added hastily.

"Confound their politics," quoted Brooke pleasantly. "I'm afraid we're excellently bad citizens, you know! Ah, Adrian, be thankful that you've escaped from Oxford; that you're not a don, as you might be if you hadn't been afflicted with riches. I despair, absolutely, of my common-room. Politics and whist, and 'varsity tittle-tattle;—whist, Adrian, has anything ever been so wearisomely perfect? I'm sure Aristides would have delighted in it!"

The speaker had risen now, and, in spite of a deprecating gesture and murmured protest on the part of his host, was gathering up his hat and gloves, with an air of imminent departure. He paused for a moment, smiling whimsically, seeking, with the instinct of his training, for some unerring shaft to give point to his retreat.

"*Eh bien*, I have my revenge," he added genially. "I hibernate, *là bas*; I live on the accumulated reserves of my proper wit. I think out the most brilliant things, and keep them for future use, just trying them, perhaps, discreetly, at undergraduate breakfast-tables. If they only knew, Adrian! Good-bye. I hope you have not put me into your novel; I have the greatest possible confidence in your art, but, all the same, you would inevitably make me so much less amusing than I really am. You know, even I can hardly do myself justice, sometimes. Good-bye."

When he was alone, Adrian sank wearily back into the easy-chair which his visitor had abandoned, and fumbled for some minutes, aimlessly, with a cigarette. A packet lay on the writing-table, addressed, in a neatly illegible handwriting, to his publishers; he eyed it listlessly. What had it all come to? he asked himself for the hundredth time, yielding to that love of self-torture which was so essential of his temperament. Where were his hopes of yester-year, his expectations, his ambitions? To make a figure in the great world, as his imagination had pictured it; to win laurels in contest with great men: that had been his dream in the old days at Underwoods. How they had dwindled, that great world, and its great . . . ! He told himself, sometimes, that it was only because he was so intimately in their midst, that the turrets and spires which had loomed tall for him across the plains now shrank to insignificance behind the tavern roofs; if he could isolate himself again, perhaps once more they would menace the sky. Perhaps— The word, so intimate of hope, so germane to despair, set his thoughts adrift upon a wandering tide; and he tantalised himself awhile with a perusal, half contemptuous, of the familiar pages of his journal of what might have been. He turned from the prospect, wearily, to find himself confronted with one already no less tiresomely familiar, as he summarised, relentlessly, the brief record of his married life; so brief, compared with the future that seemed to stretch its length before him; so brief, and yet so infinitely long. A scornful pity filled his heart—pity for himself, pity, at moments, for his wife: and if he could find no precise justification for either of these feelings, at least, his indulgence in the latter of them was impervious alike to his logic and his scorn. She had loved him;—he could admit that to himself, dispassionately, without a thrill; she had loved him, and he had sacrificed her, deliberately, of set purpose, almost, upon the altar of his art. At times, perversely, he derived a certain pleasure — a sense of fitness—from the manifest rejection of the sacrifice; and now he asked himself, with a sincerity not too profound, whether the moment had not come for a reversal of the parts played by his injured wife, and his contemptuous mistress. Since for him, under present conditions, happiness seemed no longer among things attainable, why should he not make tardy amends, and do his best to make Marion happy? He recalled, with a passionate resentment, difficult of analysis, moments when he had detected in her face, ordinarily rather a mask than a mirror of emotion, a wistful expression, a fugitive, restrained appeal, dispelling, hardly for his pleasure, the doubt as to whether she loved him still. Impartially, and coldly as any curious bystander, he weighed the evidence; it would have pleased him to conclude that his wife's love for him was dead; he would have been less inclined to resent her hatred; and his shame and despair were multiplied tenfold, when he remembered how plausibly he had simulated the passion which his heart had never harboured. Was not her love an answer, sufficient and convincing, to any impeachment that he could bring against her; her case as solid as his was baseless? Such was his mood to-day. At other times, he had consoled himself, as he doubtless would console himself again, taking refuge in a certain philosophy of worldliness, in the tenets of which one might trace the teaching of such counsellors as Lord Hildebrand and Gerald Brooke; when he argued, cynically, that marriage was a compromise; that his wife's love for him was no compensation for the lamentable want of tact of which it seemed easy to convict her. She had made a mistake; let her recognise her position, and bow before the inevitable, even as he was learning to prostrate himself.

CHAPTER XXVII

In the afternoon of one of these late autumnal days, Corbyn had found Adrian in his study, with a face so blank, and a manner so desultory, that he imagined this man of tortured moods had fallen upon one that was more than ordinarily perplexing, that hardly promised a favourable answer to the suggestion he was making. But he nevertheless unfolded his project in a few words, and was surprised to find it acceptable.

"No, I've no engagement," Adrian replied, with a reluctance that was only half feigned; "and if it will give you the least pleasure—well," he broke off abruptly, and with a smile which had in it, perhaps, more of scornful self-criticism than of ironical intention towards the dramatic enthusiasm of his friend, " I will come with you; I will even sit through four acts of an impossible transpontine drama, in an impossible transpontine house, for the sake of your company. After all, it is you who will be disappointed, not I, who expect nothing, least of all from the stage, and less still to find the golden actress of your dreams—you appear to want a budding Bernhardt, or at least the blossom of a Lina Munte—in your young lady of the Surrey-side. My poor Peter, why be so difficult, when Viola Lucerne would do anything for you? At any rate, she's a lady, and has a mind!"

Peter Corbyn winced a little; he went on quickly, with a nervous laugh, "Oh, I don't expect a paragon;

I've never seen Miss Arden on the stage, you know. By the way, she is a lady, in spite of her impossible surroundings. Did I tell you, it was at Brixton with—"

But Adrian interrupted him, with a gesture of indifference. " Well, let us go and see her, this belle of Brixton—at least, I may hope she is *belle*."

Corbyn reflected for a moment. " Yes, she is singularly pretty," he said ; then he went on with a certain accent of regret, " but I'm afraid it is a prettiness that is lost on the stage."

" Perhaps that's the best kind of prettiness," Adrian remarked, as he paused to light a cigarette ; and, with the half-consumed match, he cast away the subject, as they emerged into the square.

The late autumn tinged the air with something cold, and dusky, and sad ; it was not much after five o'clock, but the lamps were already lit, and struggling ineffectually against an increasing mist, which, by the time they had reached the river, had taken the proportions of a fog. They stood for a moment on the Embankment, looking at the livid river, and the tangle of green and ruby-coloured lamps on the railway bridge. Corbyn, chilled and depressed, pulled up the collar of his overcoat, suggested a cab; but the other demurred, absently.

" Let us walk, if you don't mind ; it's not far, you say ; " and as Corbyn fell in with his suggestion, and paced leisurely along by his side, he went on, in a tone of soliloquy—

" I like—no, I don't like, but I tolerate London in a fog. It gives me a sense of distance, and of inclusion— of being included in the distance. That's what one lacks so much—the sense of something new. One lives behind a ghastly iron grating, made out of the foolishness one has done. And so, I like a fog : it gets inside the grating, suggests (of course it is a lying suggestion) something beyond itself. I express myself very vaguely,' he went on abruptly, with an accent of indifferent apology; "it seems to me that I have quite lost any knack of expression that I used to have; but I like a fog."

He seemed to Corbyn, who, in effect, missed his meaning, to speak with an air of cheerful misery; it was plain that his nerves were very tense.

They were turning into the Kennington Road, when Corbyn halted before a flaring building, half restaurant, half public-house.

"We had better have something to eat here," he said; "it's not famous, but it's about the only possible place we are likely to fall across this side of the water. But we might sup somewhere after the show."

"Let us go here, by all means," said Adrian; "I only want a chop."

They had ordered, and were discussing their simple fare; and Adrian had been almost silent, listening with the faintest show of interest, while Corbyn discoursed of his vague and expansive plans. He taxed his companion at last with a more than usual lethargy. Adrian smiled listlessly. "I am all attention," he said; "you think of having a month in Paris, when your Geërtje is launched. You will divide your time there between the Théatre Français, La Bodinière, and the Théatre de l'Œuvre,—I wish anything in the world interested me as much as you are interested by the stage,—but nevertheless, you will have a charming time. I should like to be going with you."

"Why not?" asked the other. "There's nothing in the world to prevent it. If you're hipped, there's nothing like Paris to—"

"To drive away the dragons, as Madame de Sevigné calls those beasts of multiple names. Mine lie too close to my door; and there's everything to prevent it. Let us be moving; we will drive, if you like, and you must talk to me. If I talk, I shall say horrible things; it is bad enough to think them. Talk to me of Paris; I was happy enough there for a month or so, after I left Oxford."

And then, indifferent to what was said, his mind harked back to the period of which he had spoken. Paris! What a glamour there was about the name, and the time in question. He had been there with Brooke, and they had lodged, not too sumptuously, but with a pleasing and recreative carelessness, in the quarter of the Luxembourg. What novel, irrevocable days and nights! For to Adrian, at least, the society was new, and Brooke's company was a passport into its most diverse sections. And the regret was formulated in his mind which his tongue had not dared to utter. The nimbler Gallic spirit, the gayer charm, the utter lack of responsibility, and the freedom—ah, yes, the freedom of it all! And he reminded himself, with a smile at once bitter and whimsical, of the coming generation of genius introduced to him by Brooke, in many a literary *café*, between Procope and the Francois I$^{ier.}$; the audacious *feuilletonistes*; the poets of twenty, with three books behind them and a dozen projected; their gay and amiable affectations, their beautiful self-satisfaction, and their innocent immorality, yet conjoined so quaintly with how much enthusiasm and almost ascetic sacrifice to the muse. To be sure, there were the others, the more distinguished, the "arrived," to whom Brooke had also presented him, who haunted the greater boulevards in a very limited routine, whose heavy lids pouched beneath dulled eyes, which only fired at a present malice, or an unmentionable recollection of the past.

But they, too, were nimble, if they were caustic, with

achievement to look back upon; and whatever grim passions had burned themselves into actual ashes in those disinterested eyes, at least a certain passion for amusement had remained . . .

Here the cab stopped, drew up with a jerk, interrupting his memories; and they alighted before a building, larger and more brilliantly illuminated, but not less uniformly ugly, than the grocer's shop which adjoined it on one side, and the public-house on the other, and the repetition of such establishments, which carried a sordid and monotonous line into the charitable vagueness of the fog. With but a bare glance at the flaring posters, which depicted a not unfamiliar struggle between a highly-coloured young lady and a gentleman in evening dress, Adrian followed Corbyn through a somewhat unsavoury crowd, into a lobby that was no longer in the flush of fresh decoration. Adrian waited on one side, whilst Corbyn spoke for a moment to a man whose back was turned to him; then, following his lead down a narrow corridor which smelt of gas and oranges, he stumbled into a stage box, a blaze of light, and, as it seemed to him at first thought, into the very heart of the orchestra.

"Will you excuse me," Corbyn murmured apologetically, "while I just run behind? I won't be long. The band is at its last gasp; and in the meantime run your eye over the house; surely there must be 'copy' in it."

In effect, Adrian obeyed this suggestion; and even after the curtain had risen on a conventional village, and the stage had been for some time occupied by a pair of comic lovers, his attention was still turned, though somewhat indirectly, on the audience. It was not beautiful, but it set him thinking. It was composed— that part of it nearest his view, in the more expensive parts of the house, of tradesmen of the locality, with

their wives and daughters, dressed in a vulgar fineness
which hurt the eye, physically, like a loud light. Those
entities of the lower middle classes, they were here in
their forces, they were here in their expansion; and
to-night Adrian, who had sometimes ached with a sort
of instinctive pity for them, as for persons who lacked a
certain subtile sixth sense, which rendered life as really
incomplete to them as to the physically deaf or blind,
was irritated into a very genuine envy of their limitations. To be happy, even in a common way; to be
frankly amused, even if one were vulgar. And, after
all, there was a vulgarity in one's fineness; and of late
that had been pressing on him. Yes, he could envy
them, their limited range, and their satisfactions: and
they were so satisfied, he was sure of it; at least, they
never wanted anything to happen. He had greatly
wanted things to happen, what he knew not—but something. And now—never, never!

A dropping salvo of applause greeted a fresh entrance;
a voice appealing to his ear, with a familiar but strange
sweetness, recalled him to the stage. A presentiment—
so he called it afterwards—made his head swim. Are
there ever any other presentiments than afterthoughts
of the greatly unexpected? . . . The girl was nervous in
her part; he could never tell what figure in the cheap
and tawdry melodrama she represented; but even her
make-up could not disguise the freshness of her pure,
young beauty; and a flood of recollection poured across
the footlights, and the scene turned into a garden full of
vain dreams, and set about with trim hollyhocks. . . .
He looked up, to find Corbyn standing over him with a
certain queer embarrassment in his eyes, even before he
had stammered out—

"I know Miss Drew—your Miss Arden, I mean. You
must have known; why didn't you tell me?"

"I beg your pardon," answered the other hurriedly. "Of course, I should have mentioned it; but the fact is, I only knew just now. You see, I never knew her as Miss—Drew; and even if I had, you see your name never cropped up till to-night. It's very curious—"

If the other had exhibited a moment's discomfiture, it was only for a moment. He interrupted him, quite easily, with a little laugh that seemed to do ample justice to the occasion.

"Yes, very. But I really don't know why I should have expected you to have guessed that your Miss Arden was an old friend of mine; it was a sort of boy-and-girl friendship."

"Yes, exactly," said Corbyn. "But you must come round and see her. She is not on after the second act."

"I should like to do that." And they fell into silence. Adrian seemed absorbed in the play; Corbyn was surreptitiously watching him; his interest in his presumptive first lady—of course she would not do, he owned with a sigh—had been transferred to his companion. He was trying to gather together irrelevant threads of his recollection, of some old story, a sort of impossible idyll. And the more he remembered, the more he suffered from an unaccountable sense of discomfort.

Was there some deeper, more intimate emotion implied, than his friend's cavalier dismissal of the subject had admitted? There was certainly nothing extraordinary in his manner; neither at that time, nor later, when in the dust and glare of the flies (for there was no green-room) Adrian found himself face to face with Miss Arden, this will-o'-the-wisp of the past, to whom Corbyn had a little awkwardly reintroduced him. But there was a bright spot on either sallow cheek, and, for once, that rare luminous quality in his eyes, like the flash of wine, which sometimes touched his queer, nondescript face with beauty. The girl had greeted him almost silently; she had put on her hat, and was obviously on the point of departure.

Absently, Adrian had shaken hands with the manager, had murmured a mechanically smiling assent to the claim of old acquaintanceship, listened to a florid compliment.

"Montague Villiers, you know—remember you quite well, Mr. Rome—flattered, my dear sir, flattered, I assure you, to see you at my little slummicking show. Won't stay? Well, I don't wonder. I'm of your opinion, Mr. Rome, if I had my own way. I like Art myself—*Tosca* or *Pink Dominos*. But I'm handicapped here; wait till I get a West End house! Besides, you would like to talk to my cousin—remembers you very well—would be flattered, flattered, I'm sure, if you'd see her a little way—known her longer than I have. Excuse me, Mr. Rome," and he turned hurriedly to Corbyn. "You will wait, won't you, Uncle Peter?—with you in a moment—just got to see a man about a cut in the third act. You can meet Mr. Rome at the station—last train to Waterloo."

Adrian saw Corbyn reluctantly buttonholed, snatched away into the mysterious gloom of the passage.

"Shall I get you a cab, or walk with you a little way?" he asked, averting his eyes somewhat nervously.

"If you'll be so good," said the girl quickly.

He followed her deft guidance, stumbling, himself, over properties, up and down dilapidated steps, through the stage door, and out by a little alley into the street again. Rain had fallen, and ceased, since they had entered the theatre; the dirty pavement glistened, but the fog had cleared. He stood for a moment silently; there was not a cab in sight.

"If you are not very tired, may I walk with you to your door?" he asked.

She did not answer for a moment; then she said simply—

"If it is not taking you out of your way. It is not very far. I have always walked from rehearsals."

They set off; the girl walking very quickly, Adrian keeping pace with her. Once or twice he glanced at her with a sort of curious fear.

"So, you are Sylvia," he said suddenly.

CHAPTER XXVIII

On the threshold of the stage door, Corbyn paused to light a cigarette at the gas which flared, with an almost birdlike flutter, within a wire cage, opposite the lair of the doorkeeper. A little way up the alley, which ran by the side of the theatre, a small group had gathered, to which Montague Villiers had already attached himself. After a moment's hesitation, Corbyn joined the party; confused introductions followed, and a slow progression, which, as experience taught him to foresee, soon found its limit in the saloon bar of a neighbouring tavern.

"Don't worry about your pal," Villiers had protested, anticipating his guest's scruples, "you will find him at the station all right; there's a good half-hour before the train goes, and I want to talk to you. Besides," he added, with a departure from his confidential undertone, "these Johnnies all want to get at you; it isn't every day that we get a representative of the metropolitan press down here, all to our little selves."

The others crowded round Corbyn, pressing drinks upon him, with cries of "after you with the critic," and a burlesque of anxious sycophancy. They were all frankly professional, as young actors are wont to be, reflecting, with no shamefaced diffidence, the honest glare of the footlights, diffusing lavishly the genial radiance in which they were nightly steeped.

For Corbyn, the trait possessed the sanctity of old

acquaintance. If it had needed apology, he would have urged that it was only fair that men who did their best to make you forget the stage when they were upon it, should be allowed to carry it about with them afterwards—if only to prove that it existed, and in common gratitude. He smiled a little, inwardly, as he remembered Rome's summary of his first impression of Montague Villiers, after their encounter at Underwoods; that he "brought the scent of the footlights over the hayfields."

At half-past eleven, Corbyn, not without difficulty, effected his escape, and Villiers volunteered to walk with him to the station.

"And you don't think she'll do?" said Villiers lightheartedly, thrusting his hands deep down into the pockets of his Inverness cape, as a sudden gust of wind encountered them at the street corner.

Corbyn hesitated. "She might be splendid in her own part; it's all there, she only wants experience. I—admire your cousin immensely—you mustn't think—But—well, she isn't my idea of Geërtje; I've said that so often that I'm afraid I must be hopelessly exacting. But you don't think yourself that the part would suit her?"

"You're quite right," declared the other, nodding his head sagaciously. "Said so myself when I heard her read it. Rum thing, *she* rather likes it. But there—don't mind telling you, I rather fancy myself in 'Hamlet.'"

"She likes it?" Corbyn raised his eyebrows a little. "I'm sorry—" he began.

Villiers nudged him with his elbow playfully. "Garn!" he said. "Between artists, dear boy! Art first, feelings nowhere."

Corbyn smiled. "You're a good chap, Montie."

The other glanced at him askance, with an elaborate show of suspicion.

"Hullo! want me to buy you a drink?"

Corbyn laughingly shook off the aspersion of his good faith.

"Remember Rome, and the last train. Miss Arden— Miss Drew—" he added, stumbling over the names. "Your cousin ought to have a part written for her. Something sympathetic — hayfields, you know, and roses, and all that. We'll make Rome do it, and take a theatre for her, eh?"

Villiers assented. "They're old pals, you know; she used to be a neighbour of his, down at his place in Berks. My aunt bossed the local stamp-foundry, and ran a corner in slate-pencils and toffee; quite the village Whiteley. We used to be no end chummy—Sylvia and I and Mr. Rome. Tea in the back garden, church bells, chorus of villagers, bless our happy home, rooks, sheep, and all that kind of thing."

"Yes," said Corbyn, thoughtfully. "Underwoods, wasn't it?"

"That's the ticket. I've said to Sylvia, time and again, that we ought to give Mr. Rome a call and cheer him up with memories of his youth, and that, but she didn't seem to cotton to it. She's kind of haughty, you know, and inde-blooming-pendent. And, of course,— well, there's Mrs. Rome,—you know what men are when they're married sometimes, a bit shy of their old pals. What? Not that I mean to imply— You must come up to my shanty some time. No good to-night; you would only have missed your train, and Flossie won't be back for another hour—she's doing a late turn at the Oxford. You must come down later on for the panto.— *Aladdin and the Safety-Lamp*; they've engaged Flossie special for principal boy, and your humble servant is going to play the widow Twankay. Great games. I say, you'll have to hump yourself, dear boy. Must go, I suppose?"

Corbyn nodded. "I'll come, like a bird. Thanks, very much. There's Rome getting the tickets. Good-night."

A minute later the train moved out of the station. Rome and his companion were not fortunate enough to secure the privacy of an empty compartment, and it was not until they reached Waterloo, and had ensconced themselves in a cab, that Corbyn began to find his friend's reticence no longer to be explained by a reluctance to discuss intimate topics before strangers.

An allusion, almost inevitable in the circumstances, to the object of their expedition, had drawn from Adrian an evasive murmur, discouraging criticism of the actress.

"It's a fact that I wasn't in the secret," Corbyn hazarded, just before they crossed the river. "I had no idea that I was taking you to see an old friend."

Adrian looked at him for a moment with absent eyes, frowning a little. Then he smiled. "My dear fellow," he said, "forgive me—I quite understand. Besides, I have to thank you: I should have thanked you for a far less pleasant surprise. A surprise—"

He hesitated, and Corbyn, a little ashamed of his insistence, was prompt to interrupt him with a quick transition, curiously responsive to his friend's diverted train of thought.

"He's not a bad sort—the volatile Montie!"

Rome eyed him gravely.

"No," he said at last, adding, almost beneath his breath: "Thank God for that!"

At a point a little beyond the north side of Waterloo Bridge, Adrian brought the cab abruptly to a stop.

"It is clearing up. I will walk from here, I think," he said. "Good-night, Corbyn—and thank you."

Corbyn saw his friend enter the gloomy stairway that leads to the Embankment, before his cab turned and merged itself in the traffic of the Strand; and he wondered, with a certain sense of indiscretion, how far Adrian's mood would have carried him before he encountered his wife. His meditations were interrupted, however, when he reached his rooms, and found in his letter-box a small, square envelope, addressed in a handwriting which during the last few weeks had become increasingly familiar. He contemplated the note for a minute, by the light of the gas that illuminated, crudely, the desolate staircase; then he raised it to his lips, and entered his room, sporting the oak quickly behind him.

"Of course, it is to say that she can't come," he assured himself, with elaborate unconcern, as he struck a match and looked about him for a candle. "Of course—rehearsals—dressmakers—oh, I know."

He propped the note against the candlestick on the mantelshelf, and passed into his bedroom to put on an old coat and slippers. This accomplished, five minutes were devoted to the lighting and encouragement of his fire (for he had a couple of hours' work before him); then he pulled a dilapidated basket-chair up to the fender, established himself in it, and very deliberately filled and lit his pipe.

When he had read the note, he lay back in his chair luxuriously, letting his eyes wander again over the written words. She would be very pleased to lunch with him to-morrow, and go with him to the *matinée* at the Royalty. She would be very pleased; she was his sincerely, Viola Lucerne. . . . He cheated himself with the sweetness of the words, wilfully ignoring their want of meaning, their stereotyped conventionality.

Half an hour passed; he recalled himself from his vague, delightful dream, shook his head as one who reprehends a folly, drew his chair closer to a chaotic table, and opened his inkpot.

He awoke next morning, at an hour nicely consistent with the exactions of his midnight labours, to a vague consciousness that the day held pleasure in store for him. His nebulous vista took definite shape presently, when his eyes fell on the little note that lay, beneath his watch, upon the rickety, japanned chest of drawers which stood at the side of his bed, and did duty as a dressing-table. And he confided this impression to Miss Lucerne a few hours later, when she sat confronting him at a little table in the *Restaurant des Bienvenus*.

"The feeling one used to have—ever so many years ago—on one's birthday, or at school, on a holiday," he concluded, as the waiter deposited a cryptic *hors d'œuvre* before them with a flourish.

Miss Lucerne contemplated, for an instant, the faint mark which a seam of her glove had left round the thumb of the hand which she had just withdrawn from it, then she raised her eyes, across the depths of which a light veil of raillery flashed before the other had time to discern the expression that was beneath.

"Good little boy," she said lightly. "It should be taken to the play, and to Buzzard's afterwards, if it behaved nicely, for an ice. Now, if only it was the pantomime!"

Corbyn laughed. "Of course, that would be quite perfect; so that I could go home afterwards to dream of the Fairy Princess. To think how one used to be able to dream!"

He sighed regretfully.

Miss Lucerne shot a quick glance at him, and let her eyes rest for a moment on his half-smiling, half-wistful face. He was so different from the other men of her acquaintance; they were so many, and he so different from them all. Fortune, and the changeful life of her vocation, had brought her into contact with almost every type of the class to which, vaguely, she assigned Peter Corbyn; she had enjoyed her share, at least, of careless friendships, of friendships that had waxed and waned, of jealous enmities. They were good fellows—"good sorts," as she might have put it—some, even most, of the men whom she had known; he was a "good sort" too. They had amused her, fallen in love with her, crossed her quick temper; she had quarrelled with them, forgotten them. But he— She shook her head and smiled, recalling herself.

"But, you mustn't be sentimental," she protested. "You—you must amuse me, you know. I didn't mean 'sentimental' quite." She shrugged her shoulders, as he looked across at her, puzzled for a moment, questioningly.

"Oh," she added, "that's your business, to know what I mean!"

Corbyn smiled. "I undertake the task, with cheerful submission and tempered enthusiasm; but aren't you going to tell me about your new part?"

"My new part?" She echoed his words, with a gesture of despair. "It's turning my hair grey; wait till I get the author into a secluded corner—he'll learn something to his advantage, as the agony column says. It's too bad of Mr. Rome not to write another play; when you see him you may tell him so, with my compliments."

"You should tell him so yourself; it might have an effect. That reminds me—talking of Rome—last night —quite a story."

He paused, and the girl looked at him enquiringly.

"We were with Montie Villiers last night, over the water. They are going to put on a pantomime; I expect great things of it."

"I shouldn't. Well, and Mr. Rome—your story?"

Corbyn hesitated for a moment. "I enticed him to transpontine wilds to see a *débutante*—a possible Geërtje, you know; and Rome recognised her as an old friend. That's all."

"That's all!" echoed the girl whimsically.

"Really," she added a minute later, meeting her companion's imperturbable smile with an impatient flash of her blue eyes, "one might imagine that you were Mr. Rome—telling his wife."

"I wish I were!" put in Corbyn quickly. "I mean—not Rome, of course!"

A faint colour rose to Miss Lucerne's face, as she quickly interposed.

"You wish you were telling Mrs. Rome, instead of—declining to tell me."

Corbyn sighed. "I think you know what I wish."

"Just imagine me cast for an *ingénue*," Miss Lucerne put in inconsequently, as the waiter served coffee, and Corbyn produced his cigarette-case. "And, my dear Peter, such an *ingénue*!"

Corbyn laughed. "As if you couldn't do anything in that line—from Juliet to Jane Eyre."

"Vastly polite," nodded the actress; "**particularly Jane Eyre.** I didn't suggest that I couldn't, you know. But, Lord, this creature! In the first place, she's cursed with a moralising old father, who quavers, and wavers, and—"

"I know," Corbyn interrupted. "Regular dodderer. Grey-hairs-with-sorrow brand. And you're the serpent's tooth, of course."

"Not at all! The prop of his declining years!"

"Well," said Corbyn, smiling, "fire away—prop him up. Nice sympathetic part; I can hear the tears dripping from the gallery into the dress circle, and the stalls sniffing."

"Wretch! Oh—and the creature is in love, if you please!"

"Never heard of an *ingénue* who wasn't—particularly the kind with doddering parents."

"Perhaps you think you're being nice, and sympathetic," the girl protested indignantly. "Of course they are; but they don't all behave as if they had a monopoly of the experience, and wanted everyone to know it. Anyhow, I'd sooner play Ibsen, any day."

"Well," said Corbyn with decision, "you would be perfect as Nora. Can you dance a tarantella?"

Miss Lucerne ignored the interruption, frowning a little as she sipped her coffee.

"Perhaps, if I were in love myself," she suggested, drumming with her fingers on the table in the most matter-of-fact way.

Corbyn eyed his cigarette intently, scrutinising the gilt letters of the maker's name at one end of the white cylinder.

"But you're not," he put in brusquely, as she paused.

The girl shot a stealthy glance at him. The lines of her companion's mouth hardened a little, as he gazed with absent eyes at his empty coffee-cup. A brief silence followed; he looked at his watch, exclaiming that it was late, and summoned the waiter.

When he had paid the bill he crossed the room in search of his umbrella, which the waiter had successfully concealed.

"Dear idiot," murmured Miss Lucerne, following him for an instant with her eyes, before she turned, instinctively, to consult a convenient mirror.

CHAPTER XXIX

WHEN he had left Corbyn, in a vehement desire to be alone, Adrian walked rapidly on, careless and uncertain of his direction: and he must have wandered long and far before a heavy torrent of rain recalled him, as from a great distance, to the lateness of the hour, the strangeness of the place. He had been threading his devious way through the purlieus of Westminster; he had some trouble to find a cab; and when he let himself into his own house, it was dark and silent. His wife had doubtless long since gone to bed. Drawing a long breath of relief that this was so, he entered his library, stirred up the dying fire, and lit all the candles he could lay his hands upon. Mentally and physically, he had need of a violent illumination. And he sat down by his writing-table, and strove to recollect himself, to focus the events of the evening.

They had been trivial enough, the things that had happened, the words he had spoken; yet he was conscious that they represented some change in his life, which had gradually come to be such a routine of ennui; they inaugurated a crisis. Nothing was very tangible, nothing was at all clear; but through a sort of mist, which had overcast his mind, one fact shone like a lantern, like a beacon of safety. "*Sylvia has come back.*"

A beacon of safety was it, or perhaps, rather, some dubious will-o'-the-wisp, to lure him into fatal morasses?

No, it was of safety, it must be so: of safety! And he repeated the name to himself very softly: "Sylvia, Sylvia!"

Yet he had said but little to her, in their brief and embarrassed progress through the teeming streets.

He was glad to see her again, she also was glad; she had heard of him, of his triumphs, of the success which she had always hoped for and prophesied; and, in a brief allusion to his marriage, she had the air, very frankly, of assuming that that was part of it. Did she notice his swift evasion of the subject, turning to herself with a few brief questions as to her life and interests? The stage? No, she pretended to no vocation for it; but she had a need to earn her living, and that seemed the most natural and simple way, since her only relations were in "the profession."

He hated the phrase from her lips, and the idea which it connoted; that was the most personal note he struck; and at her faint smile, perhaps, a trifle sad, which was her only answer to this inconsequent remonstrance, he had been quick to retract. What right, in fine . . .

At the door, she had held out a friendly hand to him.

"Of course, I must see you again," he had said.

"If you go sometimes to the theatre."

She had looked vaguely aloof, had not encouraged his request to call upon her. Indeed, her whole attitude seemed to convey a quiet assumption of their divided ways—ways grown too separate to be bridged over by any friendliness. Yet just at the last, when the gaslight over the door fell full upon his face, her eyes had seemed to dwell upon it with a glance, quickly repressed, that was almost tender, that might have been pitying—and that was all.

The door of the shabby-genteel villa had shut her in

from him. And he began to think of that house and its tenants: the fluent, vulgar actor-manager; his wife, the serio-comic lady; kind, no doubt, but, in relation to Sylvia, filling him with a dumb rage, and detestable.

Suddenly, at last, he seized pen and paper and began to write to her. This was his letter.

"Sylvia, you must not misunderstand me; that at least we owe to old days. When I saw you to-night, we were afraid, uneasy. There were things to be said, and we had no chance or time to say them. There was a shadow between us, of something which does not exist, can never exist—estrangement. Oh, Sylvia, my friend, is it any reason, because we travelled apart, that now when chance has thrown us together again, we must avoid one another? I must come and see you. I will tell you why. I beg it of you—of the old Sylvia. I want you to help me, to help my work: you once cared for it, believed in it. It is like to die without you. I have gone as a blind man, wandering. Yourself gave me light again, and put me in the way I had lost, and I seemed to see the things I had seen—and once I saw visions. And I am afraid lest the light should go out. Sylvia, write and tell me that I may come to you."

It was a little note, but the candles were flickering in their sockets before he had ended it; for, between each spasmodic sentence, his fingers had lain idle, whilst his mind span out unwritten pages. He sealed it, without reading it over, in a fear of that cold reaction which follows any effort after sincere expression, lest it should tempt him to destroy it; and it was a like dread which caused him to steal out himself to post it, in the grey morning, whilst the impression was still fresh upon him.

The house was dormant, steeped in that oppressive

silence which only a great house exhales, in a great
city, when both are slumbering. There was something
guilty about it; but as Adrian passed quietly by his
wife's door, on his way to his own room, it was with no
feeling of guilt, but with a mingled sense of pity and of
the inevitable that he thought of her. He slept a heavy,
dreamless sleep until nearly midday.

"Mrs. Rome bade me give you this, sir," his servant
told him as he descended, and he handed Adrian the
laconic note in which his wife informed him of the day's
proceedings. She had gone out to lunch; there was
this to be done; such and such guests were coming to
dinner; they had a box for the French play. "Henry
Minaret was here yesterday—was sorry to miss you
again."

There was nothing novel about this bulletin—indeed,
it had become a matter of almost daily occurrence—
except the last item, which (strangely enough, for he
loved the man) gave Adrian an indefinable feeling of
uneasiness. But this impression, and all thought of
his wife, even the almost unconscious irritation caused
by her formality, as though she would accentuate the
fact of their differences, vanished as he shut himself into
his library.

The raindrops still hung to the yellowing trees in
the square, but to-day they glistened jewel-like in a
mellow sunshine; and through the windows, when, for a
moment, he opened them, the cool odour of wet earth
filtered agreeably. The room, which he had grown to
hate, with all its memories of ineffectual effort and disheartening self-interrogation, seemed to have become
bright with promise. Sylvia had come back; Sylvia's
eyes shone to him out of the sombre bookcases; Sylvia
would write to him.

He began to sum up the possibilities, the probabilities

of a response from her; then dismissed the conjecture peremptorily as an outrage upon his faith, his certitude. And to distract himself, to avoid the tedious counting of the hours or days which must elapse before the desired line could reach him, he took out the neglected manuscript of the book which had been nearest his heart, from the drawer, into which, months before, he had despairingly flung it.

He began to peruse them—those "Sensations of Florio," forlornly near completion, never, he had come to say, to be completed; at first, with a sort of indistinct repugnance, with the *gêne* with which one encounters afresh a person once loved, but long grown distasteful; but as he read, in the new light which had been shed upon him, he found himself caught up suddenly in the warm embrace of his idea. This phrase was good, that situation contained inevitable rightness; a revision here, a compression there, and the climax which he had sought for so tediously was revealed to him in a logical and admirable lucidity; it should be tragical perfection. And he flung himself into his work, with a feverish ardour which, two days before, would have been incredible to him, covering page after page with his loose handwriting, and, against his usual habit, writing rapidly and almost without erasure.

The light waned; his man silently brought in candles, and he still wrote on, insensible to the noises about the house, voices and announcements, the coming and going of carriages. He waved aside the notion of dinner with a bare excuse; they brought in a tray of sandwiches, some decanters. He poured himself out a whisky-and-seltzer, which he drank with eager thirst, and went on writing. He was unconscious of the time, but it must have been very late, when at length, in sheer physical fatigue, morally refreshed though he was by the effort of creation, he dropped his pen, and gathering together the scattered sheets, began to read over the result of his labour. And as he read, he felt an amazed joy, not to be overcome, as on how many occasions in the past, by the reaction of disgust, which is too often the ironic reward of the deadliest travail of the artist. This time, what he had written was written; let it stand; it was vivid, it was strong, it was just. Never before had he seemed to have drawn so near to the perfect expression of that haunting, visionary idea which he had followed.

He was engaged at his task, now correcting, now erasing a word, but still flushed with that joy, grown so rare with him, of satisfaction with the accomplished, when the door opened softly, and his wife entered.

She had carnations, rose and white, in her hair; she wore an opera-cloak, feathered in whiteness, over a gown of sea-green silk sprayed with roses: she had never looked statelier, more handsome. The light from the shaded candles tinged and softened the cold precision of her beauty, and Adrian, losing for a moment his resentment in æsthetic admiration, yielded to an instinctive movement of pride in her possession. And at the same time with the artist's need of sympathy, appealing to her as he might have done to any casual comer, he held up the sheet which he was correcting, his hand trembling a little.

"See, Marion, I have had a splendid day. I have been in the vein. My book is almost finished."

She unclasped the buckle of her cloak deliberately before she answered him, drawing a deep breath.

"Yes . . . I am glad to hear it. You seem to have been a long time over it."

He could not see her quickly suppressed gesture of aversion, nor the hardening of the lines round her mouth; but the ice in her voice was a subtle indication to him, and her indifference steeled him anew to her.

"I shall be able to finish it to-morrow," he said quickly.

He suffered a moment of vexatious shame at his inconsequent appeal to her; his long fingers fumbled nervously with his disordered papers; her presence there troubled him; the strange woman! What was his work to her, or she to him? In God's name, what had they to do with one another? He wished that she would go, leave him alone with his other life, his possibilities. He began to glance over the papers again, and it was out of the distance that her voice presently reached him.

"I didn't come to talk about your book. I am afraid I have disturbed you. But I wanted to speak to you, and you give me— I have so few opportunities: I must take them when I can find them. Yesterday—"

"Yesterday, I was very busy," he interrupted hurriedly. His attention was now riveted; he had half turned round in his chair, and was regarding her with anxious apprehension. She had spoken with seeming indifference, but her eyes were extraordinarily brilliant; and he suddenly became disagreeably conscious that, under her calm exterior, she was passionately agitated.

"It's very late," he said nervously. He felt that they were drifting towards what he hated most in the world, an explanation. Hitherto, the situation had existed, but it had not been explicit. For Adrian, this was the one fact which saved it; and it was through fear of himself, and of what might come to them, if once the seal were to be set upon their estrangement by an admission of it, that he made a last effort to stay her.

"It is very late, Marion. You look tired, and I am— utterly. If you have anything to say, hadn't it better wait till to-morrow?"

She looked at him in silence for a moment, then she broke out suddenly—

"To-morrow? Yesterday, to-day, to-morrow—it is all the same. When did I see you last? How long is this life to go on?"

The cluster of blood-coloured carnations, that stained the whiteness of her bosom, surged tumultuously. It was the first time that Adrian had detected any sign of discomposure, of exaltation, through the perfection of his wife's demeanour. And this observation restored his own nerve. If Marion was going to make a scene, so much the worse; he had sought to stave it off. At least, if it was inevitable, he could face it with the advantage of self-possession.

"Won't you sit down?" he asked, with a little sigh. But they both remained standing, and he went on after a moment—"What life?"

"Oh," she cried, with a gesture of elision, "you can ask it?"

He pulled his moustache thoughtfully for a moment. Then gravely—

"Listen, Marion, and consider. I understand what you mean, what you are going to say. I beg you to pause before you say it. Why can't you let things be? There is something to me appalling about words; they can't be retracted, or glossed over; they remain. Oh! one should be careful about words. For your own sake, for my sake—you don't know what it may involve!—let us avoid any explanation; don't let us specify our position."

"Our position!" She repeated the phrase in a wrath of scorn. "It is intolerable; it's horrible! It's obvious to the world!"

"Hush!" He held out his hand deprecatingly. "If our marriage has failed, if we are as completely apart as any two married lovers ever became, is that a reason . . ." He paused for a moment; then went on suddenly—"Don't let us recriminate. I have always tried to consider you. You have had everything you wanted."

"Everything!" She drew a deep breath. "How much you must hate me!" she exclaimed. "And who is the woman?"

He grew very pale; his calmness suddenly abandoned him.

"It isn't true . . . You shouldn't have said it," he stammered.

They stood facing each other, rigid and pale, for a few seconds of exhausting silence, which Marion was the first to break. She had regained her self-control. Her smile seemed a natural thing; her voice had resumed its habitual inflexion of coldness.

"I was speaking foolishly," she said. "I came about something quite different. I have no wish to interfere in your life. It is quite beyond my comprehension. I suppose you are coming to Brackenmuir with me on the 20th? So long as we live under the same roof, we owe something to appearances, to society."

It was Adrian's turn to let fall an involuntary bitterness.

"O God!" he cried. "Haven't I sacrificed enough to it?"

She looked at him with eyes in which genuine astonishment was depicted.

"I don't understand you," and, gathering her cloak together—"I don't think I want to understand you."

"Good-night," he said wearily, and held the door for her sweeping drapery to pass through.

When she had left him, he sat down at his writing-table, and gathered together the mass of his papers, with an almost personal tenderness. But his mind had been diverted from them, and he only laid them aside. He buried his face in his hands, and sat idly. He was almost grateful to his wife for the light she had struck.

"Sylvia, Sylvia!" he murmured, and presently, exulting as it were in his new conviction—"Oh, my love, my love!"

CHAPTER XXX

THE same filial piety which had made it natural for Lord Henry Minaret to address letters, affectionate, if brief, to his mother, at frequent intervals, during his absence from England, prompted him to devote the first days of his return to an attendance upon the widowed Duchess at Turreyfield, the dower house, a stone's-throw from the gates of Towers, to which, shortly after her husband's death, she had very willingly betaken herself. His father's testamentary dispositions had left Lord Henry a richer man than his elder brother, who had encumbered so heavily the estates to which he succeeded as tenant for life, that he was practically dependent upon the dubiously acquired dollars of his Duchess. This lady seemed by no means inclined to abandon her control of purse-strings that had already become somewhat frayed in her spendthrift husband's service. She was intimidated, perhaps, by her strangely abrupt arrival at the altitude which, a year ago, had tempted her speculative eye; struck, as an unpractised mountaineer, by sudden dizziness. Retrenchment flew its colours on the battlements of Towers. Guests were infrequent; the magnates of the county perfunctory in their homage. The new Duke was not accounted seriously; a stop-gap, manifestly, whose days were numbered. He had done his worst; even scandal had grown tired of his name. It was plain that the hour of his reckoning was at hand, that at last he was to be called upon for his quota of the price which his family had grown accustomed to pay.

Lord Henry, all things considered, could afford to be magnanimous. He was polite to the Duchess, forbearing with his brother, whom, after all, it was better policy to pacify than to provoke. It is possible that his exile—admittedly disciplinary—had not been without its effect, in the direction of a certain habit of self-restraint. At least, he was philosopher enough to realise the futility of cherishing resentment against a fellow-mortal, however malignantly aberrant; prudent enough to recognise that he had nothing to gain by relinquishing a standpoint which enabled him to keep a discreet eye upon his brother's proceedings.

The invention of cards—redoubtable link of the wise with the wayward—enabled the two brothers to spend long evenings together without drawing too heavily upon a limited fund of common interests. The Duke had learned to keep sober when a game of piquet or écarté was in progress. His brother discovered the fact, and made good use of his discovery.

Some weeks before Christmas, however, the dower house was temporarily abandoned, and Lord Henry accompanied his mother to Clarges Street. Already, he had paid flying visits to town,—had dined with intimate friends, interviewed leaders of his party,—but it was from this time that he dated his formal return to civilisation; from an exile which, in spite of its brevity, had seemed to him prolonged. It had struck him at first as strange, that his advent should be so quietly accepted; that the waiters at his club should recognise him with so little of effort or surprise; that his passage along Piccadilly or Pall Mall should not be interrupted by salutations more allusive and impassioned.

The days passed, and he fell into the old routine; realised that other people were not altered at all; that he was altered, perhaps, less than he had apprehended. The House had never engrossingly engaged his attention, and it was but little that he missed the occupation which, a year ago, his position as member had provided for many idle hours. And in this direction, too, with the assistance of a ready-made constituency, and a convenient bye-election, restitution seemed imminent. As Mrs. Vesper said, summing up the situation for him one evening after dinner, he had only to ask, the world was at his feet.

"Ask—no, you needn't," she added, yielding her coffee-cup to him. "You have only to sit still—to do what is expected—mapped out for you."

"And—'we do the rest'!" Lord Henry put in, rather defiantly. "Really, it's almost too simple!"

"Ah, you young men!" Mrs. Vesper murmured, with faint reprobation. "If you only knew when to be patient, and when to strike out for yourselves! Well, I admit," she added, with her gracious smile, "for a young man, you have been patient, and—it wasn't simple. After all, I'm not sure that you are not my most promising pupil!"

She paused, glancing towards the door. Guests were arriving. Mrs. Vesper was "at home," and music was promised. Mrs. Rome had just been announced. Dalrymple Green followed her closely, and, just behind, Lady Verrinder brought the charm of her fragile prettiness.

Mrs. Vesper glanced at her guest sharply, before she turned to receive the new-comers.

"Give a man the whole world, and he will still cry for the moon!"

Lord Henry bit his lip, as he followed his Amazon of

Parthian shafts into the middle of the room. Almost before he had time to fling to the occasion the merest scrap of the consideration that it deserved—to be sure, beforehand he had considered it enormously—he found himself exchanging conventional greetings with Lady Verrinder. Another instant, and she had passed on, leaving him a victim to the imperturbable smile of Gerald Brooke—never so disconcerting as when it was least allusive. To Dalrymple Green, who rescued him from the gossamer web of the wit, he listened with a masterly display of attention, conveniently corroborated by his frowning brow. Released, presently, by the kindly intervention of music, he withdrew to a corner of the smaller portion of the double room, a point from which, through a jungle of heads and shoulders, he could catch occasional glimpses of the face of Marjorie Verrinder, who was sitting on a sofa with Mrs. Rome.

Marjorie Verrinder. Their hostess had pronounced the name in his hearing, and it had struck him, curiously, as at once familiar and strange. Now, as his physical vision came to the assistance of thoughts that for many months had not been idle, he became gradually aware of an impression—a sensation. He sought in vain for a precise definition of his feeling. Loss—change. Vaguely these features loomed in the ghost that was with him.

He buried himself in his thoughts, to be recalled presently by the murmur, breaking quickly into unfettered conversation, which marked the cessation of the music,—to be rallied on the severity of his frown. Steering a difficult course, with the skill of a practised navigator of crowded drawing-rooms, he found himself at Lady Verrinder's elbow, just in time to hear her take leave of her hostess. She had another engagement, she explained; was to call for her husband, and take him to an entertainment, which, she protested gracefully, promised to be far less delightful than that which she was obliged to abandon. She acknowledged, with a nod and half a word, Lord Henry's suggestion that he should see her safely installed in her carriage, and together they made their way down the stairs.

She turned to him, flushed, and a little breathless, when they had escaped to the seclusion of the hall.

"I suppose it doesn't matter?" she said, breaking an awkward silence rather recklessly. "People would talk, I mean, anyhow. Will you ask for my carriage? I have an uneasy feeling that I forgot to tell the man that I should be leaving early: I will go and find my cloak."

He stood silent for a moment, looking at her, gravely and wistfully, before she turned away. Five minutes later he met her again, with the announcement that her doubt was confirmed, that her carriage was not in waiting.

"So I have secured a hansom," he added. "I hope you won't mind? And—you will let me take you home —won't you?"

She glanced from him to the impassive face of Mrs. Vesper's footman, with momentary hesitation; then yielded her arm to him with a murmur of acquiescence.

The night was cold and cheerless; a pale moon floated high in a surf of broken clouds; the lamplight was reflected dankly in wet pavements, and the yellow rays seemed to swim shapeless in the liquid air.

It was Marjorie who broke the silence at last, with a trivial question, such as Lord Henry had answered daily since his return to England, about his impressions of Canada. He met the enquiry with a short laugh, almost contemptuous, and halting words.

"You did not seem so far from me when I was in

Canada," he concluded, almost impersonally. "I had to come back; I'm afraid I shall have to stay."

"Really!" she protested, arching her delicate eyebrows at his reflection, that confronted her in the little oblong mirror at her side. "That's absurd, you know!"

His gesture of assent was tempered by a smile, faintly suggestive of imperfect resignation. The horse was reined back sharply at a crossing, to avoid a reckless wayfarer. Marjorie frowned, and averted her eyes impatiently, as she encountered the gaze, at once doleful and listless, of her companion.

"I beg your pardon—" he began a little stiffly. "I have no right . . ." Marjorie interrupted him with an impatient murmur; then she sighed, with momentary self-abandonment.

"You—you haven't changed, you're just the same," she continued, half regretfully. "Oh, don't look at me as if I was a riddle! I'm not—I'm dreadfully simple. If only you would accept that! I don't pretend to have forgotten that—that a thousand years ago you—we thought we loved each other—well, yesterday, if you will. Yesterday, or a thousand years—it's all the same."

"I haven't changed," he said slowly.

"But—" He paused, then added almost brutally, "You—you're different."

She shrank into her corner, looking at him askance with deprecating eyes. Then, in a flash of swift understanding, she struck home at the heart of his misgiving. "You mean—it's not me—*me* that you're in love with! Ah, don't you see, you're in love with the little girl who let you make love to her at Towers—Marjorie Lancaster —the Marjorie Lancaster of your imagination."

She paused, breathless with her discovery, and the force of her denunciation; then went on, a little sadly, to interrupt his half-hearted protestations. "Oh, you can't deny it—and, after all, isn't it better so? I don't know—am I heartless? How strange life is—and difficult! I—like you—I always liked you. You mustn't hate me—you mustn't pity me!"

"Marjorie," he murmured. "Marjorie!"

"My husband"—she continued—"he doesn't make me unhappy ... I shall be with him presently—we are going to hear Joachim, at the Lightmarks';—music always makes him go to sleep. ... He is kind to me, —I—care for him. Oh, *please* don't hold problems at my head! I'm a trivial, frivolous wretch—do you think I have no soul, perhaps—like the mermaid?"

"No soul!" Lord Henry repeated mechanically. "Do you suppose I ever thought—or cared? I loved you; you told me that you—that you loved me."

The cab pulled up with a jerk, and Lord Henry's low tones were almost lost in the clatter. He swung the doors back, with careful deliberation.

"I shall never love anyone else," he declared stubbornly, looking at his companion askance, as he leaned forward, with one hand on the splash-board.

Marjorie sighed. "You make me feel very dreadful," she murmured, as she gave him her hand, and descended, with a nice regard for her skirts, threatened by a muddy wheel. "And yet—and yet—"

She paused, before she turned to ascend the steps of the great sombre house.

"Who knows?" she put in quickly as the door opened. "I—perhaps I shall never love anyone at all."

CHAPTER XXXI

ON the third day of his expectation, Adrian received Sylvia's answer to his letter. It seemed to him constrained, frigid, almost, in its bare acquiescence to his request. So much indeed was conceded; she would grant him an interview; she would be at home that afternoon, if he would call for her: but the thing seemed to him to be granted grudgingly. And again, after repeated perusal of the few almost formal lines, he could fancy a certain dread, an apprehension lurked beneath them, as though her gentleness had taken alarm.

She must have been waiting for him, however, for she was herself immediately responsive to his knock, and she stood before him in the narrow hall, arrayed for the street, in hat and jacket.

The jingle of a piano in the upper regions flaunted through the house—an accompaniment to a woman's voice, strong and metallic; a music-hall melody, the words of which were inaudible. Then the music stopped, and there was a buzz of voices, a clash of laughter.

A slight flush came into the girl's paleness.

"It is rather noisy upstairs. Flossie—my cousin's wife—is trying over a new song with Mr. Minchin—he's one of our friends. I thought you would sooner come out for a bit of a walk."

"That would be pleasant," he said. "Where would you like to go?"

"The Park is not far," she said—"Kennington Park, I

mean. Perhaps you have never been there?" And she added apologetically, "It's not very big, you know; but I often go there; it's quiet there, and it's just green enough to remind one of the real country."

He assented simply. As he paced by the girl's side he was studying her more closely.

It was paler somewhat, shadowed slightly under the great frank eyes, heavy-lidded, that face in which he had read the promise of singular beauty; which he had known as a child's face, as a young girl's face, and which had now strayed fortuitously across his vision in its accomplished womanhood. Moving with quiet grace at his side, slim and delicate in her plain, dark gown, she had, perhaps, an air less flowerlike than of old, bred of the town, but by no means that of the theatre; she was so simple, and so inexplicably refined. As he regarded her, the old tenderness of their relation came over him, like a sudden flood of pale sunshine on a dreary day, dissipating his first feeling of strangeness. He broke the silence, a little awkwardly.

"It is a long time since we had a walk together, Sylvia. It was very good of you to come."

She hesitated for a moment.

"I did not know what to do. Your letter made me very sorry. It is rather sad, you know. I thought you had quite forgotten me."

"Did you think I had such a bad memory?"

He put the obvious question with an attempt at lightness, which he was conscious was a weak one. They relapsed into silence; and he reflected that, perhaps, she had never known or doubted of his one ineffectual attempt to see her, after her mother's death; and fell to wondering what difference it would have made to their lives if chance had been with him then, and he had encountered her.

If she did not know, fickle and cold she might well hold him; and he was resolved on that subject, at least, to enlighten her. He was too conscious of the many vital errors which he had committed in his blind perversity—so it seemed to him—not to accentuate the one misadventure which he might account to fatality.

They had reached the entrance to the uninviting enclosure which was their destination. It was quiet, as the girl had said, and it had only the redeeming feature of its quietude. Groups of squalid children draggled about the tattered grass; a few loafers, of the class which is neither employed nor seeks employment, sat smoking, with disinterested eyes, or lay sleeping, on the benches; other frequenters there were few.

"And you come here often?" Adrian asked curiously, when they had found an isolated seat. "It isn't very cheerful. It isn't much like the country—like Underwoods." Then he resumed quickly, without waiting for her response, returning to his idea—

"Did you ever know? I went down to Underwoods just after you had left. I went down to see you, but you were not there."

She had taken off her gloves, and was smoothing them between her pretty hands.

"I never heard," she said after a moment, and he seemed to detect constraint in her voice.

"I wanted you to know; I thought I should like to tell you," he said with intention, and went on quickly: "You must have thought me very heartless."

"No, no!" she protested. "I knew you would be very busy. You were in such a different world. I couldn't expect—"

He interrupted her, following his own train of thought.

"I never could discover where you had gone. But I

was not heartless—only a fool. And, perhaps, it would have made no difference."

"Difference?" She looked at him with eyes in which quiet astonishment only was depicted.

"It might have made a deal of difference—to both our lives," he went on doggedly, "if I had found you that day at Underwoods. But the Fates would not have it, and so I went away, and—and here we are."

He took up a pebble and flung it across the grass with a gesture of aimless discontent.

"What fools men are; what a mess we make of our lives," he said listlessly.

The girl laid her hand impulsively on his arm; there was pain in her face.

"I can't bear to hear you talk like that, Adrian." Unconsciously, in her earnestness, she had resumed the old intimate appellation. "I can't help guessing your meaning, and I don't want to. It doesn't seem right; it makes me think I was wrong in seeing you. Perhaps nobody is altogether happy. I am not very happy myself; but still—"

"And what makes you unhappy?" he put in quickly.

"Oh, things," she said evasively. "Only sometimes, you know. I suppose I am happy enough."

"No, you are not," he cried, almost irritably. "And I know what the 'things' are. They are all your life: the theatre, your cousin, the Flossies, and the Minchins—does Minchin want to marry you?—the unspeakable crowd, the whole cursed environment. How should you be happy in it?"

She flushed slightly.

"I shall not marry Mr. Minchin. I don't suppose I shall ever marry." And she resumed with a dignity, half sad, half humorous, "And you mustn't abuse the poor old theatre, and my cousins—they are very kind, you know, and they are all the people I have."

"Oh, I don't abuse them," he sighed. "Only there should be a fitness in things . . . My dear," he went on abruptly, "you know it is all wrong, and you hate it. What's the use of trying to throw dust in our eyes? We might allow ourselves the luxury of being miserable —it's the only one left to us. I see everything so clearly now."

"You mustn't speak for me," she protested. "I call that unfair."

"As you like. It shall be a luxury all my own, then. After all, the mistake, the folly have been all my own, and I ought to be glad to pay the price of it alone, for both of us."

The girl shifted on her seat uneasily.

"Would it make you any happier to believe that I was —paying too? Isn't that rather unjust?"

"Many things are unjust. It would make me wretched, sublimely wretched. But am I to believe it, Sylvia?"

She was silent for a moment, averted her face, then she said gently—

"Believe it—a little, if it's any good to you."

He gave a deep inhalation, and she went on hurriedly, with a confused effort to shape an evasive idea in words: "But don't give too much thought to it. Oh, I was wrong to have spoken so! Don't — don't think of it at all. And why can't you look at things differently? It makes me sad to hear you speak so hopelessly. I had thought it was all different. When I heard your name spoken, how you were thought of, I was glad. Oh yes, glad, and proud. I liked to think of you as being a great man. And can it all be—nothing? You—you who have everything—"

He checked her, with a sudden, irrepressible gesture, caught her wrist almost fiercely, and the passion vibrated hoarsely through his voice.

"I wanted you, Sylvia. *You* are everything—my soul, and my heart, and my heart's blood, and without you it doesn't beat, and I am starved and perished . . . Yes, I have said it. Don't look at me with those frightened eyes. You may hate me, I may hate myself, for saying it, but I am consumed with love of you, and it has been so—oh, since the world began! And you—you may deny it with your lips, but your true eyes cannot; you will never love anyone as you love me—ice and snow as you are. It has got to be faced."

She had risen, as he poured out this confession, and stood facing him. And her eyes seemed drawn to his irresistibly, not so much in alarm, nor in maidenly protest, as in a piteous appeal.

Suddenly he rose, and stood at her side.

"Shall we face the world together, you and I?" he cried.

But she drew back hurriedly, pressing her hand to her side, with a little sharp cry, like a dumb animal wronged. Gradually, as he looked at her, the flame smouldered out of his eyes, his figure seemed to shrink somewhat, and his mouth was twisted into a bitter smile.

"Forgive me, dear," he said, "if I have hurt you. It was stronger than myself. I was mad, indeed. Life is so ghastly; but for a moment I seemed to see a different one stretch out, with no shadow of parting from you in it, Sylvia. But I haven't the courage—for myself, may be—but not for you. . . . Shall we go, dear?"

"Yes," she said absently, and they moved along in a constrained silence. At the gates the girl paused, looked at her watch.

"Leave me here," she said. "I have to be at the theatre."

He gave a little mirthless laugh.

"You must go to the theatre, and the rest of it. And I must go home to my dinner, and my wife—perhaps she is waiting for me. What we call the realities of life are expecting us—fools that we are. But we know in our hearts, you and I, that all the reality there will ever be for us we have just looked at in this dingy garden—looked at, and turned our backs on."

She held out her hand, which he just touched and dropped again.

"Good-bye," he said, but added inwardly, as he turned away from her, "And yet! If it is written, it is written."

The idea of his own house was hateful to him, and he drove to his club; but, on entering it, knew not whether he was glad or sorry to find it almost deserted, the smoking-room untenanted. He felt jaded and unstrung, with a notion that something of the storm which had torn him might be visible in his demeanour. The waiter, hovering near him in expectation of an order, irritated him; he fancied the man was watching him, and, to be rid of him, impatiently ordered a brandy-and-soda. He drank it at a draught, drew his chair to the fire, and a slight glow played round the chill at his heart. It gave him a moment's impulse of energy, enough to start him anew upon his homeward way. As he footed it through the crowded streets, the lassitude which had seized him was changed into a dull exasperation. The people who strolled or bustled past, well-groomed or slovenly, were transformed into a jeering and hostile crowd. Unknown and unimportant units as they were, indifferent in themselves, were they not, in the mass, the terrible force which controlled one's life, which compelled obedience, which was the slave-driver of beauty, and genius, and knowledge; blind instrument of an unknown will, to make men their own tormentors, and the victims of themselves? The very physical discomfort of noisy London on a dank winter's day, the rattle of the cumbrous omnibuses, the shrill cries of the newsboys, seemed to Adrian but symbols of his moral and intellectual collapse.

Outside his house a neat victoria was standing, which he was not at the trouble to identify; but as he opened the door the servant came to meet him, with an expression, almost of curiosity, on his usually impassive face.

"Mrs. Vesper is here, sir."

"Yes," he answered absently, delivering up his hat and overcoat; and then, somewhat impatiently, as the man still lingered, "Well, Hawkins, what of that? I suppose she has been shown up to Mrs. Rome?"

"I beg your pardon, sir. Mrs. Rome left early in the afternoon, I believe for the station. Mrs. Vesper asked for you, sir. I said it was uncertain when you would return, but she wished to see you." And he added, apologetically, "She is in the library, sir. She prefered to wait there."

Rome knitted his brows nervously.

"Very well, Hawkins. Will you tell Mrs. Vesper that I will be with her immediately."

He paused for a minute to collect himself, feeling that something new was in the air, was indistinctly heralded by a visit which had all the nature of the unwonted. But a strange flutter round his heart warned him that in his present mood disturbance was a good and salutary thing, that nothing could henceforth be more desirable than conflict.

As he opened the door, Mrs. Vesper rose to meet him with an expression of annunciation on her hard, enigmatical little face. Adrian murmured a few words of apology.

"I am so sorry. I can't imagine what has become of

my wife, and why they showed you into this den of disorder. I hope you haven't waited long?"

She waved away the inconvenience, with a little bird-like gesture.

"It hasn't mattered in the least. I asked to be allowed to stay here. I like so much to be with books—one's not alone. I hope you don't think it a dreadful piece of audacity? I went with Marion to the station, and came back to see you, and explain."

"Explain?" He looked at her blankly, and noticed that she held a telegram crumpled up in one gloved hand. "Has Marion gone away?"

"To Towers, with Henry Minaret. I see you haven't heard the news. The Duke of Turretshire—his condition is most critical. It was important to be on the field at once. There is no knowing what that woman might have done—have made away with."

"I see," he said, "Marion has gone to the rescue of the family jewels."

"They are such fine ones," Mrs. Vesper said simply; and then she added inconsequently, "And you didn't read it in the papers?"

"I never read the papers."

"No; of course you have other things to read." And she went on quickly, "It is most fortunate that Lord Henry should be at home. He will have everything, we hope—even if that unfortunate man has made a will."

Adrian glanced at her, with a certain humour.

"Poor Lady Lancaster!" he ejaculated, "she was too precipitate."

Mrs. Vesper, with downcast eyes, seemed to give assent to the sadness of the situation.

"Poor Lady Lancaster, indeed!" she said.

Adrian had remained standing, and at this juncture

he had the air of tacitly assuming that the interview was at an end. But Mrs. Vesper still remained, and, as they hesitated, he became aware that her tidings had been a pretext—she had more to say.

He steeled himself to confront her.

"Won't you sit down?" he said coldly.

She sank back, into the chair from which she had risen on his arrival.

"It is true," she said, with an attempt at lightness, "I had something else to say. I had a talk with Marion to-day, which distressed me. Oh, the merest hint, of course; I have such a horror of—of interference; but I couldn't be ignorant that there has been a sort of disagreement. I know that I have no title, no right, perhaps you will say, to intervene, but when one is an old woman one must be pardoned an—inconsequence, and I must risk one. I mean," she went on, growing desperate in the face of his chilly silence,—he would listen to her, but he would make no effort to help her,— "I mean that I am in a position to say that it is not too late. Marion will make allowances; you have both been too hasty! Where true affection exists, it is so easy! Marion will meet you half-way. Oh, I hope I make myself clear!"

Adrian favoured her with a long and studied scrutiny. Under her composure, he saw that she was ill at ease, and the sight of the little worldly woman's discomfiture gave him an odd pleasure. He felt that he had a bitter grudge against her; that she had committed the unpardonable sin against him, had seemed to like him, and had simply made use of him.

"You said just now that you had no title," he said at last.

"Oh," she interrupted, "the title given by my affection for both of you."

"I don't dispute it. You have every right to interfere in my married life." He let his great bitterness pierce through his calm. "Didn't you make it? Aren't you the cause of it?" And he went on, with the impassiveness of a judge summing up a case. "I have no mind to dispute your right; what I deny, is the utility of exercising it. Is the disagreement between my wife and myself a matter of yesterday? Mrs. Vesper, why couldn't you have let us alone? Weren't we always as remote—"

She leaned forward in her chair, interrupting him again with a little cry of protest.

"Ah, don't, don't! You can't imagine how you distress me—"

Adrian waited on her words deferentially.

Strangely calm, he found himself remotely interested, wondering, dully, and impersonally almost, whether the woman—imperturbable mistress of emotion as he had fancied her—could genuinely be moved. He watched her idly, a little pleased and distracted by the thought that his words had pierced a cuirass so finely tempered as that which he had accredited to her worldliness.

"A mistake," she murmured, dropping her eyes; "I won't—I can't admit it. It is you who are blind, mistaken. Ah, poor Marion!"

"Poor Marion!" Adrian echoed gravely.

"At least you cannot blame her."

"Never in the world!" put in the other impatiently. "My dear Mrs. Vesper, I blame no one—not even myself. That is a satisfaction which you are welcome to enjoy, but believe, at least, that it is denied to me!"

They had both risen, and Mrs. Vesper confronted him, leaning with one hand on the back of her chair.

"I don't understand," she said slowly. "This is—a mood, I suppose. Your father had moods . . . but they passed, like clouds. Was I foolish to—interest myself in the marriage of your father's son?"

Rome was silent; his eyes smouldered ominously in his pale, constrained face; it was plain to his visitor that her mediation had failed. She composed herself, smiling, a little wearily, nicely mindful of the emblems of an honourable defeat.

"Pray make allowance for the anxiety of an old woman!" she exclaimed more lightly, holding out her neat gloved hand. "Marion would never forgive me . . ."

He took her hand for an instant, bowing over it with ceremony. She turned towards him, as he held the door open for her to pass.

"And I—if it is true that I—interfered, at least you cannot suggest that I had anything to gain."

He bowed again, rather acknowledging than meeting her challenge.

"For you that is doubtless a matter of congratulation."

Mrs. Vesper threw a shrewd glance at him before she turned away.

"But you—you think that makes it worse!" she murmured quickly, as she stepped into her carriage.

CHAPTER XXXII

SOME ten days later, the door of Rome's house had just closed behind Peter Corbyn, when he was confronted by the figure of a tall and blonde young man, whose pleasant face seemed strangely, and yet distantly familiar. The hesitating recognition in his own eyes was shadowed for a moment in the other's; then they both smiled simultaneously, and gripped cordial hands.

"I am going in to see Rome," explained Lord Henry Minaret, nodding his head in the direction of the house; and there was a note curiously anxious in his frank voice, which seemed to lie in wait for the other's answer.

"You may spare yourself the trouble of ringing; I have been on the same errand."

"Oh, he hasn't come back yet? That's a bore."

He spoke with an assumption of lightness, but frowned as he fingered the buttons of his glove; and the other was the less deceived, in that, although he masked himself with more subtilty, he was himself a prey to a certain hardly definable fear. Corbyn was the first to realise that their position there, procrastinating irresolutely on the doorstep, began to partake of the grotesque.

"Well, I am afraid it is useless to wait," he remarked.

Lord Henry flushed awkwardly; then he shot a glance at the other's good-humoured face, and seemed reassured by his scrutiny.

"Would you let me walk with you? Any way is the same to me."

"With all the pleasure in the world. I am going home; I live in the Temple."

"I'll come part of the way with you." Lord Henry spoke with greater blitheness. Then, when they had gone a few paces, he burst out suddenly—

"It's deucedly odd!"

Corbyn made no feint of ignoring his meaning.

"Yes, it's odd," he said, with a little sigh.

"I think you are a great friend of Rome's. I believe he is awfully attached to you."

"We are old friends," said the other cautiously.

"Deucedly odd!" Lord Henry resumed. "There are things one doesn't like to talk about, you know; one doesn't like to go prying into a fellow's affairs. But I've got a sort of right—I mean, as Mrs. Rome's cousin, don't you know; and you can say what you wish to me. In fact," he blurted out, "I think if you know anything,— what he means, where he is gone, and so on,—for the sake of—of the family, you ought to tell us."

Corbyn reflected silently for a moment. He was glad of this opportunity, of these confidences; he was a prey to an uneasiness even more acute than that of his companion, because, if like him he was extremely in the dark, he had a point of suspicion to lean uncomfortably upon: there were incidents within his knowledge which the other might not know.

"Yes," he said at last. "It is better to speak out, and you can perfectly depend upon me. But I must begin by telling you that I know next to nothing. I was never in Rome's confidence. He didn't tell me that he was going; he hasn't told me where he has gone."

"Thank you," said Lord Henry with a sigh. "I felt at once you were the sort of man one could talk to about it. You see," he went on quickly, surmounting his scruples with a rush, "the last time I saw him, we had a bit of a row. It hasn't all been straight sailing, with his wife, you know. I daresay you remarked that yourself — that they were not a very united couple."

Corbyn maintained a decorous silence, and the other went on ruefully.

"Well, of late it has been getting worse, and I, like an ass, must needs get myself mixed up in it. My mother went at me; I think it was Mrs. Vesper who put her up to it."

Corbyn interrupted him with a little expressive ejaculation.

"Ah, Mrs. Vesper!"

"You don't like her? She's not a bad sort . . . Well, Marion had made a scene, it appeared. No doubt he has neglected her awfully. And Mrs. Vesper hinted that there was some other woman; she spoke as if she knew something—oh, very vaguely. The long and the short of it was, that I was coaxed into interfering—the word in season, you know. I am afraid my diplomacy was overrated. I didn't mend matters; probably I made them worse. I believe I lost my temper. Afterwards I was sorry. You know how queer he is; this time he was queerer than ever. He seemed like a man who was quite indifferent, who didn't care a rap for anything—any scandal; like a man who was just making up his mind to a jump."

"And you gave him the final shove?"

"That was what I was afraid of," said Lord Henry simply. "When I got cooler, I went back. That was the next day."

"And he was gone?" Corbyn murmured. "I called also." Then he went on absently. "The man was speaking the truth. He doesn't know where his master is. And there is a pile of letters; they are not being forwarded."

"You don't think—" Lord Henry stopped short, with a blank, significant interrogation, to which the other as quickly responded.

"No, no—not that! I'll tell you. I was excessively uneasy. I made some enquiries, and this much I discovered: the *Anonyma*, his yacht, left Southampton last Monday for a cruise in the Channel, owner not on board. It's meagre, but there it is." Then he went on after a moment's hesitation, "You see, I will be quite frank with you; there *is* a woman, a girl."

"O Lord! And you mean to say that Rome has run off with her?"

"I don't know; I can't make up my mind. But I think he wants to run off with her."

"But that's terrible," said Lord Henry; in his dismay he had stopped short, clasped his hand intimately on his companion's arm. "Think of the scandal—think of Marion. I say," he added, with a sudden inspiration, "surely there's time. My cousin—fortunately she is at Towers, with my mother. And this woman—you know her? If it's not too late, couldn't you see her, couldn't we frighten her—buy her off?"

Corbyn shook his head.

"It's not as you think. She is not the woman one drives. She's your only hope." His own words seemed to strike him trenchantly, and he repeated them, "She's your only hope!"

"That brings a gleam of comfort," said Lord Henry, after cogitating for a moment on this obscure remark. "But see the girl, my dear fellow, see her, and tell her how it stands."

"See her, not I," protested the other. "And Lord

knows how it stands, I don't! And perhaps," he was unable to resist this shaft of irony, "there has been too much arranging—interference—as it is."

Lord Henry reflected a moment, allowing the full effect of this reasoning gradually to penetrate him.

"Then you mean—to do nothing?" he enquired presently, with a touch of coldness.

Corbyn shrugged his shoulders.

"To help Rome—anything I can," he said shortly. "But I don't see what can be done, and I doubt whether you can tell me?"

They had reached the broad terrace on the northern side of Trafalgar Square, and Corbyn halted, with an unconscious suggestion of his wish to close the interview. Then, as the other confronted him, eyed him with a troubled frown, he added deliberately—

"You see—it's quite natural—you are thinking more of your cousin—the family—yourselves. My concern begins and ends with Adrian."

His companion nodded silently, with grave perplexity.

"It's difficult to speak of it . . . One wishes, of course, that their interests were identical. But—"

Corbyn hesitated; then continued, stumbling—

"As things are, haven't I already exceeded . . . ? It's conceivable, at least, that Adrian might blame me."

"You couldn't have done less," protested the other.

"Or more," put in Corbyn, smiling ruefully. "After all, there is such a thing as discretion! Of course, one wants to help. Oh, it's damnably difficult!"

Lord Henry assented, holding out his hand.

"I'm sure we can count on you," he said weakly. "I'm glad I happened to meet you; you will give me your address—in case—"

A minute later, after exchanging cards, they parted; and Corbyn, as he let himself drop into the tide-race of the Strand, wondered, a little, whether to ascribe to a strange oversight, or to an unexpected delicacy, Lord Henry Minaret's omission to demand the name of the woman who seemed to have come between Adrian and his wife. He was the more inclined to congratulate himself, on his escape from the indiscretion which would have been involved in a voluntary surrender of the information, when he remembered, curiously, that Lord Henry's intimacy with their friend dated from the days of their association at Underwoods—an association in which the girl had participated.

And while they conjectured and were perturbed, to Adrian, waiting, in the tension of his purpose, at a little seaport on the Dorset coast, all this surmise and anxiety would have seemed incalculably trivial and remote. So conscious was he—and it was almost the beginning and end of his consciousness—of the memorable leagues which his mind had traversed, separating him, far more than any mere physical distance might, from all their concern in his life.

Even now, he could not remember precisely how he had taken the leap. People had been stupid, crass, insolent; and because they were so many, and spoke with authority, for a little while he had walked servilely in their ways. And then an illumination had come to him, and a sense that a man's folly should not be final; that if one had been imposed upon, even if one had oneself largely contributed to the imposition, one had nevertheless the right to set oneself free, to begin again. Was not selfishness a bugbear, after all, and not the real devil that superstition had painted it?

And so, there had been that last passionate interview with Sylvia, when his irrevocable utterance had borne them high and far upon its wings. He would never forget that utterance, nor the plenitude of her response, of which the unshrinking truth was at once his crown and torment. Sincerity had flashed from the clouds, and by its light he had read her soul, as even she had never dared to read it. The softening of her eyes to his appeal, to his confession of all the weakness of his strength, the failure of his success if she was not to share it,—was that to prove the ultimate reward of his endeavour? Just then, through all its reservations, her love had seemed to envelop them, as consummately as if there had been no shadow to separate them.

And the haunting spell and sweetness of that moment had carried him, as a man in a dream, through all the practical details of his departure. Mechanically, almost, as a man in a dream, he had set his house in order. He had spent a long hour with Mr. Featherstone in Lincoln's Inn; perturbing, ruthlessly, his discreet adviser, who had never found him so clear of purpose, sane, inscrutable. For once, he had not sought advice, but given instructions. Remittances should be made to him, at such and such dates and places; two-thirds of his income must be paid to his wife's banking account; secrecy was significantly enjoined; no word of explanation was forthcoming. He had cleared the ground with the unfaltering directness of a captive breaking prison; each step taken with a sure precision which proclaimed premeditation, seemed strangely incompatible with the freshness of his purpose.

At first, while he waited, in this place of incurious strangers to which he had betaken himself, the long days had been beguiled by the same enchantment, the charm and thrill of that dear possession, wrapped close in his heart, where no too sudden breath or touch might reach and shatter it. He had waited for Sylvia's answer, for Sylvia's self. A week had passed since he had shaped his appeal in writing. From the first, when he had believed himself secure of her consent, it was to the sea that he had turned, of his yacht that he bethought him, as the most natural means of bridging over the gulf they needs must cross. Safe on board the little ship, with her white wings spread, and her prow pointing to the South, would they not be out of reach of the lash of tongues, their love sanctified, as it were, by the primitive benediction of those heaving waters? To the South: for the South must call them, as it calls all the lawless ones, children of passion, rebellious against accepted bonds. Yes, it was there that they lay, whatever fortunate islands the world might hold, for these fugitives from the world.

So he had waited, happy in that cherished treasure of her love. At first, until, on the third morning he woke to discern, from the window of his little hostelry upon the quay, the *Anonyma* swinging her riding-light under the rose-flushed canopy of the dawn, his expectation stood firm in the background of his happiness, steadfast and unshaken by either hope or fear. With the yacht came Salvesen, frankly rejoicing in his escape (none too soon, it seemed) from the dram-shops of Southampton, in the prospect of a cruise. The man, keenly impatient for the sea, chafed visibly at delay; and as the days passed, and brought no word from Sylvia, Adrian's impatience, too, caught fire, and at once his expectation was tarnished by uncertainty. Had he done wrong, perhaps, to commit his ultimate appeal to the untrusty mediation of written words; wrong to bid her take time for her reply? And yet, each day, at noon and evening, as he left the post-office empty-handed, he was vaguely troubled to find his disappointment tempered and alloyed, by a sensation to which he shrank from assigning too close a definition. Was it in her strength, or in her weakness, that his hopes were centred—his hopes, or fears? Was convention right, then, and selfishness the hideous monster of accepted precept? He loved her with his whole heart and being; with his heart and being he yearned and longed for her. And love was strong, with wings to outsoar and tire the heavy pinions of remorse. If her love was as his love, where should doubt find foothold at all? Would not her love, too, tend its sweetest flower in self-sacrifice? In sacrifice — ah, but where was his?

And now Sylvia's answer had come. It was on the high cliff that he had read it, above the wheeling sea-gulls, where the sky seemed near; and afterwards he had walked far and aimlessly in the exceeding bitterness of his thoughts; until, long after the light had failed, hunger and weariness reminded him of the practical needs of life. As he wandered, the crumpled letter nestled in his hand, and now, while he retraced his steps, the final phrases of that piteous renunciation besieged him still, seemed almost visibly imprinted on the dark background of his mind.

"You must forget; you must not give up; you must be strong. It is so cruelly hard to say! But I have known always that I cared for you. And that it could not be, that I have known too, always. Nothing is changed. I can't; oh! I can't ... I should make you suffer; I should reproach myself, even if you did not reproach me. You must pity me, and forgive me and forget—no, I can't write that! Forgive me, think kindly of me—be strong. Don't make me feel that I have spoiled your life. Let it be as if we had not met again ..."

The wind had risen since the morning, and Adrian looked down, over the sheer cliff, at an angry sea, a dark waste from which sudden swirls of thrilling whiteness glimmered ominously. Yes, it was time to go.

"So be it," he murmured drearily, breaking the long silence of his thoughts. "And perhaps, my poor child, you are right. It isn't a new thing we should have tried. The world is so old, its precedents so hopeless. Those others who have tried—have they found happiness? But we, Sylvia, my love—are we not strong enough . . . God!—to think that anyone has loved as I love—I'll not believe it! And—you love me, Sylvia—you have always loved me, and forgiven me!"

An hour's rapid walking brought him at last to the jetty, under shelter of which the yacht's dinghy lay tugging at her painter. Of Salvesen and the boy, who had received orders to wait his coming, there was no visible sign; but presently, in a lull of the wind, the voice of the Scandinavian skipper, upraised in a boisterous sea-song, betrayed his presence in the little tavern on the quay. For a few minutes Adrian waited, peering seaward through the shifting darkness which hid the yacht's lights from him. He pulled himself together with a start.

"A dirty night," he said softly. "Would you have been frightened, Sylvia?"

He found Salvesen in the taproom of the tavern, making merry; and opposite him the boy, eying the wild-eyed sailor with awestruck admiration, over a big mug of cocoa. A few minutes later they followed him to the jetty. He shrugged his shoulders patiently, with a touch of self-reproach, as he noted his skipper's eloquently clumsy gait, and watched him fumbling aimlessly with the dinghy's painter.

"I'll take an oar," he said rather sternly, as he stepped into the boat. "And, Salvesen, we shall sail to-morrow. After the post comes in," he added, half to himself.

A new boat-cloak, warmly lined, lay folded in the stern-sheets, and he eyed it forlornly, remembering for what service he had destined it. And then he bent to his oar, calling on Salvesen, and bidding the boy steer carefully.

CHAPTER XXXIII

At half-past eleven on the morning of the following day, Sylvia sat in one of the corners of a third-class railway carriage, her eyes fixed remotely on the horizon of the country through which an express train was bearing her to Dorsetshire. To nerves keenly alert, after many sleepless hours, and missing the calm domination of her newly-shaken steadfastness, the rhythmic sweep and clangour, the suggestion of strength and inevitability, brought an incredible sense of respite and repose. Just as her eyes rested on the motionless tranquillity of the far blue hills, hardly conscious of the nearer detail and reality of the hurrying fields, and her ears ignored the shrill gossip of the country-women who shared her carriage; so her thoughts, too, overshot the obvious problems of the present, and hovered, almost restfully, over the abyss, wrapped and sheltered in the comfortable dimness which her anxiety no longer essayed to fathom. They had warred so furiously of late—that ordinance of self-denial which had become the heart and motive of her life, with her woman's longing to love, to be loved; to make complete surrender, and cast her all upon the divine hazard. Too generous to be selfish, too humble to expect much at the hands of Fate; and yet, withal, exceeding proud, with a pride finely primitive and wild; in these qualities her purpose had found staunch allies, such as it needed more than ever now, if it must prevail against the dear enemy within her gates.

It was so hard to seem unkind! And so, after she had despatched her reply to Adrian's appeal, misgiving had found her an easy prey: the peace which, for a brief moment, spread its wings over the battlefield of her doubts, was succeeded by a fierce riot of rebellion and regret; a tumult to be quelled, it seemed, only at the cost of some concession. That concession Sylvia was making now. What its limits might be, she had not cared to ask herself too curiously. Only, she would see Adrian again; would be able, in some degree, to soften the cruel finality of her denial.

She would see Adrian again: there her thought stayed itself, poised in anticipation, in worship of the bright moment. Beyond lay the abyss, vague, unfathomable.

The train hurried on: it had passed Salisbury now, and Yeovil, nestling close among its downs. The sweet, formidable hour drew near, and already Sylvia's apprehension stirred uneasily in its sleep. She ceased to wonder, absently, which of the ultimate hills sheltered her lost Underwoods; fresh doubts assailed her, as the familiar struggle was renewed, and she thought, with dim foreboding, of what should be the manner of her return; the manner, and the time? She half dreaded, half hoped, to hear from Adrian's lips that his determination (to make a new beginning, as he had phrased it) was irrevocable; that he had burned his ships, and definitely withdrawn himself from the heights on which her imagination vaguely enthroned him; from the realisation of those ambitions, of which, in her solitude, she had felt so proud to have, however imperfectly, a part and understanding.

To deny herself had become easy; for in what other

practice had her life been spent? And the belief that she had helped Adrian—had, at least, not stood in his way; this had been her fine solace and reward. She had cherished this rose ever more closely in her breast, braving its thorns in her yearning for its sweetness. It was not until her lover's insistence stirred dissension in her heart, that her love sprang up in rebellious arms to challenge her devotion. Her love; had it been a folly in the old days; was it worse than folly now?

She shivered a little, turning in her seat, and withdrawing her eyes from their weary contemplation of the wooded banks, and bare, wintry fields, over the hurrying procession of which a wild wind drove mists of rain. Presently the train drew up at a station; it was Axminster, where she must alight and find a vehicle to carry her to the coast. She gathered up her wraps, and made her way out of the station; called back, to her confusion, when she had already passed the barrier, to receive the unused half of her return-ticket. Half an hour later, a dilatory omnibus, the interior of which she shared with a sleepy commercial traveller, was bearing her over the hilly roads that lie between Axminster and the sea.

For the first time, now, her anxiety took the shape of a fear lest she should prove too late, lest Adrian should already have set sail for those vague regions of which his letter spoke. She chafed at the delay which each acclivity imposed upon the cumbrous vehicle; counted the milestones, leaning forward restlessly in her seat, curiously beset by the impression that the speed of her progress depended intimately on the alertness of her will; as if a due exertion of her volition could lend wings to the horses, and lift their patient trot to swiftness.

It was still early in the afternoon when Sylvia

realised, not without a touch of incredulity, that she had reached her destination. She lingered for a moment at the spot, outside the little post-office, where the coach had set her down. The rain had ceased. Overhead the wind whistled in the telegraph-wires, tearing the grey fleece of the sky, as it fled inland with a dismal moan. From her feet, as she stood, half-way down the hill, the steep roadway, flanked with low houses, swept downward in a curve, breaking off abruptly in the very face of the restless welter of the sea, which alternated rhythmically the thunder of its onslaught with the sonorous rattle of its retreat, on the unseen shore below. As Sylvia made her way down the hill, the wind buffeted her, stinging her cheeks, and tugging unexpectedly at her skirts. She felt weary and dishevelled; and was half conscious, among her real anxieties, of a fear lest Adrian should find her so.

Reaching the seawall, she turned instinctively towards the jetty, which stretched its blackness through a surge of breakers at the further end of the desolate "promenade." A few ships (all alike, to her inexperience) lay heaving at their anchors in the harbour; she eyed them eagerly as she hurried along the road, which ran, slippery with spray, between the face of the cliff and the wet seawall. The tide was high, and the spray towered from the crest of each successive wave as it dashed against the rough-hewn granite: the air was charged with tingling spindrift, through which faint gleams of sunshine made fragmentary rainbows.

The quay gained, Sylvia paused to recover her breath, and lingered for a moment, forlornly, among the piles of timber which yielded shelter from the wind. The coastguard, whose uniform at last attracted her inquiry, glanced at her sharply, then fixed his eyes on the horizon in a perturbed silence.

"Mr. Rome?" he said gently, "the gentleman who owned the *Anonyma*?"

Sylvia's answer was impatient.

"Mr. Adrian Rome; he owns the *Anonyma*—he hasn't gone—started?"

The man shook his head, plainly embarrassed; and inviting her to follow, led the way to a little building of official aspect, outside the open door of which a few fishermen and sailors were talking, eagerly and gravely. Their eyes turned to her—curiously, she thought—as she followed her guide into the office; and she heard one of the sailors (he was in the centre of the group, and the breast of his jersey was marked *Anonyma* in a scroll of red) murmur a few words, which sounded like "No—not his wife."

"Not his wife—not his wife!" she repeated softly, as, with a chill at her heart, she confronted the burly, grey-headed harbour-master, who looked at her over the top of a wooden desk littered with blue papers.

"You're not Mrs. Rome?" he assumed, when she had refused the chair which he pulled forward for her. "The telegram says that she can't make—she can't get here before night."

"No . . . but Mr. Rome expects me," she put in nervously, as he hesitated.

The man folded a strip of paper clumsily. "You don't know, then . . . You haven't heard . . . You see, there's been an accident . . ." he stammered, and paused helplessly, eyeing the closed door.

Outside, the siren-whistle of a passing steamer hooted, hideously plaintive; and the chain of a derrick clanked and rattled to the accompaniment of the stifled gasps of its engine. Sylvia threw her foreboding from her with desperate courage.

"You mean, he's hurt?" she said quietly, in a voice

that she seemed to recognise, oddly, as her own. "Please tell me—he would wish it."

"Ay, poor soul!" said the other, with gentle brusqueness. "Hurt—you'll need your courage if I'm to tell you!"

He turned his eyes away, with a shake of his head, as they met her gaze of urgent enquiry, of apprehension.

"He's dead—he's dead!" she moaned; then waited, agonised for the denial that the cruel, black silence withheld from her. The whole world—the very light and air, grew dark, and full of a quivering stillness, as Sylvia leaned against the ink-stained wooden desk, wondering, impersonally almost, why she did not faint; praying, without hope, that she might awake from the horror of this benumbing dream.

With tearless eyes she watched the clumsy masts of a departing collier swing round and creep across the window, obscured from time to time by the smoke that poured spasmodically from an unseen funnel. The voice of the old harbour-master sounded dully and remotely in her ears, torturing them with almost the meaningless persistence of the ticking of a clock. His laboured story had been told, and she had not lost a word of it. To her imagination, it had all been pictured, vividly and memorably, as he spoke; the stormy night; the little boat tossing on the dark waste of water; Adrian—ah, that was like him!—struggling to save the drunken sailor—"a foreigner, name of Salvesen," who had fallen, or madly thrown himself, into the water after his lost oar; the capsized boat; the struggle; and all the grim horror of the sequel;—to the rescue of the one survivor, clinging to the boat,—and the finding of the dead, hardly an hour ago, on the shore where the tide had left them—the dead body of her lover . . .

Adrian was dead! The sea that he loved had given

him death; the sea that he had so loved; and the woman. And the triumph of the waves thundered, relentless, in the woman's ears; and the window on which her tearless eyes were fixed was wet with spray. A passionate resentment filled her heart, that the God whom she had been taught to love could be so cruel, fashioning out of her very obedience to His laws so terrible a scourge.

It would have been so sweet to yield to Adrian's entreaty; and if she had yielded, she would have been far away, and Adrian with her; they would have been happy. Happy? she repeated the word dully. It had never seemed possible, that happiness; a thing no more to be grasped, or even essayed, than the inexorable serenity of the furthest star. And it was precisely this quality, indeed, this hopeless remoteness, forbidding hope, which had made Sylvia content for so long to realise what pleasure she might from an almost unconscious contemplation of the radiant unattainable.

And now this terrible thing had happened; and her sacrifice was ignored.

It was true; and her last hope fled, when, presently, they left her alone with the dead body of her friend. Adrian was dead; and she must leave him there, within sight and sound of the faithless waves which he had trusted. She must not stay with him; she must not take him with her.

It was not for the first time that she looked upon the face of death. She had seen her mother die, and her mother's sister: there had been others, too, at Underwoods, to whom this great change had come, for the most part as a release, long expected.

And Adrian—was he now more irrevocably withdrawn from her life, from the reach of her love, than he had been at that time when, on a sudden, the pleasant paths which they had so long paced together seemed to branch in sundering ways, and she, at least, had been resolute to choose that separate path to which her devotion pointed? Was it not then, when that momentous choice was made, that for her, as her lover, if not as her friend, Adrian had ceased to belong to the world in which she lived?

But this was Death. How trivial, by comparison, was all that before had seemed so final, irremediable! While Adrian lived, she could picture him happy, and owing his happiness, in part, at least, to her; successful, and harvesting his success from those fields which, humbly, she had helped him to till. No; it was no mere physical distance that could separate their lives. One thing only could really intervene: and that had come. And he had not found happiness, after all. The pity of it; and, ah, the cruel phantom of reproach that must lie in wait for each empty moment of her life. . . .

On the quay, outside the tavern, a bell clanged noisily, and a clock struck four. Sylvia remembered, drearily, that other people were expected to arrive before nightfall; people who had rights; one, at least, who would look at her askance, with eyes that she must not encounter. There must be no scene, no scandal. She must go.

For the future, was not her course simple, inevitable as the daily routine of a prison?

She must go back; she must accept the inevitable, just as when, years ago, Adrian's life first diverged from her life, she had patiently accepted it.

She must go back. She must gather up the grey threads of her existence, dropped when that transient gleam had crept from the far horizon to beguile her, in spite of herself, with dreams of sunshine, of flowers. A rainbow, was it, that had spread its brief radiance across the greyness of her prospect—or the treacherous glimmer of some marish light? Will-o'-the-wisp, or rainbow, it had passed; and before her lay the straight path, and the greyness.

THE END

www.ingramcontent.com/pod-product-compliance
Lightning Source LLC
Chambersburg PA
CBHW030743250426
43672CB00028B/382